THE HIGH ROLLERS OF THE TURF

COVER PICTURES

...ver: From left – Noel Furlong, Barney Curley and J.P. (The ...ce Kid) McManus, three of the most prominent and fearless of an ...igh Rollers of the present era and (below) Destriero, with William...s in the saddle leads into the home straight on his way to ...ory in the 1991 Trafalgar House Supreme Novice Hurdle and in the process lands a £1 million coup for Noel Furlong.

Back Cover: GOLD CUP DAY IN THE SNOW . . . Caroline Norris's graphic picture from the 1987 Cheltenham Festival meeting when the start of the Gold Cup was delayed by snow. Eventually when it got under way, Cleeve Hill in the background presented a Christmas postcard-like scene as Cybrandian, the eventual runner-up, led the field on the first circuit.

THE HIGH ROLLERS OF THE TURF

By

RAYMOND SMITH

SPORTING BOOKS PUBLISHERS
DUBLIN
1992

THE HIGH ROLLERS OF THE TURF

First published 1992

Copyright © Raymond Smith, 1992

Published by Sporting Books Publishers, Dublin.
Print origination and typesetting by The City Office, Dublin 2.
Printed by the Leinster Leader, Naas.

CONTENTS

AUTHOR'S NOTE

I have long been fascinated by the High Rollers of The Turf. It's not merely the fact that among them you find characters who are prepared to put £10,000 "on the nose" on a prime fancy of theirs. More important, some of them have become legends in their own lifetimes and the stories surrounding their names are an integral part of the lore of racing. They live by the motto: "Better one day as a lion than one hundred years as a lamb."

There was a need, I felt, to bring the most famous of the modern High Rollers together between the covers of the one book. I thought it essential too to contrast the philosophy of the winners with the compulsiveness of the losers; on the one hand men whose primary goal is to "stay alive" and retain enough ammunition to go into the trenches the next day to continue the battle with the bookies and, on the other hand, those who, in contrast to the professionals, see the last race as the "getting out stakes" and who suffer the consequences.

Many people contributed to making it possible for me to meet the pre-Christmas '92 deadline for the publication of this book.

I am especially grateful to Michael O'Leary and the City Office, 14 Fitzwilliam Place, Dublin 2, to Helen and rest of the staff, especially Des Swords and Jimmy Cuthbert, for their professionalism in the preparation of this book for printing.

My thanks also to Maurice Moore of Independent Newspapers who designed the cover. I thank all the photographers, including Ed Byrne, Caroline Norris, Jacqueline O'Brien,Bernard Parkin, Peter Mooney, Laurie Morton, Colin Turner and Liam Burke (Press 22) who supplied prints for the book. Also Independent Newspapers.

I am deeply indebted to Eugene Webber, News Librarian and the other members of the Press Association Library, Fleet Street and also the staffs of Independent Newspapers Library and the Cork Examiner Photographic Library.

My thanks also to the editors of the other newspapers, racing papers and magazines, and other publications for permission to quote from various interviews, reports and features and for the photographs which were made available to me.

Special thanks to the Mercier Press, publishers, for allowing me to quote from "The Gay Future Affair" by Larry Lyons.

I express my deep appreciation for the help and assistance I received from Tony Sweeney, an acknowledged expert on racing facts and statistics, for so authoritatively answering the queries I submitted to him, going back decades.

I record my gratitude to the *Leinster Leader* for another job well done in the printing of the book not forgetting my very good friend, Michael Kane, with whom I have worked closely now for over a decade.

My thanks also to Dr. Michael and Sheila Mangan, Terence and Annette Sweeney, Denis and Mary Ward for providing me with facilities to meet the writing deadlines.

Lastly, I could not have devoted the necessary time to writing without the understanding of my wife, Sheila and I am grateful too for the patience of Stephen and Bairbre.

RAYMOND SMITH

Dublin, 1992

INTRODUCTION

'Banana' Scott and the Garden of Eden

Over dinner one evening in Dublin, Terry Rogers brought me back to the days of 'Banana' Scott and the Garden of Eden.

Terry himself was dubbed "The Red Menace" in his heyday as one of the most colourful rails bookmakers and born characters in the Irish ring. It was not simply because he had a shock of red hair that he was given that nomenclature. No, it was because his father was also named Terry and when they went to Point to Point meetings, other bookmakers when they saw "Terry Rogers" up on a board near them would inquire automatically: "Is it the old man or 'The Red Menace'?" Terry Junr. was seen as a threat to business as he commanded so much attention around his pitch.

The Garden of Eden was in a laneway between Dublin's Eden Quay and Lower Abbey Street, just around the corner from Wynn's Hotel. This hotel is still as popular as ever today with people 'up from the country', including priests and nuns who find its atmosphere more congenial than perhaps the Shelbourne, the Berkeley Court or the Conrad Hilton.

You could hardly imagine a more apt name for a betting shop than the Garden of Eden, especially at a time when S.P. offices were still illegal (having a bet on a horse in a bookmaker's premises was akin, I suppose, to eating the forbidden fruit in 'The Garden').

They didn't legalise betting shops in Ireland until the issue of licences under the Betting Act of 1926. And even then they laid down strict regulations about no loitering and nothing being on offer in a betting shop like a radio commentary on a race that could induce people in from the street to have a flutter.

If it had been the legal era, there is little doubt that 'Banana' Scott's gamecock would have been judged as an inducement to step inside the Garden of Eden and I reckon 'Banana' would have found himself in the 'slammer' for it.

'Banana', whose real name was Charlie Scott, was a breeder of gamecocks apart from being a bookie. "Normally cocks crow at dawn but the particular bird that 'Banana' kept in his betting emporium never crowed before midday or coming up to it or after the clock had struck 12," Terry explained to me.

"They would run a sweepstake on the time they felt the cock would crow. I don't have to tell you the kind of characters who frequented that betting shop and invested their money in trying to read the mind of the gamecock. Some of them could have stepped straight out of *Juno and the Paycock* and *The Plough and The Stars*, born Joxers and Fluthers!"

"A crazy kind of a mixed up bet," according to Terry Rogers, who went on to reveal to me that when no one won the sweepstake on a particular day, the pool was carried over. "You could call it a Cockpot instead of a jackpot carry-over," added Terry, bursting his sides with laughter.

The story of 'Banana' Scott and his gamecock proves beyond any shadow of doubt that the Irish have always loved a gamble and, furthermore, there are intrepid characters who are prepared to bet on anything.

And it illustrates another point — there have always been eccentric bookmakers to match the kamikaze punters.

There was a bookie in Belfast around the period after the First World War, Hugh McAlevery by name, but known simply as "Bo" to his many friends and admirers. "Bo" spent so much time sailing to and fro across the Atlantic in luxury liners that the seagulls nodded hello to him!

2

Once he dressed up as a Chinaman to win a challenge with side stakes on it, according to Sam McAughtry, the Northern Ireland author, playwright and columnist in a contribution to Finbarr Slattery's excellent book, *Horse Racing*. He walked into the *Belfast Telegraph* office and introduced himself to the Editor as "Mister Mo". Having been summarily dismissed from the august presence, he stood outside in Royal Avenue shaking hands with passers-by and introducing himself to all and sundry as "Mister Mo", the Chinese bookie. The incident became such a popular anecdote throughout the North that "Bo" used it to coin his famous motto: "SP All Races in China".

As I have indicated already, the Irish will bet on anything. I have seen them in the early hours in the days when big poker games were played openly in the lounge area of the Queen's Hotel in Cheltenham, getting involved in head-to-head pitch and toss battles (it has its own set of strict ground rules and you cannot, for example, bring your hand above your shoulders in the act of tossing). I have seen up to £4,000 changing hands on "heads" or "tails". Crazy you may say but it's true.

And I have seen them on Friday mornings in the Long Day's Journey to the Last Flight Home, as we partook of buck's fizz, pointing the champagne bottles at the chandelier in the bar and trusting their aim that the popping corks might knock off not just one but two crystal "ear-rings" as a trophy to bring home. Fifty pounds a go. You know they became quite expert at hitting the target though, fortunately, the chandelier was solid enough to withstand their onslaught.

Everything was possible on Friday, always the most relaxed and hilarious day for me and the one that seemed to leave the funniest memories... memories that made one conclude that if a specialist gave you the word that you had the "Big C", at least you could say you had lived and all you would ask for was one more year, so that you could get in one last Festival meeting and more of the "crack".

In The Cotswold pub, when the incomparable Con Carroll, who hailed originally from West Cork, was 'Mein Host', I remember Jimmy Whelan, a true-blue Dubliner

3

telling me back in 1983 that he was having an ante-post bet on a 'dark one' that he expected to win the Gold Cup of pigeon racing. My God, and I missing out on Bregawn that same year!

If that was not enough, Jimmy had Liam Dillon and other friends and myself holding our sides in laughter as he regaled us with the art of how to breed a black canary and a finch mule (as far as I can recall, you cross a goldfinch with a canary) or a linnet mule (in this case you cross a linnet with a canary). In trying to get a black canary, it's all about breeding down to the weakest link in the genetic line to achieve the required specimen which, of course, is so weak that he can only hang there off his perch, like someone in the last stages of consumption.

That same year a Kerryman walked through Customs at Birmingham carrying a bag containing 60 lbs of uncooked ham and three bottles of poitin — though one Irish jockey who flew in on the same plane was stopped by the Customs men and had his bag searched. The Kerryman was bringing over the ham and poitin for relatives in London.

What self-respecting bookie would have laid a price on his getting through with the uncooked ham and poitin!

In 1981 some Irish punters stepped in and took 10/1 — a real "overlay" — that Prince Charles would not complete the course on his mount Good Prospect in the Kim Muir Memorial Challenge Cup. Of course, his prospects of getting round were much less than that but you see the bookies concerned didn't want to insult the Royal family by quoting the true odds which would have been no more than 2/1; besides it was more of a fun bet and they were not taking big money. The Prince, in scarlet and blue silks, was still there coming to the tenth fence and then the course commentator was heard to say: "Good Prospect has made a mistake. The Prince is down…"

The Irish punters, sporting their shamrocks, proceeded to the bar and lifted their glasses to "Bonny Prince Charlie", first for lining their pockets and, secondly, they were applauding his courage. They were quick to acknowledge that although the Prince had not the

4

experience at this level to really compete with professionals, he still deserved credit for being man enough to face the testing Cheltenham fences. And then he came a cropper, he could easily have been hit by any of the horses thundering up behind him.

The concentration on the horses and the cards and the betting can become so intense at Cheltenham that men think of nothing else. I remember in the seventies a task force from Bristol leading the "invasion" of the "armies of the night", under the impression that there were rich pickings to be had from the Irish. But they hadn't reckoned how unresponsive the male of the species could be when there are cards to be played or the form book to be studied for another tilt at the ring.

Two ladies of the night were overheard exchanging views and one remarked: "Those bloody Irish are useless — all they think of is cards and horses."

The Kerryman's response to that, as he contemplated the vision of four beautiful Queens coming up before his eyes, was: "There's a time and a mood for everything."

Cheltenham has always been special to the Irish since they really discovered it after the Second World War. They were the days when lovers of the National Hunt racing travelled to England by boat armed with steaks and bacon and eggs, sausages and black puddings and all of these were virtual currency in a country where no one talked of the dangers of cholesterol.

Even though Britain was on the "winning" side in the War, the food shortages of earlier grimmer days — the days of the Blitz, the black-outs and V.2 raids — continued right up to 1950. It may seem impossible to imagine it now, but the traditional full English breakfast, now taken for granted by those who form the annual exodus from Ireland to Cheltenham and Liverpool, was a luxury in the 1946-'50 period. The innovative Irish brought the 'makings' to their regular "digs" and friendly landladies viewed like gold dust their treasure.

Incidentally, the front-line troops of the invasion force brought liberal quantities of Irish whiskey also to fortify themselves for the boat journey and for the convivial gatherings after racing that went on into the early hours, as they sang and played cards and simply talked horses and form. Thus were the traditions born that were to live on into the Nineties.

In the golden seasons of the initial invasion period, they came home with pockets full of money as the Irish winning roar was heard again and again at Cheltenham and Liverpool also. It seemed that there would be no ending to those happy, winning days — days of the famous Prince Regent winning the Gold Cup in 1946 for Tom Dreaper and J. V. Rank and then Vincent O'Brien taking the Gold Cup three years running with Cottage Rake (1948-'50) and the Champion Hurdle three times also with Hatton's Grace (1949-'51) and a fourth Gold Cup with Knock Hard (1953). Meanwhile he was hammering the bookies with a succession of spectacular betting coups as he almost made the two legs of the Gloucestershire Hurdle his own through the fifties.

Distel, trained by Charlie Rogers for Miss Dorothy Paget and ridden by Bobby O'Ryan, took the 1946 Champion Hurdle to crown a memorable meeting for Rogers who saddled four winners.

In 1964 Arkle won the first of three successive Gold Cups and the "Irish roar" that greeted his triumph over the mighty Mill House was not matched again until that unforgettable March day in 1986 when the gallant mare Dawn Run rallied from apparent certain defeat at the last to take the Cup for Paddy Mullins. Jonjo O'Neill's arm-aloft victory gesture to the heavens as he passed the winning post still remains engraved in the mind.

Yes, memories are made of moments like that...

The English have always been fascinated by the Irish at the Cheltenham Festival meeting and the legends they have helped to create.

Gaynor Shutte produced a 45-minute documentary for BBC radio ("Cheltenham the Irish Favourite") and one of the people she interviewed for her programme was Templeogue-based Fr Sean Breen, a regular at Cheltenham every year and no mean judge of the form book. The BBC crew was allowed to record Fr Breen saying Mass on St.

6

Patrick's Day morning in 1988 in the restaurant of the Golden Valley Hotel for a group of intrepid Irish punters.

The most memorable moment of all was when Cavan-born Fr Sean thanked the Lord for giving the Irish the gift of being able to socialise and enjoy themselves. And when he prayed for guidance for his flock in their battle with the bookies. And as he put it himself to journalist, John McEntee: "I also prayed for winners."

Gaynor Shutte and her crew were somewhat taken aback. All she could exclaim was: "It was absolutely amazing. I'd never seen anything like it.."

Cheltenham features a lot in this book as I detail successful coups and failed gambles at the Festival meeting.

Racing has stirred the Irish for as long back as one cares to go. Indeed, Tony Sweeney, one of the greatest authorities on Irish racing, maintains that its origins can be traced back to the dawn of time. "Records of early races are lost in the mists of antiquity, but we do know that horse and chariot races formed part of the programme for the Aonacht Tailtean in pre-Christian Ireland," he wrote in a contribution to *The Horse In Ireland* in 1967. The significance of the role of the horse is indicated by the frequent references to them in the Brehon Laws, the statutes which governed life in Ireland down to the time of the final conquest by England in the closing decade of the 17th century. It was ordained that a foster-son should be 'supplied with a horse at the time of the races'.

The Tudor King, Henry VIII, was a great supporter of racing. Various sums were paid to people who competed against the Royal stable and amongst those mentioned in this connection is Gerald Fitzgerald, the 9th Earl of Kildare and a man who in his day was known as the 'uncrowned King of Ireland'.

King Henry VIII had his own trainer, jockeys' fees were laid down and he may even have had his own colours. He took great care to ensure that only those who could afford to do so were allowed to gamble. Labourers laid themselves open to a fine of forty shillings for breaches of anti-gambling laws.

7

But nothing could deter the Irish from gambling, whether they be blue bloods or ordinary folk.

The 17th century saw the emergence of some outstanding sportsmen and unique characters. One of the most famous of all was one Thomas 'Buck' Whaley (a night spot in Dublin's Leeson Street is named after him today). As revealed by Fergus D'Arcy in his excellently-documented history of the Irish Turf, *Horses, Lords and Racing Men,* "Buck" Whaley won £20,000 in a famous wager over travelling to Jerusalem and back in two years and, believe me, that was a lot of "bread" in those days. However, he lost it all and more in reckless gambling.

Indeed, in a comparative short space of time he ran through a fortune of £400,000. A member of the Jockey Club at Newmarket and owner of some excellent bloodstock in Ireland, "Buck" described his own record thus: "In the course of a few years I dissipated a fortune of near four hundred thousand pounds and contracted debt to the amount of thirty thousand more without ever purchasing or acquiring contentment or one hour of true happiness."

He had a brother, John who led a much more controlled existence. In fact, he had a very successful career and made an immense contribution to the Irish Turf Club.

Such was the passion for racing in Ireland that the sport had become so widespread in the eighteenth century that *Dickson's Dublin Intelligence* of August, 1731 reported that "horse racing is become a great diversion in the country".

Places great and small throughout the land had their own organised racing. Mallow offered six consecutive days of racing in the first week of June, 1771 and two weeks later, Tralee had a full week's racing "interrupted only by the Sabbath". July saw the six-day Down Royal meeting; Rathkeale also had a six-day meeting while Cashel, Enniskillen and Belturbet were running race meetings as far back as 1704.

By 1750 Dublin newspapers were advertising approximately 70 race meetings throughout Ireland. Even though many of them were badly supervised, it was still a staggering figure.

8

The Rising of 1798 may have affected continuity and caused disruption but it could not kill the lasting love of the Sport of Kings.

In the mid-eighteenth century Dublin (population 130,000) was one of the most elegant capitals in Europe with its lovely Georgian residences for the gentry. The ownership of horses was primarily a sport for the rich and racing and hunting formed the pastimes of the wealthy. The peasantry and poorer sections of the population enjoyed racing as a spectacle and found in it an escape from the daily grind.

The young bloods in their distinctive brightly-coloured and patterned waistcoats, with silver buttons on their coats and at the knees of their breeches (fastened outside the stockings to show off the gleaming buttons) and low-cut black shoes, set off with brass buckles, with tall hats completing the ensemble, gambled heavily at the races.

Matches between different horses were a highlight of that era. As much as £1,000 — a fortune by the standards of today — could be wagered on a single match, with the minimum normally £100. The distance of one of these matches ranged from four miles to five and even six miles.

Prior to the 1914-'18 World War one of the most prolific gamblers in Britain was unquestionably Robert Standish Siever, known to his friends and acquaintances as simply "Bob". He was the owner of Sceptre, perhaps the greatest race mare of all time, who won all the Classics except the Derby in 1902.

Geoff Hamlyn, who was 45 years Starting Price reporter with the *Sporting Life* and observed in his time some of the greatest characters ever seen on British racecourses, noted in the course of a special feature in the 1983-'84 *Irish Racing Annual* that Siever was an outstanding example of Damon Runyon's edict that "all horse players die broke".

In the words of Hamlyn, Siever was "one of the most profligate gamblers of all time" and died penniless just before the Second World War. He had the distinction, however, of revolutionising the system of betting in Australia, where before his arrival it was customary to bet only on double events and every layer was his own clerk.

9

When Siever started quoting the odds on single and not double events and paid out immediately after the winner had weighed in, he caused a sensation and not alone did he do a roaring trade, but others were forced to follow suit.

If he had remained a bookmaker betting to a rounded book, he could have ended his days a wealthy man but his gambling instincts were too strong and the bug proved fatal to him in the end.

A punter who bet immense sums was James A. de Rothschild. At one stage in his career he was reputed to have lost £100,000, the equivalent of a million pounds by today's values. When this was reported to his uncle, Leopold de Rothschild, he remarked: "Oh, is that all? I thought you were going to tell me something serious."

Such was the Rothschild wealth that James A. survived as an owner and gambler for half a century.

A professional punter of terrific courage, racing knowledge and integrity was the peerless Charlie Hannam. Meyrick Good, the Man on the Spot of the *Sporting Life* for sixty years, told Geoff Hamlyn that "there was never a man like him". He asked no one his opinion and offered none himself.

He had an unbounded admiration for the riding ability of Sir Gordon Richards. If Domaha, ridden by Richards, had won the Cambridgeshire in 1938 instead of finishing fourth, Hannam would have been set up financially for life. But that's racing. After the failure of that gamble, he departed the scene the following Monday. He had graced it with his presence for forty years. Ironically, he was owed at least eight times what he was "knocked" for.

"Scotch" Johnny Marr, whose claim to fame was that he executed commissions for many of the nobility, was one of the best judges of the form book of his day while at the same time he was a first-class judge of odds and invariably looked for value when having a cut. Nor surprisingly, he left £260,000 in his will and if you translate that into 1992 figures he was a millionaire a few times over.

Tommy Westhead was a bookmaker-turned-backer who landed two tremendous coups when his own horse Punch won the Cesarewitch in 1937 and on Langton Abbot when

10

he won the first post-War Lincoln in 1946.

Ben Warner, who died in 1974 at the age of 84, was a bookmaker-cum-owner-cum professional punter whose greatest claim to fame was that he master-minded the "Oyster Maid Coup" at Tenby in 1927. The members of the betting fraternity who were not in the know, were taken to the cleaners. They claimed subsequently that the horse should have started at 5/2 instead of 100/6. But Warner, it was alleged, connived with certain bookmakers on the inside to see that it went off at 100/6 and the "killing" was brought off at those S.P. odds.

The period after the Second World War produced gamblers who wove legends around their names that live on in racing lore to this day.

Joe Sunlight... Dorothy Paget... the Aly Khan...

These were but three punters who, by today's money values, bet in astronomical sums.

For forty years Joe Sunlight was locked in battle with the bookies and, even though some of his biggest attempted coups went wrong, he still left over £5 million in his will.

Geoff Hamlyn takes up the story about this amazing personality: "Joe Sunlight probably had the biggest annual betting turnover of all outside of Dorothy Paget. But then he had the readies with which to bet. Of Russian origins, he was a highly-successful architect and surveyor and Sunlight House in Manchester, once the highest building in Britain, was a monument to his professionalism.

"Racing and gambling were his real loves. He would often back several horses in every race, every day and his daily turnover would often exceed £10,000, and this was equal to twenty times that amount when translated into the values of a half-a-century later.

"Yet he was parsimonious in other matters and travelled second class by train and bus to meetings, although he owned a handsome Rolls-Royce.

"He had his big wins on the racecourse. I remember when Noel Murless won the 1,000 Guineas with Queenpot in 1948, Sunlight told me that he had had £30,000-£3,000 with a number of bookmakers.

"I remember too a wet afternoon at Manchester, this

well-known bookie was going around with a broad smile despite the fact that five favourites had won. I asked him why he was so cheerful. He replied that Sunlight had given him a cheque for £7,000, a lot of money in those days. I asked him if that was in full settlement. 'Oh no', the bookie replied, 'he really owes me £35,000, but I have accepted £7,000 in full payment!' Many other layers could tell the same tale."

Miss Dorothy Paget became a legend in her own lifetime as the woman who bet in telephone numbers. It was a double-edged way of explaining her approach to gambling. For example, she was a very superstitious person and if someone rang her up in the morning whose phone number happened to be 1582, Miss Paget would invest exactly that amount on her horses in the afternoon.

But to say that she bet in telephone numbers was also another way of saying that when she went for a "touch", it was nothing to her to have £10,000 on one of her horses and double that amount, if the mood struck her.

She had the wealth to gamble, having inherited an immense fortune from her grandfather. Inordinately shy, she went to special lengths to avoid being bothered by strangers or media representatives. She used a bevy of female secretaries as a screen, especially when she went racing.

For the last twenty years of her life she lived as a recluse but even away from the racecourse, she maintained her love of betting and there is little doubt that, as an owner she enjoyed far more singular triumphs in the National Hunt sphere than on the Flat.

She was the only owner in racing history to win the Derby (Straight Deal), the Grand National and Gold Cup (Golden Miller) and the Champion Hurdle (Insurance). She undoubtedly won a lot of money through her tilts at the ring on these champions. But, of course, anyone betting at the awesome level at which she punted lost heavily also. However, it has to be said that on the days of her successful coups she really stung the bookies and left them feeling very sorry for themselves.

Yes, she has to go into racing history as one of the most

outstanding owner-punter personalities of all time and it was not for nothing that she was dubbed "one of the great eccentrics of 20th-century racing" by the *Biographal Encyclopaedia of British Flat Racing.*

Another lady who, as a gambler, attained the same level was Mrs J.V. (Pat) Rank, who never hesitated to have £10,000 on one of the horses running in her husband's colours. J.V. Rank will be best remembered as the owner of Prince Regent, who but for the intervention of the Second World War would certainly have won more than one Gold Cup and at least one National as well. This great chaser was eleven when he won the Gold Cup in the hands of Tim Hyde in 1946 and he was third, beaten seven lengths, in the Aintree Grand National the same year carrying 12st 5lbs.

Prince Aly Khan was one of the biggest punters of the immediate post-War period.

You couldn't have personalities like Dorothy Paget, Pat Rank and the Aly Khan (in 1959 the latter had £1,000-£80 six times as a saver on Petite Etoile in the 1,000 Guineas when he thought his other runner, Paraguana, was sure to win) unless there were bookmakers of steely courage to take them on. And the ring certainly threw up men whose fearlessness became a by-word.

The legendary Percy Thompson was already an established figure in the ring when along came William Hill, who in time was to become the undisputed "King" of the racecourse bookmakers.

Thompson, rated by Geoff Hamlyn as "undoubtedly the greatest board bookmaker of all time", would tap his board at Royal Ascot and say quietly: "Any horse to win £5,000."

And that was back in days when £5,000 represented a fortune by present-day money values.

Hill's strength was that he could do double the business in half the time of any other layer one cared to name. The fact that he became undisputed leader of the ring in an era when it had such strong figures as Willie Preston, Percy Thompson, Albert Williams, Laurie Wallis and Hector MacDonald and others, proved beyond any shadow of a doubt the impact that Hill made up to the time of his retirement in 1955.

Hill left the running of the S.P. business to his lieutenants. His personal metier was the rails.

He never flinched in the face of four or even five-figure bets. He could stand horses in the big ante-post betting races for £100,000 or more.

The arrival of professional punters of the calibre of Alex Bird and Phil Bull saw the never-ending "war" between those who bet for a living and the bookmakers become more sophisticated in Britain. As will be seen from the chapter on both these two, they disproved Damon Runyon's edict that "all horse players die broke". Not alone did they die wealthy men but their life-styles must have made them the envy of many a man who slaved all the day in the City.

Bird was unquestionably one of the most successful professional punters after the Second World War and with his totally unemotional business-like approach, he ensured that he would have at the very least a 7% to 10% profit on a turnover of £300,000 to £400,000 a year.

Phil Bull adopted the same approach. He, of course, was the man who will always be remembered as the founder of *Timeform* which added to the edge that those, who bet strictly from knowledge both of form and the clock rather than hunches, have over the bookies.

Betting tax became an insuperable obstacle to the racecourse operations of men like Alex Bird and Phil Bull. It meant that well before his death, Bird had drastically reduced his betting.

And, frankly, the days of punters betting in "telephone numbers" at the scale of a Dorothy Paget or Pat Rank were past.

However, there will always be those who will go into the trenches for hand-to-hand combat with the rails bookmakers and likewise there will always be those who will try to mastermind coups that will add to the storehouse of racing legends whether they fail or are successful. Ireland has produced a succession of fearless punters since the 1939-'45 World War, among them

14

outstanding characters. One has only to mention "The Gay Future Affair" and you are talking immediately about an episode in racing history that is relived in all its detail wherever racing men gather. Naturally it merits a chapter in this book.

We turn the spotlight too on J.P. (The Sundance Kid) McManus, Barney Curley and Noel Furlong. Furlong, living by the motto that "you may only get one chance of a real killing", would have netted a cool £4 million if The Illiad had won the 1991 Smurfit Champion Hurdle at the National Hunt Festival meeting (Destriero had already completed the first leg of the double by taking the Trafalgar House Supreme Novices Hurdle). It was not to be. But seldom in all my years going to Cheltenham have I seen such a stir engendered by Furlong's attempted coup which had the representatives of the big bookmaking chains going pale at the thought of the pay-out facing them had The Illiad obliged as he had done when landing a "morning board prices" gamble for Noel Furlong in the Ladbroke Handicap Hurdle at Leopardstown earlier that same season.

We turn the spotlight also in this book on men who lived true to the immortal phrase of the English eighteenth century bookmaker, Fred Swindell: "There's a mug born every minute."

"Mincemeat" Joe Griffin and Terry Ramsden were just two who qualified for this category and who were casualties of the war with the bookmakers. Their bones were picked clean and they were left with only bitterness.

We contrast the born losers with those whose motto it is to survive at all costs — men like J.P. McManus and Barney Curley.

What emerges is that the true professionals operate to clear-cut ground rules — to maxims which they will not desert under any circumstance.

The losers aim for the moon. And in the flush of a few successful gambles, they think they have unlocked the secret. When the tide turns, they bet heavily to try and recover their losses and become victims of a failure to control their emotional impulses.

The one secret they have not learned is to "know when to fold", to operate to the dictum that there is no such thing as a last race or a getting out stakes.

Professionals like J.P. McManus and Barney Curley will coldly close up shop knowing there is always another day — that if you are not to be left defenceless and picked off by the enemy, then you avoid at all costs using up your remaining ammunition defending a last unstrategic hillock, so to speak.

To have ammunition for the next day's battle with the bookies is what keeps you continually in the trenches.

Above all The High Rollers of the Turf are born characters, and whether they emerge from the pages of this book as winners or losers, they certainly have left their footsteps on the sands of time.

The very fact that this book has given permanency to the amazing stories surrounding their names will continue the cycle... for we have no doubt that a new generation will seek to emulate them.

There will always be those who will want to outstrip the legend of Butch Cassidy and The Sundance Kid.

PART ONE

BARNEY CURLEY
The Man in the Beige Fedora

1

"Barney's Having A Go!"

There I was in the kitchen of Barney Curley's seven-bedroom mansion with its own indoor swimming pool and snooker table at Stetchworth on the outskirts of Newmarket on a lovely sunny morning during the July '91 meeting.

The smell of frying bacon and eggs, sausage and black pudding, cooked by his wife, Maureen permeated the atmosphere.

It seemed a far, far cry from the whirl of the ring at Cheltenham during Festival week in March – Cheltenham that stirs Curley to the marrow of his bones as it stirs J.P. McManus and which he describes as "one of the great meetings." It makes him note with total satisfaction that when he goes down the line of the rails' bookmakers "there's a buzz that you won't even get when Sheikh Mohammed runs one of his million-dollar horses." And he delights as the chorus goes up: "Barney's having a go!"

"Barney's having a go!" means one thing and one thing only – that he is wagering at least £10,000 on the nose on one of his prime fancies.

We weren't talking at that particular moment about the great gambles landed by the Man in the Beige Fedora, who has been the scourge of the bookmakers for years and nowadays is something of a folk hero to everyday small punters in Ireland and Britain.

I had brought the subject round to his concept of Heav-

19

en. Hell also.

The reason I had done so was that it intrigued me that he had started out in life with the vocation to become a Jesuit – an Order priest spurning worldly possessions and dedicating his life solely to the poor and underprivileged in society.

Then the Destiny that shapes our ends stepped in and he was forced to give it all up when he contracted tuberculosis. Surviving that in an era when "they were dying like flies around me," he got the call of the secular world and managed pop groups on the road before drifting into betting-shop ownership and then becoming a professional gambler and racehorse owner and trainer.

"Life would be meaningless to me if I didn't believe in a God and there was no after-life," he said simply. "It's not something I treat lightly."

But what kind of God does he believe in? "For me he's a merciful God. At the same time, let me make it clear that I am not the sort of chap who thinks that you will go straight to heaven if you spend half-an-hour every Sunday inside the door of a church. As far as I am concerned belief is a very searching and personal business."

The searching side of his belief was fully tested in 1981 when one of his mares died in childbirth. With no foster mother available, Barney bottle-fed the foal himself. "After two days the vet told me the case was hopeless," he told Brough Scott.

But then his faith came into play. He strode out into the field, knelt down on the grass and looked up into the driving rain. The foal survived against all the odds. And two years later when Brough Scott met Barney Curley to talk to him about his life and times, the foal was a thriving fleet-footed three-year-old called – Answer to Prayer.

Now I asked Barney Curley about his concept of heaven? "I visualise it as a place that you can count yourself very lucky – if you get there. I like to think of it as a great peaceful garden where you never have to worry about anything anymore."

"And Hell, Barney?" I asked tentatively.

"I think it must be very, very hard to get into hell," came

his reply. "I mean you would have to be an intrinsically evil person – I mean very evil – and unconcerned about doing the most terrible things against your fellow-man before you would be consigned by what I view as a merciful God to eternal darkness.

"Most people have the best of intentions. The just man falls not just seven times but seven times seven, we are told. So I can only conclude that about one in a million – the ratio might even be higher – end up in hell."

Now some hard-boiled cynics of my acquaintance who go racing day after day and for whom gambling is the very essence of life will wonder what the hell I was doing in Newmarket talking about heaven and the hereafter to a man who has made it pure hell in this life for the bookies on more than one occasion. Especially when they reflected on the manner in which he masterminded "The Yellow Sam Coup" in 1975 – a coup that has gone into the records as one of the boldest and most brilliantly-executed gambles in racing history.

That's the very aspect of Barney Curley that makes him DIFFERENT. It makes him a character out-and-out who can turn hours into seeming minutes as you converse with him over a typical English cooked breakfast, taken at a time of day when it can more reasonably be classed as brunch, without the champagne or wine.

The very fact that he lives in the sumptuous residence formerly the demesne of failed financier and gambler, Terry Ramsden brings you right up face-to-face with the stark reality of the game. And that is why Barney Curley, professional gambler-cum-racehorse owner is the first to admit that he lives from day to day.

The five years he spent studying philosophy in Mungret College in Limerick – where Vincent O'Brien and his brother, Dermot went to school, incidentally – gave him a depth of outlook that one doesn't associate in the normal course of events with those who frequent the race-tracks and dog-tracks as professional gamblers.

To Barney Curley, taking on the bookmakers and making them squirm causes the adrenalin to flow in a manner that he could never experience if he spent his life chasing

wealth for wealth's sake and accumulating all its trappings.

It could be a Buddhist monk talking when he looks at
you intently with those deep-set eyes under the shaven
domed head and elaborates on his beliefs. "I don't believe
in gathering a whole lot of earthly possessions that I know
I can't bring with me to the after-life.

"Answer me this – have you ever seen anyone cross the
Divide carrying antiques and oil paintings and line draw-
ings and share certificates and anything else you care to
name that is associated with having money in the bank?
No bookmaker will quote you a price on that happening!"

It wouldn't cost him a thought if he cleaned out a particular bookmaker and sent him to the poorhouse. And I suspect that nothing would give him greater pleasure than if
he overwhelmed Ladbrokes – if that were possible – in
one glorious strike as Stormin' Norman so swiftly won the
Gulf War.

But the same man would be spontaneous in his generosity to a broken bookmaker and his family. You see, just as
belief in an after-life is an integral part of his make-up, so
is helping charitable causes and lame-duck individuals.

"In giving you receive," is how he puts it. "But what you
must NEVER do is to patronise the person to whom you
are giving. There is a lot of patronising done under the
heading of charitable giving. I have no time whatsoever for
that."

His critics – and he is certainly not without them –
assert that it is the outsize ego of the man, who likes to
wear camel-hair coats in winter, that makes him support
charitable causes that have a way of hitting the headlines.

But such accusations and insinuations bring a flush of
anger to his cheeks and he contends that the caring part of
him has cost him heavily financially on occasions.

For example, he organised a raffle at the end of 1988 in
aid of the Great Ormond Street Children's Hospital in London. The idea was that the ten winners would each have a
Curley-trained horse running in their name for a year with
no fees to pay.

Ticket sales did not go as well as expected. In fact, there

was a drastic shortfall. Curley did not welsh on the prizes and, furthermore, kept his promise of a guaranteed £100,000 donation to the hospital. With all the costs – including advertising and administration – he admitted to me that it set him back £350,000.

"I don't think it was properly marketed," he added in cold retrospect. But then a shrug of the shoulders: "As I have said already, it is in giving that we receive. I have survived."

Terry Ramsden was down on his luck, broken by the financial markets and the bookmakers, when Barney Curley bought his Stetchworth home from him. He purchased it before it went to public auction and he admits he got it for "a reasonable price."

"No, I wouldn't have had the money to buy it if I had to bid the price it would have gone at an auction."

As he brought me on a tour through the house and the adjoining stables and showed me the spot in a back lot where Ramsden once had his helicopter pad, he turned suddenly and remarked: "The name of the game is SURVIVAL. I have managed to survive – so far."

"When I used to meet Terry Ramsden at race meetings and saw the way he was gambling, observing none of the rules that true professionals observe, I told him again and again that he was a madman and that the bookies would get him without fail. He wouldn't listen. They cleaned him out as the vultures pick the bones of a dead body lying under a hot desert sun."

Now that I had established that Barney Curley was a believer and a philosopher to boot, I was beginning to almost see a halo around his head and wondered if there was ever a time when ice water ran in his veins instead of blood (as the professional poker players put it in Las Vegas when they go all in on a hand which they reckon to be the "nuts").

"When I walk into a racecourse I am walking into a jungle," he explained and now his eyes had taken on a cold, diamond-hard look. "It's a dog-eat-dog world where there are no rules. Unless I am as tough as the toughest individuals who frequent the tracks, especially those in the bookmaking business, I will not survive.

"In battling to survive you have to be careful not to do anything that is morally wrong. What I mean by morally wrong is – to quote you the ultimate example – owning all five runners in a five-horse race, then stopping the four seen to have any chance and fixing it to win with the complete outsider.

"It's morally wrong also if you can manage to stop the clock and you lay a bet on the 3 o'clock race when the bookmaker thinks it's 2.55 and you already know the result. That's stealing money from the bookmaker. Yes, daylight robbery is morally wrong and you have to answer for it.

"It's morally wrong also if you fix races by squaring jockeys to do what is totally out of bounds. Again you have to answer for that."

But would it not be morally wrong, I ask, to get a horse down to a very low handicap mark by giving it a succession of "easy" races and then hitting the bookmakers for six when you knew the animal in question had a stone in hand and was a proverbial "good thing"?

"The bookmakers aren't fools," he replied. "They didn't come down in the last shower. They are up to every trick in the game. They have their lines into the big stables.

"If you have a horse and you can keep something up your sleeve from them and then go to the well and draw at the right odds, I believe there's nothing morally wrong in that.

"It's your ability against the bookmakers in the jungle of betting where, remember, gambles come unstuck as much as they come off.

"The horses in my stable are fourth-division performers and unless they get down to the handicap mark that gives them a chance of success I am not going to make it pay as a trainer.

"You don't hear the bookies weeping in sympathy when the punters are hurt. They only weep crocodile tears in public when they are hit where it hurts most."

It was inevitable then that I should bring up "The Yellow Sam Coup".

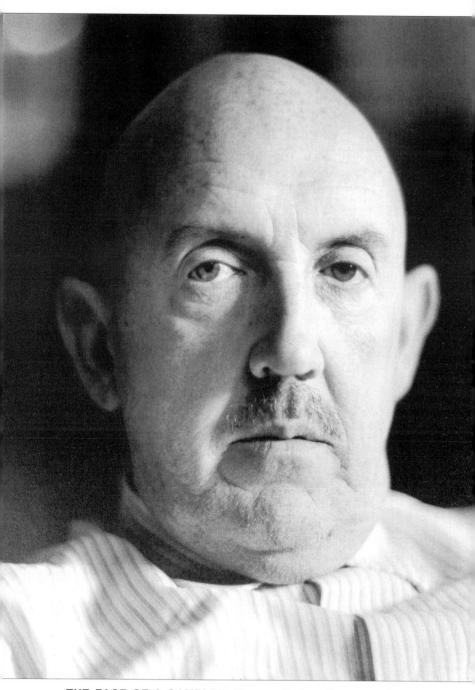

THE FACE OF A GAMBLER: Barney Curley, the man who once studied to be a Jesuit priest, talking under the shaven domed head to author, Raymond Smith of heaven and the hereafter.

Barney Curley, the race-reader, goes to a meeting, in the words of his wife Maureen, as another man will leave for his office and the gambling money is totally separate from the household money and that for the college fees for the kids.

Curley at home in Newmarket with "friends" before leaving for what he describes as the racecourse "jungle" – "a dog-eat-dog world where there are no rules."

IN THE TRENCHES . . . Curley, pictured (above left) doing business on the rails and (right) in pensive mood as he contemplates the odds on one that may carry £10,000 of his money. He once lost £350,000 in a week but survived to retain the trappings of wealth, including a magnificent home and a Mercedes Benz with the distinctive "I BET" plate.

THE FACE OF THE MAN WHO WENT FOR A £4 MILLION COUP:
Noel Furlong, who stood to win a cool £4 million in double bets
had The Illiad won the 1991 Champion Hurdle at Cheltenham.

Noel Furlong (top) caught in the front lines doing battle with the bookies at Leopardstown and (below) talking to the racing writers after Destriero had finished second to Trapper John at Navan.

Noel Furlong and his wife, Betty in the parade ring at Leopardstown on the day The Illiad landed a major "morning board prices" coup on the 1991 Ladbroke Handicap Hurdle at Leopardstown.

On the gallops at the Curragh watching Destriero being prepared for a 1992 Champion Hurdle bid that did not materialise.

Pat McWilliams acknowledges the "Irish roar" as he comes in on Destriero after landing a massive gamble for Noel Furlong in winning the 1991 Trafalgar House Supreme Novices Hurdle and (below) it's champagne time as Betty Furlong (second from left) shares the joy of victory with trainer, Andy Geraghty and Pat McWilliams. Geraghty later broke with Furlong.

THE MILLION POUND GAMBLES: Destriero clears the last safely in the 1991 Trafalgar House Supreme Novices Hurdle to win £1 million for Noel Furlong while (below) Betty Furlong gives a congratulatory pat to The Illiad (with lad, Declan Behan) after he had cleaned the bookies for £1 million in the Ladbroke Handicap Hurdle the same year.

I suggested to him quite frankly that there were aspects of it that not everyone would agree with. Like the S.P. bookies being thwarted from getting any money back to the track and thus the horse went off at 20/1 when, if the "blower" had been operating properly, or more correctly had been allowed to operate, it would assuredly have been returned at odds-on?

He laughed, as if I was naivety personified in even suggesting that there was something wrong in bringing off an S.P. "job" at odds that held all the way down to the wire.

"You see there was only one phone line to the Bellewstown track," he explained. "There was this heavily-built man, a tough sort of guy, who suddenly discovered that a close relation of his was seriously ill and he had to keep in constant touch with the hospital. Once he had the phone in his hand he was not going to let go. He was broad enough in the beam not to permit anyone past him into the box. You could trust him with your life in a situation like that!"

Barney Curley's Yellow Sam hadn't shown any form in his nine previous outings.

It wasn't surprising that he should be unconsidered in the betting for an ordinary handicap hurdle event at one of Ireland's smaller tracks.

Curley had his trusted "troops" lay bets on the nose in the S.P. offices – bets of £30, £40 and £50 mostly. In all, the bookies were cleaned to the tune of between £250,000 and £300,000.

By 1975 levels it was an awful lot of bread.

Dublin bookmaker, Terry Rogers was one of those who was hit in the gamble but, as he put it to me: "I paid out like a man" – even though he was badly stung. Terry, to his eternal credit, paid out also like a man in the case of "The Gay Future Gamble".

Rogers has his own reservations about "The Yellow Sam Coup", in particular how Barney Curley's horse came to be put up on one board on the rails at 20/1. He contends that Curley can use his Jesuitical training in theology to explain away happenings on that occasion and salve his own conscience.

But Curley flatly rejects all insinuations that there was

anything morally wrong with what he claims was a beautifully-executed "stroke".

"Look, if the bookies had got even the slightest hint that
money was being laid in the offices, they would have been
forewarned and it would have been a case of 'no show'
Yellow Sam.

"Because we thwarted them in getting a whiff of gun-
smoke in the air as we went for the kill, they moaned afterwards. Naturally, they'd moan. They always do when you
go for the jugular and leave them gasping.

"They know as well as I do that the Yellow Sam Coup
could not be brought off today with the more sophisticated
blower system for getting money from the offices back to
the tracks. It was because of that very coup that they had
to learn to update the system and that when there is only
one phone into a racetrack, some guy is going to discover
that his dear old granny is dying and he just has to hog it
for the duration!"

With the money from "The Yellow Sam Coup" and other
successful gambles, Curley was able to move from Ashford, County Wicklow and buy Midleton Park, a 30-room
stately Georgian mansion set in almost 380 acres of County
Westmeath countryside, 50 miles from Dublin. It was once
owned by the Boyd Rochfort family, trainers of the Queen
of England's horses and it had family connections also
with Lawrence of Arabia. The house came complete with
50 horse boxes and sheds for 300 cattle.

Maureen Curley, a woman of generous and warm-heart-
ed nature, remembers Midleton Park with mixed feelings.
On the one hand the big house was well-nigh impossible
to keep heated but against that she admits she will never
forget the friendships forged by Barney and herself in the
area. "We have come to settle in Newmarket. We like it
here and have made a lot of new friends but the Mullingar
area was special, yes very special and I retain very happy
and abiding memories of my days there."

Nothing has ever matched the headlines commanded by
Barney Curley when he decided to raffle Midleton Park –
and ran foul of the law in the process, bringing Michael
O'Hehir, who performed the act of drawing the winning

26

ticket, into Ballinacargy court with him for a case that seemed to have a global spotlight on it.

The outcome of this extraordinary episode in the career of this colourful character was that first he was sentenced to three months in prison, then on appeal to Mullingar Circuit Court it was reduced to one of probation, Judge Peter O'Malley ordering that Curley donate £5,000 to the local branch of the St. Vincent de Paul Society. So delighted was Curley at escaping jail, that he promptly announced that he would go for a double and make it £10,000.

It all started so innocently. It involved selling 9,000 tickets at £200 each. Barney Curley produced a spectacular promotional video which was shown on television all over the world and an equally taking brochure.

The question was: Did it breach Section 21 of the Gaming and Lotteries Act, 1956 to put the mansion up in a raffle?

In the no-nonsense language of the law, the Act states: "It is contrary to law to promote or assist in promoting a lottery, or to print, publish or distribute or sell, offer or expose for sale, invite an offer to buy, or to have in one's possession for sale or distribution any ticket, counterfoil or coupon for use in a lottery, or any document containing any information relating to a lottery."

Curley, however, described his lottery as "A Private Limited Subscribers Draw". The Act states that if the sales are confined to the members of a club or society, it is legal.

Everyone buying a ticket for the Midleton Park lottery was enrolled as a member of the Ballinagore GAA Club before they were given their ticket (you had Englishmen and Americans who had never seen a hurling or gaelic football match and hadn't even the faintest knowledge of Ireland's national games who were now members of the Ballinagore GAA Club!).

In addition, after seeking legal advice, Curley contended that it would not be a lottery if an element of skill was introduced. So, everyone who bought a ticket was asked a number of questions, like: "Name the winner of last year's Derby".

He sold his 9,000 tickets. It was estimated that the raffle

27

netted a gross £2 million, allowing for an extra £200,000 garnered from currency fluctuations. After allowing for costs, Curley was reported by the media to have cleared £1 million and, taking into account what he originally paid for Midleton Park, he would have banked £500,000 at least.

But the court case that followed brought a lot of worry to a man who could normally take gambling losses in his stride. He was worried especially that Michael O'Hehir might end up in prison like himself. "The week before the draw when the legality was questioned, I told Michael that I wouldn't mind if he withdrew. But he said he would go ahead and draw the ticket. He told me: 'I gave you my word'."

On the night of February 7, 1984 ticket No. 41877 was drawn by Michael O'Hehir and it saw a syndicate headed by Tony Ray of Bungalow Farm, Fiddington, Tewkesbury, Gloucester duly win Midleton. The members having come to view their dream stately Irish home soon decided to put it up for auction and it was sold this time in orthodox fashion to Noel and Thelma Langan from Lucan, County Dublin, who in the summer of 1992 put it up for sale again, this time with a reserve of £285,000 through Hamilton, Osborne, King, the Dublin auctioneers. It was withdrawn at £260,000 and sold afterwards at a substantially higher figure.

But not before Barney Curley and Michael O'Hehir walked in together into a packed courthouse in the little village at Ballinacargy where Curley heard District Justice William Tormey state that he had intentionally and deliberately flouted the laws of the State. Michael O'Hehir was charged with assisting in the lottery promotion – a charge subsequently withdrawn.

The press benches that normally would hold only one reporter were crammed to capacity.

Barney Curley walked out of the courthouse on July 5, 1984 with a three months jail sentence hanging over his head. He lived on with his wife, Maureen and family in Midleton Park pending the hearing of his appeal against the sentence. At one stage Maureen was contemplating moving into the Gate Lodge with the children and Barney himself had to face up to the thought that he might be spending Christmas '84 in prison, as it was November by the time the appeal was heard.

With the application of the Probation Act by Judge O'Malley, Curley left Mullingar Court breathing a big sigh of relief – but when first he left Mullingar to start training in England he had to deal with a problem of a different kind.

He lived in a modest room above the stables. "I used to take a heavy pair of boots or shoes to bed every night. I'd leave them beside my bed because at two or three o'clock in the morning the orchestra would start – you know, the rats and mice scurrying about the room. The boots were my only protection. Yes, I think you could say it was a spartan existence."

The wheel had come full circle for the man who had started out in life wanting to be an Order priest in the Jesuits. Listening to the "orchestra" of the rats and mice at night he was doing his penance in a way he could never have imagined.

2

"I Have To Bet Big To Cover Expenses"

Barney Curley is unquestionably one of the biggest gamblers of the current era and at the same time one of the shrewdest and most coldly calculating. He seldom bets less than £10,000 when he decides to put down the "readies" on a horse he really fancies.

Curley lost £250,000 by backing against Golden Fleece winning the 1982 Epsom Derby for the Vincent O'Brien-Pat Eddery combination and the same week gave a further £100,000 to the bookies in losing wagers.

Rather than being tempted to take an overdose, he flew with his wife and family to California for a holiday and came back refreshed in mind and spirit and "rarin' to go".

Curley took £200,000 out of the ring when he trained Assultan to win the Snow Hill Handicap Hurdle at Ascot on November 19, 1988. The four-year-old carried 10st 1lb in a field of 13 and was backed down from 4/1 to 5/2 favourite. It was one of Curley's most fearless gambles.

"The Inland Revenue people were after me for some back tax I owed," he recalled. "They were even threatening to make me a bankrupt. We got most of our money on at 4/1. As I trained my glasses on the runners cantering down to the start, my heart nearly stopped when I saw Assultan's saddle slip and, as he bolted, Declan Murphy had difficulty in pulling him up for almost a mile and they nearly ended up in the bushes.

"I said to myself 'that's that' and was resigned to failing

with the gamble that was going to put me right with the Tax Man. However, Assultan was brought back to the start and managed to get away okay with the rest of the field.

"We knew he had something in hand. I didn't think he had that much as he coasted home by one-and-a-half lengths and I smiled afterwards as I saw the way the race-reader of *Chaseform Note-Book* put it – 'won with something in hand'."

Why bet at such an awesome level, I asked?

"I have to bet in substantial five-figure sums to cover expenses. Most of the twenty or so horses in my stable I own myself. You don't keep them and feed them on nothing. You have to have money coming in – all the time.

"It would be no good for me having £500 on a horse I judged to be in with an outstanding chance on the book and particularly if I felt I was getting a point or two above the odds.

"If I did not have such high expenses to meet I would be much happier, believe me, betting £200 or £300 on a horse.

"You win at the level you invest, you lose at the same level if things go against you. I have had losing runs. The true professional, however, learns to scale things down at such times and not to chase his losses. He works to the dictum: 'There is always another day's racing.'

"It's no use being a professional gambler and adopting a Post Office savings bank attitude, as it were, counting every penny you have in your pocket and seeing it as something to be put away if you do not require it there and then. No, the professional gambler sees money as the weapon he uses when going to war with the bookmakers.

"At the same time he separates the gambling money from the household money, the money for the groceries and the College fees for the kids.

"Maureen, my wife, doesn't have to worry that there will be no money tomorrow to pay the milkman or the telephone account.

"I could be a banker going to the office as far as she is concerned when I head for the races.

"Gambling is a job to me devoid of emotion. I might bet on the first two races at a meeting, then take a cup of tea

31

and head home if I think there is nothing worth backing in the remaining four races on the card. The ordinary every-day punter will find it extremely difficult, well-nigh impossible to discipline himself to do that. More often than not he will try and 'get out' on the last race if he has had a bad day up to that point.

"Professionals NEVER bet on the six races on the card simply for the sake of having a bet. They don't see the last race as the 'getting out' stakes, should they be behind at that point. They will bring the shutters down if their main bet of the day on one of the earlier races is a losing one and look forward to the next day or the next opportunity to apply their judgement of form and the homework they will have put in. They know that their knowledge must inevitably pay off once they can control their emotions and not chase losses."

Maureen Curley comes in with the coffee and I cannot resist asking her if she finds it a very unusual life and one living constantly on the high-wire being married to a gam-bler?

"Not at all," she smiled. "As I see it, it's just another job that Barney is doing, the same as someone going to the City each morning and coming home at night. Or if I might put it another way, he's like any professional doing a pro-fessional job, whether you liken him to a professional jock-ey or a sportsman in any field.

"What distinguishes him, to my mind, and which causes me not to be worried that we will ever be heading for the poorhouse is the fact that he is a TOTAL professional when it comes to gambling, an utter out-and-out professional.

"The key word, as I see it in all this, is being a profes-sional as against an amateur.

"He never allows sentiment to enter it. He's not in it for fun. It's a business to him and he operates to the same principles that any professional will operate to in running a business."

The Curleys have three children, Katherine (23), who is making her life in journalism; Marie-Louise (17) who has completed her A-levels and is going to College and Charles (15) who has no other ambition but to pursue a career in racing and who in time could well become a trainer (he already gives a lot of assistance to his father around the stables when home from school on holidays).

Back to Barney Curley. He accepts that ordinary people would regard him as crazy perhaps to be putting £10,000 and even more on a single bet in one individual race.

"I would be the last to deny that if I took £10,000 and counted it out in £20 notes, it would buy a hell of a lot of groceries and other goods. I mean if I were to begin thinking that way I would lose my nerve completely.

"You have to have nerves of steel in this business. Emotion and sentiment play no part in it.

"I won't back a horse at Cheltenham simply because it's Irish-trained and I want to join in the 'Irish roar' if it beats what may be a more-fancied English-trained contender up the hill.

"I am not influenced one iota whether the horse I pick on form to win a particular race is Irish-trained, English-trained or even French-trained. I am only influenced by what I have seen myself of the horses comprising the field and by what my judgement of the form book tells me. Any other approach is the road to ruin if you are betting big as a professional."

The 1992 Cheltenham Festival meeting, for example, was kind to him. He got in early to back Royal Gait at 10/1 ante-post for the Smurfit Champion Hurdle before those odds quickly evaporated in face of inspired support for Sheikh Mohammed's horse. Assuming he had his normal £10,000 on, he would have collected £100,000.

But Barney admitted that he was really sweating during the Stewards inquiry. "I feared history was going to repeat itself with Royal Gait," said Barney, noting that in 1988 Royal Gait was first past the post in the Ascot Gold Cup but was disqualified and the race awarded to Sadeem, owned ironically by Sheikh Mohammed.

Curley had a right "cut" on the Wednesday – said to be at least £20,000. The winner of the National Hunt Chase, Keep Talking, was returned at 5/2 but I know that Barney got in at a much better price than that.

Between the Tuesday and Wednesday he could have

taken between £200,000 and £250,000 out of the ring and, where generally Irish faces were glum because of the setbacks suffered by Irish-trained runners, the Fermanagh-born professional was being true to his own philosophy of not being swayed in any way by sentiment.

I asked him whether he would lay off to at least save his stake when he had a goodly sum coming off a horse like Royal Gait or Keep Moving? Would he make a 'backer's book', so to speak, by backing more than one horse in a race, assuming the odds were in his favour?

"If my judgement tells me that one horse looks outstanding, then I am not inclined to dilute it by backing another horse or other horses in the same race.

"Let's say that in my case it's whole duck or no dinner!" he added.

Barney Curley's own father was 'skint' at the dogs. Engraved indelibly in Barney's mind is the memory of the evening at Belfast's Celtic Park when his father lost everything on one make-or-break tilt on a dog he owned himself.

"He had £300 on at 7/1. Sheer disaster befell him when the dog broke its neck at the first bend. I can still see my father carrying the dead dog up the track and inside I knew he was weeping for his shattered hopes."

Barney Curley was home on holiday from boarding school when that happened. Being the eldest of six children (his parents ran the local grocery store in Irvinstown, County Fermanagh), he was taken out of the school and crossed to Manchester with his father to raise the money to clear the gambling debts.

"We lived in one room together, working double shifts in a plastics factory for fifteen months until we had raised enough money to allow my father to come home with the knowledge that he could hold his head high again in the local community because he owed no one anything. But it had affected him so deeply, it had caused such an inner wound that he wouldn't return to Irvinstown until he had bought himself a new suit. And even then he couldn't face the challenge of walking through the town. He got a friend to pick him up in his car and drop him home."

Barney Curley swore he would never be broken by the bookies. In a way every time he has hit them for six with spectacular coups, he has been settling that old score for the way his father was made suffer, especially in those long grinding days of work in Manchester – the days that Barney had shared and which proved a university of life that was incomparable in its own way.

He was a gambler as long as he can remember. And he even gambled when he was studying to become a priest.

He won't deny that his grandmother can shoulder the blame for passing the gambling bug on to him. "She used to send me to place the bets for her – three sixpenny doubles and a treble each day. One day I had a bet myself. I won £4 which in the Fifties was an absolute fortune as far as I was concerned."

The near-escape he had from death from tuberculosis taught him the salutary lesson that life itself is a gamble.

At the time he contracted T.B. he was well into his studies at Mungret College, Limerick to become a Jesuit. "One day I was out playing soccer when I got these terrible pains in my chest," he recalled for me. "They rushed me to hospital thinking I'd had a heart attack. But the x-rays revealed that I was riddled with T.B.

"I was sent to a special hospital in Northern Ireland and had to lie on my back for twelve months. They were dying like flies all around me. But I was young – I was just 21 at the time – and fortunately for me they'd just discovered a cure. The older folk and the bad cases died. I was lucky enough to pull through.

"It took me another eighteen months to get back to health. During my time in the sanatorium and the weeks and months of recuperation I formulated my own philosophy. I concluded that I wasn't going to worry about unimportant matters and that every day I woke up feeling fit and well was a bonus and that I might as well enjoy myself. For all the world like a person who wins a battle with cancer and gets another chance."

He returned to the Seminary briefly. Soon, however, the realisation dawned that he would never be strong enough to finish the gruelling studies to become a Jesuit priest. He was 24 when he packed it in.

Then despite his inherent shyness he took on the job of managing a pop group and ended up with three under his care. It is still a source of immense pride to him that under his management Frankie McBride was the first Irish showband singer to get a record into the British Top Ten.

Do you recall the number, I asked? "Recall it," he retorted. "I can never forget it. It was *Five Little Fingers*."

The Ballrooms of Romance era saw Barney Curley experience the grind of maybe leaving the Town Hall in Skibbereen at 3.30 a.m. or 4 a.m. in the morning, driving all the way back to Omagh and reaching it around 11 o'clock or midday the next day.

"The dance would finish at 2 a.m. but by the time you had put the instruments away in the wagon and had something to eat, it was well into the early hours of the morning. The main roads weren't as good then as they are now. Neither were the vehicles as good. We certainly earned our money the hard way."

He met and married Maureen who was from Cheshire of Irish parentage and the daughter of a bookmaker.

Barney was still gambling even when he was on the road. He hit a lucky streak. It saw him take a cool £100,000 from the bookies. He was able to buy three pubs with the money. But that didn't satisfy him. Neither did the life of running a betting shop.

One night Maureen and himself were lying in bed and Barney asked her if it would affect her attitude towards him if he became a full-time professional gambler? Her reaction was that whatever he decided was best, she would go along with it. She had faith in him. She trusted him.

So Barney Curley became a professional gambler and has been betting big now for almost a quarter of a century.

Now 52, he doesn't see himself still gambling at his present level when he gets to 70.

Neither would he wish his son Charles to follow in his footsteps. "I wouldn't stop him if he really wanted it but at the same time I wouldn't encourage him. I've seen too many people go broke at this game. To succeed as a professional you've got to be out of the ordinary."

There is a part of Barney Curley that is a throwback to the days when his desire to serve his fellow man steered him towards becoming a priest.

Nowadays he sees himself as the champion of the small men of racing, the ordinary little guys who have no one to fight their corner, the Willie Lomans.

He may not be the Patron Saint of Punters as such. But the manner in which he has taken on the big bookmaking chains and also the Jockey club undoubtedly added to his image of a Don Quixote, who will stop at nothing when he feels there is a wrong in racing that has to be righted. "If I see a wrong I'll fight it, no matter who it hurts or what I might lose financially," he told me.

His complaint to the Jockey club in 1987 over the way in which Graham Bradley had ridden Maureen Dickinson's horse, Robin Goodfellow in a novice hurdle at Ascot – Curley had invested £12,000 on it – became a *cause celebre*. The Jockey Club threw out Curley's complaint and then four months later he became the subject himself of a disciplinary hearing over alleged "threats of a serious nature" he had made to Bradley. He was disqualified for two years for causing "serious damage to the interests of British racing."

He had not been legally represented at the Jockey Club hearing. Now he engaged the top barrister, Richard du Cann and at a High Court hearing won an injunction lifting the ban and gaining a re-hearing of his case by the Jockey Club. The Disciplinary Committee found that while he had caused distress in phone calls to Bradley and Mrs. Dickinson, he had not breached the rules. He got his licence back.

In the euphoria of that historic victory, Barney Curley backed himself to win £275,000 if he could turn out ten winners before the end of 1987. It was a bet that caught the imagination of the public, small punters in particular.

He achieved the feat when Experimenting came home an easy winner of the Sellindge Handicap Hurdle at Folkestone on December 22. As Experimenting took up the running in jumping the last, the cry "Come on Barney" went up from the cheering crowd. Never had there been such a reception at the Kent course for a hurdle winner and the trainer.

"It's tremendous how the public latched on to my bet," said Barney who that day had the last laugh on the Jockey Club. When he originally applied for a licence to train in Britain, he had been turned down on the grounds of inexperience.

Then in a throwing down of the gauntlet to all and sundry in the bookmaking profession, he offered to put up his winnings and original stake, a total of £401,000 if anyone would lay him 2/1 against his training another ten winners inside the following three months.

There were no takers.

His jousts with the Jockey Club continued to make headlines.

He was fined £1,000 for "willful disregard of racegoers" for the late withdrawal of Ardbrin at Ascot – an action that he contended was in protest against bookmakers not offering fair odds about another of his charges which had won earlier at the same meeting.

That had no effect on him. He called the Catterick Stewards "buffoons" after he had been fined £400 over the running of his selling plater Urbi Et Orbi. The Stewards reckoned that Curley's 10/11 favourite – backed to win £17,000 on the course – "was not ridden to obtain the best possible placing." Jockey Declan Murphy, who pulled the ten-year-old up before the second-last hurdle, was also fined £400.

"That's the worst decision ever," stormed Barney after learning of the fines imposed on himself and Declan Murphy. "What they (the Stewards) know in there is about as much as I know about cricket and all I know is it's played with a bat and ball. They are just getting by on buffoonery.

"What really hurts is that the public will read it in the papers and think I've pulled a fast one."

Barney told the Stewards that Urbi Et Orbi – a winner at Market Rasen ten days previously – was not going well from the first hurdle in the back straight.

He told the racing writers after the inquiry that he was satisfied with Declan Murphy's riding and added: "That horse has a history of leg trouble. What did they want Murphy to do? Abuse him and finish 15th?"

His attack angered the Catterick Stewards. Lord Ronalishay said: "I am surprised at Mr. Curley's abuse. Nobody who watched the race and saw the film afterwards can have been in any doubt that the rules were broken. Mr. Curley's jockey made no effort whatsoever to maintain or improve his position in the race from a long way out. And, by the time he did give his horse a slap, all chance had gone."

Amazingly enough, Barney Curley will tell you that he has nothing personal against the Stewards of the Jockey Club. In fact, he respected the way he was given a re-hearing after bringing the High Court injunction in the "Bradley Affair" and then being given his licence back. In a word, he believed that there were battles he just had to fight and when he proved he was right, then the Jockey Club for their part didn't hold anything against him. "I can say that they are honourable men," he said, adding that he has been so many times in the Jockey Club building he should be made an honorary member!

Meanwhile he came into open conflict with Satellite Information Services (SIS), being highly-critical of betting shows relayed by them to betting shops. He was very critical too that the bookies had such a powerful share in SIS.

SIS flatly rejected his accusations and went so far as to announce that they were considering taking legal action against him in order to clear their name. SIS also made it clear that writs would be issued if the media continued to publish Barney Curley's allegations against the organisation.

Nothing it seemed could stifle him completely. I have no doubt that the crusader in him will go with him to the grave.

The fact that he wasn't born with a silver spoon in his mouth has allowed Barney Curley to walk with kings and keep the common touch.

He may have many of the trappings of wealth but he takes them for granted and cannot be said to be ostentatious. For example, for a long time he was driving what he describes himself as "an old banger", so much so that his family advised him that he was a danger to himself and to others on the road.

So he bowed to them and bought a new Mercedes and then with that mischievous element in his make-up he got the lettering put on the number plate: "1 BET".

But he has never forgotten the lessons of the time he spent in Manchester with his father. "It was the toughest period of my life but if I had my time all over again, I wouldn't try and run away from it.

"If you don't go through hard times, you don't appreciate the good. I feel many youngsters today miss out on life. Things are too easy for them. It gets to the stage where they appreciate nothing."

That is why, I reckon, Barney likes to see his son, Charles doing manual work around the yard. The last thing he wants is to see him growing up soft.

When Barney Curley is out working horses in the back he can never escape seeing the spot where Terry Ramsden once had his helicopter pad.

That was before the crash in the financial sense, before the bookies picked his bones clean.

Barney Curley will never allow the bookies to do the same to him.

The memory of his father carrying a dead dog down a track in Belfast after losing every penny he had in the world is far too vivid.

Barney Curley had a narrow escape from death on Friday evening, July 11, 1992 when the Cessna six-seater which he was sharing with South African jockey, Michael Roberts and Irish-born lightweight, Jimmy Quinn, who earlier in the year had won the William Hill Lincoln Handicap on High Low, ended up in a dyke after pilot Neil Foreman was forced to abort take-off when a wheel came off.

Curley, Roberts and Quinn were returning to Newmarket from the Chester evening meeting.

Foreman, who six years ago received the Queen's award for gallantry after being shot in the stomach by a bank robber when he was an off-duty policeman, performed miracles to "soften the crash."

"We ploughed through the edge of some trees and hedges and the plane started spinning, but Neil managed to avoid the big stuff and held on to it and guided us into a dyke, said Michael Roberts.

"We found ourselves in stinking green water, well above the waist and my first thoughts were to get out before the plane exploded.

"Jimmy (Quinn) could not swim, so Barney (Curley) carried him on his back to safety. It was a terrifying experience, and for those few seconds I could feel the whole world turning round. I never want to go through that again."

The aircraft ended up a total write-off, while its four occupants were taken to Chester Hospital with superficial injuries. Quinn had four stitches inserted under his left eye.

Curley, pale and drawn and visibly shocked, said: "We were feeling hungry outside Chester and asked the driver to stop for some kebabs.

"When the shopkeeper saw us walk in wearing pyjamas, he wanted to call the police, thinking we were escapees from a mental asylum!"

Curley made headlines again in the racing press a week after his escape in the plane crash, when he announced that he was giving up training. "My stables are closed and I am no longer prepared to burn money," he said.

It appeared that he was going to concentrate all his efforts on his favourite pastime – taking on the bookies as a professional punter.

Then in another surprise development, it was reported early in August that Barney Curley was to continue training after all. He leased half of Eve Lodge stables from close friends, Lester and Susan Piggott and planned to train from there, although he and his family would remain at Exning.

He explained that he had no other choice but to keep going as a trainer as he had failed to dispose of all his horses once he put them on the market. "In fact, I've sold only one horse since I made the announcement that I was giving up training – for the princely sum of £1,350."

He had about 40 horses in all, most of them stores. The bookies didn't greet the news with any marked enthusiasm.

They had cause to remember a Curley "sting" or two.

PART TWO

NOEL FURLONG
"You May Only Get One
Chance of a Real Killing"

3

The Secret Gallop that Killed a £4 Million Dream

I met him in his world of carpets, some of them made to his own specifications as far away as Pakistan. His office, in no way ostentatious, was like an oasis in the giant warehouse in the industrial estate off the Naas road where you turn right at Joe Wong's restaurant. As I entered, one of the employees driving a forklift was moving rolls of carpets and I jumped out of his way as I went to greet Noel Furlong, standing there like a thick-set American airforce commander in the vastness of a hangar housing the planes of war.

All the time big trucks that you wouldn't like to meet on a hairpin bend in Ireland's rural heartlands were coming and going, either supplementing supplies or heading off to meet orders that had come in from various parts. He would be flying out from Dublin Airport next morning to expand his outlets in Britain.

Noel Furlong is a BIG man. He is big and swarthy physically. They knew him simply as "Big Noel" in the days when he was deeply involved in dog racing in Belfast. "It was natural, I suppose, when there seemed to be so many small guys frequenting the tracks," said a friend who added with a smile: "No, you could never describe him as a *wee mon*".

Now in his early fifties and father of three daughters, he has been one of the biggest 'players' in the Irish ring since he turned his attention to horses.

His big, hearty laugh impresses when he talks of the way he caught the bookmakers with their pants down for a cool million pounds on The Illiad in the 1991 Ladbroke Handicap Hurdle at Leopardstown.

He laughs even more heartily at the way he had them literally shaking to the soles of their feet at the prospect of facing the biggest pay-out in racing history globally — £4 million in fact — if the same horse had won the 1991 Smurfit Champion Hurdle at the National Hunt Festival meeting.

He is big in his vision of what represents a real coup. "You may only get one chance of catching the bookies for the kind of gamble from which they will not easily recover. I went for that kind of touch in doubling Destriero with The Illiad on the first day of the Cheltenham '91 meeting. I knew that Destriero was as near a good thing to win the first race on the card as there can be in racing. I had already won enough on The Illiad in the Ladbroke to make it so that I was playing with bookies' money in going for the jugular and the kill.

"So really it came down to whether The Illiad would win the Champion Hurdle and complete the double. On top of what I had won on him in the Ladbroke I had my winnings, coming to over a million pounds from Destriero in single bets.

"As it happened there was nearly £500,000 going on to The Illiad at varying odds in the doubles. If it had come off, it would have netted me £4 million. I don't think it made that much difference that he hit the fourth flight and ruined any chance he might have had. To draw an analogy from Flat racing, he ran his Derby on Ladbroke Hurdle day.

"But even though he failed, I won money — big money — on the day as a result of Destriero taking the Trafalgar House Supreme Novices Hurdle at returned odds of 6/1. Anyway, I gave the big English bookies a fright they won't easily forget. If they had never prayed before, they were certainly praying that Tuesday at Cheltenham and it would have been their 'unlucky 13th of March' with a vengeance. Who was it — Ladbroke's man, I think — who

45

said afterwards: 'It was a wonderful advertisement for the power of prayer'."

Whereas J.P. McManus makes no bones about it when he tells you frankly that he is a professional gambler whether punting on the horses or laying the odds, Noel Furlong will tell you simply: "I am not a professional Punter."

And he confesses that the thrill for him in in going for a "killing" and bringing one off — as in the case of The Illiad in the Ladbroke and Destriero in the Trafalgar House Supreme Novices Hurdle — and not in laying off so that the risks involved will be reduced to the minimum.

I quoted to him the maxim of the professionals that the only good bet is one where the element of risk can be all but eliminated. For example, if you had an ante-post bet on Shahrastani at longer odds than the 11/2 the Aga Khan's colt started at in the 1986 Epsom Derby and concluded on the day that the only real danger was Dancing Brave, then was it not the obvious thing to lay off — to ensure that your stake on Shahrastani was covered? I told him I had done just that — and, in fact, the ante-post odds I got on Shahrastani meant that I was going to win anyway, whichever of the two colts came out on top on the day?

Noel Furlong replied: "I know a professional or one adopting the approach of a professional would naturally lay off in such circumstances. It might seem crazy not to do so. But let me repeat — if I believe, as I did in the case of The Illiad in the Ladbroke and Destriero in the Supreme Novices Hurdle, that a horse of ours cannot get beat, then I don't look for dangers in the race and start to lay off. Now in the case of the double I had on Destriero and The Illiad, it was different. I knew that once Destriero won, the money going on The Illiad would be such that I was in line for the biggest killing in racing history for no outlay on my part. The winnings I had from the single bets on Destriero ensured that and in addition I already had £1 million in the bank from The Illiad's win in the Ladbroke. I was, in fact, £2 million in front of the bookmakers as The Illiad went to the post for the Smurfit Champion Hurdle and the double bets were a bonus if they came off."

Noel Furlong admits that he is not interested as a punter

46

in small, steady winnings through a process of what you might describe as "risk elimination". And as an owner he is not turned on either by the thought of picking up a small race at Bellewstown or Sligo, for example. Leopardstown on the big National Hunt days and Cheltenham in March is his kind of scene.

He prefers to go for a touch in major events where the market is likely to be strong and he will get a price to his money. Thus he was attracted by the Ladbroke Handicap Hurdle and, despite their liabilities on The Illiad, there was no way the bookies were going to make him favourite ahead of the two English invaders, Wonder Man, which started 3/1 favourite and Riverhead, which went off at 9/2.

He was also very attracted by the Supreme Novices Hurdle because again Destriero, even though he had won quite impressively at the Leopardstown Christmas meeting, was not going to displace the Martin Pipe-trained Granville Again from 2/1 favouritism while the weight of Irish money was going on the Dermot Weld-trained General Idea, which started second favourite at 5/1 and the Jim Bolger-trained Nordic Surprise.

In the wake of the 1991 Cheltenham Festival, Noel Furlong on his own admission gave back £100,000 of his winnings to the bookmakers but set against overall winnings of well over £2 million, it wasn't a body-blow, considering the scale of his punting. He was taking a temporary holiday from serious betting at the time I went to interview him in April '91 and it was being felt in the Irish ring.

He holds firmly to the view that by being a careful student of the form book you can make racing pay. This means being able to judge how certain trainers operate and when the horses in their charge have reached the point of fitness that they are in with a real chance of winning — in a handicap, for example — and should win, assuming all goes according to plan. In reading the form then, you must be able to get into the minds of the trainers and be able to figure out from experience their *modus operandi*. The skill in that was fascinating in itself. It fascinated Noel Furlong.

47

On that very basis he first hit the big time in 1985 when he won £50,000 at Royal Ascot by putting £5,000 each way on Time Machine which was thrown into the handicap as a result of an error by the handicapper. Later he was reported to have grumbled to a friend: "I wish I had bet £25,000 each way but I lost my nerve at the last minute."

No one would accuse him of having lost his nerve when he asked Ladbrokes to take enough on The Illiad in the 1991 Ladbroke Handicap Hurdle so that he would win £2 million. They would only facilitate him to the extent of a £10,000 bet each-way at 33/1. You don't need a calculator to tell you that this single bet stood to win him over £400,000 — if it came off. But he didn't stop. He went for what you would call "a morning board prices killing".

On the morning of the race itself — Saturday, January 12, 1991 to be exact — The Illiad was being quoted at 10/1 in the S.P. offices. Agents of Noel Furlong hit the offices with a vengeance. They took all available prices down to 7/1. Meanwhile too, the whirlwind action reached Ascot racecourse where J.P. McManus was on the spot to see his horse contest and emerge a convincing winner of the Victor Chandler Chase. In fact as a result of the bets laid at Ascot, where J.P. was right in the middle of the action, some of the bigger bookmakers stopped taking bets on The Illiad.

The phenomenon of 'morning board prices' give the S.P. job operators an opportunity of beating the bookies in another way — but at the same time it can alert the bookies and allow them to take the necessary precautions. In a highly-competitive business there are bookies who like to be ahead of their rivals by offering a price on every horse running at an Irish race meeting and seeing to it that it is available when their string of offices open in the morning. Now if you had an office in Kildare or Newbridge or Naas, you could have stable lads or friends of work riders dropping in to have a "cut" on a good thing. The £30 or £50 bet from someone in the know on a two year old that had never been out before could alert Head Office to the fact that this particular colt or filly was "on the job". And instead of being hit on the course itself, the bookmaker in question would put up an opening price on his board in the ring that would ensure that he was not going to be taken to the cleaners.

By backing The Illiad at the morning board prices of 10/1 down to 7/1 Noel Furlong knew exactly what he was getting to his money. As one friend of his put it to me: "He had the bookies strangled. It was a beautifully-executed coup, as good a gamble as was ever brought off on a big race in Ireland."

You see, if he had made it an S.P. job, the money would have been blown back to the course and the starting price reduced considerably. In this instance it would have been no use reducing the price say to 3/1 or even 5/2 as Furlong had already got 10/1 right down to 7/1 to all his bets. The reason that The Illiad started at 7/1 was that the bookmakers were simply laying off to cover their own liabilities and not spreading money around the ring to compress the starting price.

I have confirmed from Noel Furlong himself that he cleared over £1 million pounds as a result of The Illiad winning the Ladbroke. Pat Williams brought the Bonne Noel–Star Vision gelding up on the inside of the leader Bawnmore Lad on the turn for home to win by 2½ lengths from Bawnmore Lad with Riverhead third.

Already at the Leopardstown Christmas meeting he had a nice little cut on Destriero. He knew he had "the goods" in this one for the Cheltenham Festival meeting.

The price was going to be right for him also as the word from England was that the Martin Pipe stable couldn't see Granville Again beaten, especially after the manner in which he had hacked up by fifteen lengths when winning the Dovecote Novices' Hurdle at Kempton the previous month in the hands of Peter Scudamore in a field of fourteen.

And Dermot Weld was really confident that General Idea would follow up his impressive six-lengths win in the Le Coq Hardi Novices Hurdle at Leopardstown by taking care of Granville Again. Likewise Jim Bolger had high hopes for Nordic Surprise, which had three lengths to spare over Nomadic Way, the runner-up to Kribensis in the

1990 Champion Hurdle, when taking the Wessel Cable Champion Hurdle at Leopardstown on Saturday, February 3rd. That certainly was form — good enough to impress any professional.

Again I have confirmed with Noel Furlong that he took £1 million out of the ring as a result of Destriero's four-lengths triumph over Granville Again with Gran Alba third, Nordic Surprise fourth and General Idea fifth.

Now in the count-down to the Cheltenham Festival meeting he tried The Illiad and Destriero in a final gallop. They came out level. It convinced him that if Destriero as a novice could come out equal on level terms to the Ladbroke Handicap Hurdle winner, then he was even more of a certainty for Cheltenham — whatever the opposition and whatever was emerging from the stables of Martin Pipe, Dermot Weld and Jim Bolger.

No one knew about that gallop only Noel Furlong and his wife, Betty and a few intimate friends. Furlong 'went to war' accordingly on Destriero to take the Trafalgar House Supreme Novices' Hurdle and coupled him in double bets with The Illiad that effectively had a massive six-figure sum going on the gelding at odds of 16/1 down to 12/1 when on the day of the race itself he was to start no less than 11/2 because of the bookmakers' liabilities.

Unfortunately the rehabilitated "crock", The Illiad left the Champion Hurdle behind him when he performed so well in that final gallop — on top of his brilliant performance in winning the Ladbroke. A young horse like Destriero, who could only improve, was able to take it and go on from the question asked of him in that gallop. The Illiad couldn't.

On the morning of the Smurfit Champion Hurdle, Betty Furlong told her husband that she didn't think The Illiad was right. It was not a question of him not being able to run or being off colour. No, it was that the woman whose healing hands had ensured that he would land a £1 million gamble for her husband in the Ladbroke knew now that he was unlikely to reproduce his Leopardstown run on the first day of the National Hunt Festival meeting.

If Noel Furlong was a professional gambler he would

there and then have hedged his double bets. He could easily have offered a price about The Illiad to punters of his acquaintance who would have been happy to get better odds to their money than was available from the on-course bookmakers at that point. He could even have backed the favourite Morley Street — if he saw Toby Balding's charge as the only danger. he had enough options to eliminate all risk — and add substantially to his winnings on Destriero.

But he was no professional punter and he wasn't thinking like a professional punter at that point in time. He was playing with bookies' money and to hell with it, why lay off.

He knew that after Destriero had justified his confidence by winning the Supreme Novices Hurdle the big bookmakers would realise the level of their commitments on The Illiad. He knew that they would go pale around the gills at the thought of a £4 million pay day.

There was nothing for it then only to back The Illiad back which saw him start at a price that was ridiculously short considering that he was a rehabilitated crock who might have won a big handicap hurdle but which the professionals hardly judged as a potential Champion Hurdle winner.

And they started praying.

Meanwhile Noel Furlong was laughing heartily in private at their discomfort. If he had come in out of the skies on a magic carpet to Cheltenham racecourse, he couldn't have made such a story for the racing writers.

On the one hand there was action in the ring on the Illiad as the big layers cut their commitments. On the other, there was whirlwind action in the Press Room as the writers got wind of what Noel Furlong stood to win and learned also that he had settled for £500,000 with the Inland Revenue in Britain over proceedings that had been initiated against him some years earlier ("it was my customers who didn't pay the VAT and now I've had to pay it for them," he insisted) just to be there to see Destriero take the Supreme Novices Hurdle — and cheer The Illiad home if he triumphed in the Champion.

It was not to be — but, my God, how the bookies

51

shivered in the count-down to the third race on the card on that first day of the 1991 Cheltenham Festival meeting. And how they cheered when they saw him hit the fourth hurdle and kill whatever chance he had of winning the race.

Noel Furlong wasn't crying over the lost opportunity. It was not his way. For, as we shall see, there was from the very outset a streak in him that saw him cut out to take risks — and go for the jugular.

4

Married to the Girl With the Healing Hands

Noel Furlong does not attempt to conceal the pride in his voice every time he talks about his wife, Betty and the amazing way she has with those healing hands of hers.

He acknowledges that the fact that he took a cool million pounds from the bookmakers over the Illiad's success in the 1991 Ladbroke Handicap Hurdle had to be put down almost solely to her uncanny skill and to the way she brought this 'crock' back to the point where he could land such a spectacular gamble in a highly-competitive event.

But then he had reason to know her capabilities long before she turned her attention to the horses.

It was during his sojourn in Northern Ireland that he fell in love with dark-haired Betty, with the Elizabeth Taylor looks, meeting her first in fact when she was just sweet sixteen. She hailed from Portstewart. Theirs in a way was a meeting of kindred souls. In the world of dog racing and on the coursing circuit she was admired as a genius when it came to applying her gifts as an animal therapeutist in instances where a greyhound needed the healing touch and on her own admission she "loves animals". At coursing meetings her services were frequently in demand. And more than one successful owner had reason to lift his glass in a toast to her contribution. Those same hands were to help restore The Illiad to health.

Some years back she told Noel to buy three saplings —

she didn't care at what price he would purchase them but guaranteed to him that to prove a point about her theories she would make all three winners — if not champions. In time Ger McKenna, rated one of the best trainers in the business by shrewd judges of greyhound racing in Ireland and Britain, asked to buy one of them. He wasn't prepared at that point to pay the price being asked but came back later and paid £20,000 for the same dog.

Little wonder that Noel Furlong decided that rather than have his horses with public trainers he would train his own — or rather Betty would be at the helm. So having acquired a yard and put a string of close on twenty horses together, he had Betty apply for a licence to the Turf Club. She was turned down — a bitter setback for the Furlongs.

No reason was given. In such instances the Turf Club doesn't have to give a reason. No doubt Noel Furlong speculates to himself in private the reason why — but he won't say anything publicly.

Andy Geraghty was called out of virtual retirement and he had no problem in getting a licence to train the Furlong horses. All the requirements on a proper yard and access to gallops were met, for Noel and Betty Furlong were not sparing any expense.

But if Andy Geraghty's name went into the racing records in parenthesis as the successful trainer in the case of the Leopardstown successes of Destriero and The Illiad and Destriero's victory at Cheltenham, Noel Furlong impressed upon me that he wanted Betty to take most of the credit. "Without her contribution, especially in the case of The Illiad, there would have been nothing," he said.

In the case of The Illiad racing men had written him off and at one stage it didn't seem likely that he would race again. Betty Furlong corrected the back ailment and got him to the point where he was not alone fit to win at the Leopardstown Christmas meeting but that he hit a new peak for the Ladbroke. "A lot of people can spot an old injury but she will be able to identify a new problem that turns up and which can set a horse back if not worked on and put right," Noel told me. "The Illiad would be regarded in racing circles as brittle and that was why I was able to get that £10,000 each way on him at 33/1 with Ladbrokes. But the bookies hadn't reckoned with Betty's gifts."

Fitness, he contends, in horses as in humans can be about the well-being achieved when any physical problems have been FULLY corrected. Any trainer, no matter what his ability, could go out with his charges on the gallops for first lot and second lot or even third lot, depending on the size of the stable in question and the patronage it commands. Putting the horses through their paces and galloping them in the count-down to the races they are targeted to win, can all be meaningless and fruitless if there are hidden injuries in instances that prevent a horse from giving 100 per cent on the day.

Furthermore, there is the necessity once a horse has achieved a winning level to maintain that level — if one is to go on to greater things. Once again the emergence of a small problem between one race and the next can spoil everything.

Noel Furlong explained that The Illiad was being laid out for the Ladbroke Handicap Hurdle. The victory at the Leopardstown Christmas meeting was but a precursor to that. It revealed to Betty and himself that the gelding was right — "but we both knew that more improvement could be achieved, far more. It was here that Betty scored — in ensuring that The Illiad, having come through the Christmas test successfully, didn't have any re-occurrence of earlier problems but was brought to an even greater pitch of excellence for the day that really mattered.

"If I had been a Vincent O'Brien, I might not have subjected The Illiad to the final gallop with Destriero — a gallop aimed at telling me exactly where both stood in the lead-up to Cheltenham. I would probably have foreseen that a gelding that had come back from serious ailment could leave his best on the gallop. You learn from your mistakes. I learned from this one. If we hadn't had that gallop I am convinced that The Illiad would have put in a run on Champion Hurdle Day comparable with his run in the Ladbroke. I am not saying he would have won it, for he had his one BIG day in the Leopardstown event.

However, as Betty spotted and conveyed to me before Champion Hurdle Day, the horse wasn't right — and that was that."

Noel Furlong allowed Betty to take the giant share of the acclaim in the unsaddling enclosure at Leopardstown after The Illiad had won the Ladbroke Handicap Hurdle. He allowed her also to bask in the sunshine of the adulation of friends and admirers after Destriero had taken the winner's spot following his impressive victory in the Trafalgar House Supreme Novices Hurdle at the National Hunt Festival meeting. He was content to stand to one side and take it all in. Men like the intrepid Mick O'Toole and legendary bloodstock agent, Jack Doyle were among the first to seek him out and shake his hand. They realised the level of achievement in Destriero accounting not alone for Granville Again, the hope of England, but for General Idea and Nordic Surprise, the two more fancied of the Irish challengers.

Noel Furlong had come a long way from the time in his late teens when his father, a Sergeant in the Garda Siochana in Dun Laoghaire, wanted him to get a steady job at home. Noel's father retired early from the Garda — at 40 in fact — and ran a snooker and billiards hall in Dun Laoghaire. Noel could have been of help to his father in the business but already he was attracted by broader horizons.

The sea called — for a time. One day he was on a boat that arrived in Belfast and he began to play the dog tracks. Soon he had said goodbye to life on the ocean wave and had, in effect, entered the world of gambling.

He teamed up with the renowned 'Major' Bobby Dahl, feared by the bookmakers for the manner in which he could plan and execute a coup. The Major soon had Furlong doing the commissions for him; if Dahl were to try and bet on a dog in 'readies' any board would be swiftly wiped clean.

Later Noel Furlong and his wife had their own dogs. The bookies came to fear a Furlong runner which was 'expected' as previously they had feared him when he was 'doing the business' for Major Bobby Dahl.

Noel Furlong in time would get out of the dogs because

"he couldn't get on", to quote one of his friends.

"Immediately a Furlong dog went up on the boards, it would almost inevitably open at 4/6, if not less."

Another friend told us: "If Noel was £10,000 down going into the last and wanted to have £15,000 to £10,000 on a 6/4 shot or even £30,000 to £20,000 on a 4/6 shot to get out, there was no way he could get that kind of money on. Really, it was hopeless."

In horse racing, of course, it was different. At least when it came to the big handicap events and the major Festival meetings of the National Hunt scene like Cheltenham and Liverpool and great occasions on the Flat like Royal Ascot. It was a case of how much you were prepared to invest and at what odds you wanted to your money rather than a case of how much you could get on. The market at Cheltenham is so keen, for example, that if you had a horse that was not in the first two in the betting, you would get real value for money and that was why Noel Furlong could get 6/1 about Destriero and better on the course as the weight of money was for Granville Again, General Idea and Nordic Surprise. There would be no 6/1 about Destriero in a novice hurdle at Naas or Navan. Not if Noel Furlong was putting the money down in the ring.

Those who know the betting business and the machinations of the Irish ring are agreed that Furlong is a fearless gambler — one of the most fearless that has ever hit the scene. When the mood takes him, he is wont to go in with the 'head down' for a real old-fashioned cut on a horse he cannot see beaten.

"Where you will find professional gamblers looking for every reason NOT to bet on a horse and prepared to hedge if necessary to cover their stake, Furlong will just not hear of defeat if he thinks he has the goods. That explains why he went for a £1 million killing on The Illiad in the Ladbroke. In his case he will aim for the moon and nothing less in the gambling sense," said a friend. "He simply has no nerves in the normal sense."

Subsequent to Cheltenham '91 there came the parting of the ways between Andy Geraghty and himself. He applied to the Turf Club for a licence to train his own horses, was granted it and now Destriero and The Illiad, instead of being listed as trained by Andy Geraghty, were prepared for their engagements by Noel Furlong with the assistance of his wife. Some contended that the Furlongs might have been wiser to have appointed an experienced private trainer for the close on 20 horses in the stable.

Destriero's principal target was the 1992 Smurfit Champion Hurdle. He ran second behind Trapper John on his initial outing of the season in a 2m 3f hurdle at Navan on December 14, 1991.

I went down to the Curragh to interview Noel and Betty Furlong in the count-down to the Leopardstown Christmas meeting. I saw at first hand her expertise in dealing with any horse that had a problem. You could see immediately that she knew exactly what she was about and could pinpoint with precision where the trouble spot was and what was required to correct it. For example, she revealed to me that at one stage there were those who were convinced that The Illiad's problem was "in his mind" and that he could never be trusted to "put it in" again in a race when the money was down.

"I discovered that it was in his back rather than in his mind. The result was that when we eventually got him right and really fit for the 1991 Ladbroke Hurdle, we were able to land a gamble that many pundits had deemed impossible with what they judged to be a crock at one stage in his career."

Already Noel Furlong was contemplating a killing on Destriero in the Champion Hurdle, though obviously he deeply respected the reigning champion Morley Street. As he put it to me — "a champion is a champion and until he is beaten, you cannot ignore him." Furlong had a cut on Destriero in the Bookmakers Hurdle at Leopardstown on December 29. In fact, as I entered the racecourse, I met Noel and, displaying total confidence, he said: "We'll win this one."

The gelding, which was on the boards in the ring at one point at 4/6, started at 4/5. He was close up when falling at the third flight, the Victor Bowens-trained Galeville Express taking the race by a short head from Clippie Lad.

In the Paschal Butler Champion Hurdle at Leopardstown on Saturday, February 1, '92, Destriero started second favourite at 7/2 to Morley Street, which went off at 8/11. Mistakes ruined whatever chance he had and he finished second last of the nine runners as the Jim Bolger-trained 20/1 chance, Chirkpar got up to pip Morley Street by a short head in a photo finish.

Destriero, after all, did not make it to the '92 Cheltenham Festival meeting.

The day I talked to him at the Curragh, Noel Furlong told me that he would be aiming The Illiad at novice chases in the New Year, because, after the Ladbroke Handicap Hurdle win of the previous year, he realised that he would not be shown any favours by the handicapper. I was surprised then to see him running in the '92 Ladbroke Hurdle. And even more surprised to learn that Noel Furlong had gone for another fearless gamble, even though the gelding was carrying 11st 9lbs and on the book could not be said to have anything like the chance he had the previous year when he had 10st 13lbs on his back.

There were conflicting reports as to what Furlong would have taken from the bookies had The Illiad triumphed for the second year running. Some estimates were that he would have won far more than in '91. Suffice it to say that Corals admitted that their ante-post liabilities alone would have come to £250,000. So you can conclude that Furlong had really "gone to war" on The Illiad.

In mid division most of the way, The Illiad was being ridden three out and eventually finished tenth behind the John Brassil-trained How's The Boss (10st 2lbs), another dream ride for Jason Titley.

It cannot be taken from Noel Furlong that when he really believed that a horse of his was going to win, then there was no one to equal him when it came to putting down the readies to support his own beliefs. And he had to be admired also in that he didn't cry in his cups in defeat. He took his successes, like the spectacular winning gambles on The Illiad and Destriero in 1991, in the same fashion that he took his setbacks. A gambler all his life, he knew you had to be able to take the heat in the kitchen.

The gambler's life wasn't one for wimps.

The career of this most colourful of characters could fill a book in itself, as it involves chapters of history from Northern Ireland to South Africa, Britain to the gambling halls of Las Vegas and back to the private roulette tables and poker games in Dublin. And fearsome tilts at the ring.

Friends talk in awe of how, after he had become Irish poker champion at the Texas Hold 'Em game, he took on the cream of the professionals in Las Vegas, including Stu (The Kid) Ungar and Doyle (Texas Dolly) Brunson, both dual world champions, and a host of others and actually reached the final table in the 1989 World Championship with over one million dollars in prize-money, of which the winners would receive 755,000 dollars.

Hold 'Em Poker — often called "Texas Hold 'Em" because it originated in that American State in the late 1800s — sees the dealer dealing each player two cards face down (known as "hole" cards). The dealer now deals three consecutive cards face up in the middle of the table. These cards are called the "flop". They are community cards used in common by every player still in the hand (for example, if you had an Ace in the first two cards dealt to you face downwards and one came up in the "flop", you would already have a pair and this is where Hold 'Em differs sharply from draw poker).

The real excitement comes in the dealing of the last two cards face up in the middle of the table — known as "Fourth Street" and "Fifth Street". There is, of course, betting on each round and matters can change very quickly. You could have two Aces after Fourth Street only to be outdrawn by another player who ends up with three Tens after Fifth Street. It is the player who commands the best hand between the two in his hand and the five in the middle who takes the pot — unless, of course, he is bluffed into folding or an opponent happens to have an equal hand, in which case the pot will be split.

Now Noel Furlong had been winning the commendation of the commentator calling the action in Binion's by his "aggressive play throughout". At one stage he said: "The Irishman is betting on garbage hands but

facing down opponents who think he has the nuts —
opponents with far more experience of the professional
circuit."

Now Noel Furlong draws two fours and, looking across
at Johnny Chan, reckons that the world champion may in
his "hole" cards have had an Ace/Jack or Ace/Queen at
best, anyway an Ace with something or other.

As it was, Chan had a pair of Queens and there was a
half a million dollars in the pot when they both went all in.
Nothing came in the flop to help Furlong build on his
hand — and the crucial four that would have saved the
day for him and seen him in a winning position for the title
itself, did not come either. He was the first of the final six
players to be eliminated, ending up winning 52,850
dollars.

The aficionados of the Texas Hold 'Em game will argue
that he made a mistake in going all in on a pair of fours.
He agrees in cold retrospect that he was "obviously
wrong" to do so.

But he explained to me what had made all the
difference. "I was on song with everything going my way
and I had visions, in fact, of going all the way and lifting
the crown when a break was called. It shattered my
momentum at the crucial juncture. I am certain of that
now. Anyway, when play resumed I said 'to heck with it'
and decided on an all-or-nothing break. All right, it didn't
come off but if I had drawn a four, I would have been
credited with out-drawing the world champion and I
would have been a hero. It has happened on Fifth Street
before but it didn't happen for me in this instance.

"Boil it all down in the end and I was effectively an
amateur at this level playing against the most hardened
professionals in the world — and playing too for a lot of
money all of the time. Frankly, I was a bit out of my class.
It's very, very difficult to come into Las Vegas and pull it
off, especially when it comes down to the last table and
experience can count for so much. All told, I think I did
well in taking sixth place."

Noel Furlong went back to Las Vegas in 1990 and was
tournament leader with 10,000 in chips at the end of the

first day.

His gambling instincts don't permit him to stop at poker or betting on horses. He has been known to wage thousands at roulette, no doubt concluding that one can get 'an edge' as the ball spins, but your true-blue professional who gambles only on horses would NEVER allow himself to be a victim of the spin of a wheel or the toss of a dice.

Likewise he has been known to go from the poker table in Las Vegas to the crap tables, where again the odds are inevitably stacked against the gambler.

The born professional will see himself as an investor and not a gambler, being happy with definite percentage winnings overall on the money staked over a year. With Noel Furlong there is no such thing as a 'safety' out. The instinct is go for a killing — aim for the moon as with that 1991 Cheltenham double with Destriero and The Illiad.

Again he stresses that he's not a professional punter. He emphasises also that while the scale of his betting might seem awe-inspiring if not frightening to ordinary people trying to survive on a fixed income in face of crippling PAYE in a country like Ireland, he has not allowed his business to be affected by his gambling.

He can meet his commitments to the bookies when he loses and that is why he could get a bet of £10,000 each way on The Illiad with Ladbrokes and why he was able to get such big money on Destriero at Cheltenham.

Up in Belfast the small men who frequent the dogs and who knew him from his days as a fearless layer talk with new respect these days of 'Big Noel'.

And of Betty Furlong, the girl with the healing hands.

PART THREE

J. P. McMANUS
The Man They Know As
"The Sundance Kid"

5

J.P. And The Attainment Of Maturity

It's a grey day in January, 1992. The Galtees in the distance are shrouded in mist and there is only the sound of the jackdaws in the trees to break the silence.

Over lunch in the dining room of his spacious home at the Martinstown Stud Farm near Kilmallock, County Limerick, J.P. McManus, who would celebrate his 41st birthday during the '92 Cheltenham Festival meeting, talked to me about his attainment of maturity as a professional gambler.

There is no racing in Ireland on this Tuesday, so he has time to develop on his theme and on the principles and ground rules by which the true professionals operate. The main piece of advice to those who are serious about their gambling and who are prepared to observe the ground rules is: (1) "Never chase your losses" and (2) "There is never a last race".

Chasing losses, he asserts, is the bane of many a punter's life. There is always tomorrow. One must scrupulously avoid seeing the last race as the "getting out stakes".

"The professional operates differently from the amateur. His approach is to get the very best out of a good run and when in a bad run, to ensure that he lives to fight another day," is how J.P. McManus expresses it as he pours the white wine.

He also expands on his liking for the challenge, which he views as an integral part of life and which he finds annually at the Cheltenham Festival meeting as one finds it nowhere else in the world.

That love of action has also seen him play in major backgammon tournaments in Monte Carlo, Florida, the Bahamas and other centres around the globe. There could be up to 700 or 800 players involved, from all parts of the world.

On one occasion he won the World Championship Consolation Tournament. Apart from the actual tournaments, one invariably found terrific action in side games and very serious gambling. "I have seen more heavy wagering on those occasions than I have seen on the racecourse. However, I always seemed to get my expenses when I took part in major tournaments," he recalled.

The compelling need for action and the liking for a challenge can also be seen in the way in which he will test his ability as a golfer (and he is reckoned to be no mean performer off his double-figure handicap) in head-to-head fourballs, partnered maybe by his friend, Coolmore Stud boss, John Magnier, another player not to be underestimated off his handicap. The "big match" may be against local men Eric Browne and Michael Nagle over the Ballybunion links and for J.P. always, more important than the money involved would be the prestige of winning.

Then again the major test might be in an international setting as when John Magnier, Dermot Desmond and himself teamed up together to take part in the Annual Charity Golf Outing at Sunningdale on the eve of Royal Ascot '91 and backed themselves at the same time with Surrey Racing Bookmakers to finish in the top spot, bringing off a nice "touch" in the process.

He has invariably graced the Vincent O'Brien Golf Classic held in recent years at Thurles for the Irish Equine Centre.

And, of course, he is right in the thick of the action too in the Charity Pro-Am run at the Sandy Lane course in Barbados each January by another of his close friends, Robert Sangster.

The world is J.P.'s oyster when it comes to answering the need for a throw of the dice in the figurative sense.

The man to whom they gave the name "The Sundance

Kid" in the Seventies because of his awesome tilts at the ring, especially at Cheltenham, has on his own admission "grown older" but that does not mean that the legend has diminished in any way. He is now more selective. The recklessness that marked his betting in his twenties is a thing of the past. Yet when he goes in with the proverbial "head down" on a prime fancy, you can be certain that he has lost none of his steely courage or his willingness to have a real old-fashioned cut.

However, he prefers nowadays, if he can manage it, to avoid centre stage when planning and executing a stroke.

"What is the best stroke in racing"? is the rhetorical question he poses across the table as he tops up my glass. Incidentally, he doesn't take a glass himself – in fact, he never touches wine with a meal. However, he may take a whiskey occasionally before dinner with friends or afterwards as he finds that it makes him more relaxed in conversation.

"The best stroke is the one that no one knows anything about," he asserts.

"It's not a properly organised coup if the whole world knows about it, and of course, you may need to use it again."

"I like to think I am now more controlled and have a better chance of surviving as a result of the learning process that has extended over the past twenty years," he went on.

I didn't have to remind him of how he first came to the attention of the media, not alone in Ireland but in Britain too. I didn't have to recall the legend of "The Kid" strolling into a bookie's office in Cheltenham on a morning in the mid-Seventies with a satchel of money and putting it all on a horse in the Gold Cup. It lost.

On the other side of the coin, I didn't have to recall the headlines he commanded when he was reputed to have severely punished the ring at the Festival meeting in 1982 when his own horse, the Edward O'Grady-trained Mister Donovan won the Sun Alliance Novices Hurdle. The horse was backed from 7/1 down to 9/2 on the course and looking back on it, J.P. McManus remarked succinctly: "Yes, we were in real trouble at the meeting before that one was landed."

No one knows the pitfalls of the gambling game better than he does and few can articulate as well the philosophy of the full-time professional, as he alternatively wears one of his two hats, that of the bookmaker or the punter.

As a big-time on-course bookmaker he has pitches on the rails beside the Graham Boys and David Power but that does not deter him, when the mood strikes, from leaving his pitch and "going to war" with his fellow bookmakers when he judges the odds are in his favour on a particular horse, which he believes will win.

In a word, he has the advantage of being able to see things clearly – from both sides of the fence.

He constantly keeps before him the piece of advice he got from an old English bookmaker friend some years back: "Beware of the certainty." A piece of advice this, he emphasises, that has saved him a lot of money.

J.P. was "skint", not just once but twice, after he first set up as a bookmaker. "It would be wrong of me to say that there is no possibility that I will ever be skint again. In this game you can never take anything for granted," he stressed.

When he had finished school he left the family Plant Hire Business run by his late father, John James or, 'Johnny' to his friends. Roscommon-born Johnny McManus had moved from Dublin to Ballygar before eventually settling in Limerick in the early Fifties. He had a small farm but the main source of income to support the family of five was the Plant Hire Business. As the eldest son, J.P. went to work for his father on leaving school. He used to operate all kinds of machinery and was paid roughly a tenner a week. "I actually cleared the site for the house I now live in, though, of course, it was then being built for somebody else."

He quickly realised that he was never going to make a fortune driving a bulldozer and so he decided to become a bookmaker, having already cut his teeth as a punter from his school going days.

"I went broke twice as a bookie shortly after I started and had to return home. The second time I went back, my mother lent me a few hundred pounds. I told her 'if I take it and Father gets to know about it, he won't be too pleased,' as the last thing he had wanted me to do was to become a bookmaker. She replied 'he won't know a thing about it.' So I took the money and I suppose I had more respect for it than for any money I ever had before or since in my pocket. Strangely enough, I have never been skint again. Granted, I was often very, very, short of money but there is a world of difference between having just a little in your pocket and being flat broke with nowhere to turn."

He says with deep conviction in his voice: "Once you have been skint in life and come through it, you come to respect money and you certainly never want to be flat broke again."

"One of the great things in life is being able to do what you enjoy doing every day of the week – and getting paid for it. I have managed to survive in what I love doing. I would do it as a hobby if I wasn't doing it for a living," sums up his philosophy.

The maxims which he acquired over twenty years and which saw him stay alive when others were so stung that they had to gather up their tents and creep into the night, led to a situation where today he has all the trappings of a successful entrepreneur.

Indeed, I suspect, no one appreciates more than he the motto of the late Jack (Treetop) Straus from San Antonio, Texas, World Champion Poker Player who, having shot a lion in Africa, always wore the inscription on a chain around his neck – "Better one day as a lion than one hundred years as a lamb." J.P.'s wry comment on that is "the lion was hardly the winner in that parable."

Nevertheless, J.P. is like a lion when he really "goes to war" with the bookies. He is happiest when savouring the excitement of the ring and being in the thick of the action. He feels it is wrong to talk about good or bad bookmakers and believes that good punters make good bookmakers in that they feed off each other. If the big punters are missing then the volume of business done on a race is mundane and you often get a false market. If the percentage for the bookies is so small, then there is no point in standing and he very often gets down and becomes a punter as he feels, that way, he gets a better percentage return on his money. In this situation, his brother Kevin takes over, marking the board and calling the odds with J.P.'s long-standing friend and confidante, Jimmy Hayes from Fethard, Co. Tipperary occupying a key position always.

"I consider myself a professional gambler whether I am punting or making a book," he went on to explain. "but I am not an addictive gambler. If I didn't have a bet at a particular race meeting, it wouldn't bother me."

"Gambling is a state of mind. The gambler who doesn't operate to strict ground rules, and who chases his losses and cannot shut up shop when his tank for the day is gone, is like an alcoholic who cannot control his drinking. Only that the gambler can destroy his whole life in a half a day while it can take years to destroy your life with drink.

"You should remember when you are winning that there is another fellow losing i.e. the bookmaker. He is just as affected by losing as is the punter. The bookmakers will start to chase their money and that is when they offer better value as they are working to much tighter margins.

"There are some punters who adopt a safety-first policy when they are winning. These are not the real professionals who always look for value especially when the bookmakers are losing as they can possibly get a point or two over the odds. This doesn't often happen, but that is where the real professional, going with the streak, will hit the opposition when they are at their most vulnerable."

The most successful punters, he contends, are those who believe in the form book and know how to interpret form. They are not swayed by tips from owners, jockeys, trainers or connections.

Betting big or in five figure sums does not make a professional in the strict sense of the term. "I know men," he said, "who may never have more than £50 or £100 on a horse and who make a nice living out of the game. I like to see these men having a bet with me, even though they will come off winners at the end of the year, because I know they are not betting blindly and their judgement may influence my opinion."

He recalled a time when the results hadn't been going well for him and he did not yet have the discipline in his gambling or the ability to stop when he should. He wrote to the big English bookmakers and told them he did not want credit and they would give it to him at their peril. It meant that he didn't leave a racecourse owing any money and very quickly acquired the necessary self control and discipline.

That discipline is never more obvious than when he visits a Casino. The arrangement is that he can cash only one cheque for the night when he arrives. The amount of the cheque automatically sets his limit and cannot be exceeded. The Casino Manager will have received a letter to this effect and in no way can more credit be extended.

I ask him if he has ever regretted becoming a professional gambler-cum-bookmaker?

"If you analysed everything and tried to allow for all that might go wrong, you would never have a bet. I don't have any regrets about life in the overall sense. All right I made mistakes, who hasn't? One mistake can make all the difference in life itself – just as one mistake can cost you dearly in gambling. It's the same in any sport or any business. But I like to think that, having made my share of mistakes, I still won 51% of the battles."

He also emphasised that he tends to think more of the future than the past. "You can't alter the past. It's done with, finished. Even when I lose at gambling I stick to the principle that it is no use dwelling on it. You must look ahead to the next day and the next battle."

His philosophy can best be summed up: "Don't bother me about yesterday, it is what is going to happen tomorrow that interests me."

After lunch we adjourned to his study for coffee as there was racing at Lingfield and Folkestone on the SIS Channel on television. He allows all the races at Lingfield to go by and four at Folkestone and then picks up the phone, and having ascertained that the odds about the Nicky Henderson-trained Calabrese, ridden by Richard Dunwoody in the 5th, a 3-mile-two-furlong chase, are still at 4/6, he has what I would describe as an "interest" bet. Calabrese duly romps home by three lengths.

"It was really only a question of his jumping around," he remarked, not showing too much sign of emotion.

I asked him to bring out the backgammon board, as I reckoned I could gather a few hints from him even though he admits to being "below the world's best players".

Backgammon, he explained, is a very personal game. "Unlike cards, it is the move to follow rather than the move beforehand that you have to think about. It's a game which, when you think you have mastered, you realise that you don't even know it."

Elaborating he went on: "You will know you are making progress when you can recognise a player who is better than yourself, especially when you thought you had reached a stage when there was not all that much more you had to learn. Your opponent will make a move that brings the immediate reaction inside your head – 'that is better than I could have done'."

Stressing that until you have come to understand the use of the cube in backgammon, then you cannot be numbered among the top players, he said: "It's the most important piece on the board as you can at an early stage challenge your opponent's courage by in effect doubling the stakes so that he has either to fold or accept the challenge."

Frankly, I was only a novice in the face of J.P.'s mesmeric movement of the pieces on the board and when it came to the use of the cube, he told me exactly the odds on the various options facing me and I was happy to fold.

As he put away the board he said: "I love the game. There was a time when I played a lot of backgammon at a very serious and intense level, much more than is the case nowadays."

His bungalow-style office building, overlooking the lawn, is a model of its kind, replete with books on breeding, and sales catalogues going back over a long number of years, and also back numbers of racing magazines and sports publications from all parts of the globe. His outlook and approach to racing, as it is to sport in general, is global rather than insular. Some of the pictures and framed prints catch J.P. in action on the golf course, as when competing in the Annual Charity Golf Day at Sunningdale in 1991 with John Magnier and Dermot Desmond.

When you step inside the front door of the imposing Martinstown House, you are met by an eye catching painting done by Peter Curling of J.P.'s Blitzkreig beating Young Snugfit in the Victor Chandler Chase at Ascot on Saturday, January 12th, 1991.

You immediately ask yourself what is special about this picture? The grey, Desert Orchid wasn't concerned in the final battle for honours with Blitzkreig, Young Snugfit and Katabatic but the artist has allowed himself the licence in this instance of stretching racing history somewhat to get Desert Orchid looming into view just behind Blitzkreig and Young Snugfit.

It's there for all to see – the Irish horse had beaten the 1989 Gold Cup winner and the pride of England.

It gives him immense pride that his recent winners on the domestic front like Gimme Five and Time For A Run were bred at Martinstown Stud from mares that had run in his colours.

He confesses that he has known no greater satisfaction than seeing his colours carried to victory at Cheltenham. "I have been lucky to have had three winners there already, Mister Donovan (1982), Bit Of A Skite (1983) and Danny Connors (1991). There are owners who have given a lifetime hoping to win even one race while others simply want to have a horse good enough to run there."

His greatest ambition would be to win the Gold Cup, to watch a chaser of his, jumping the last safely and storming up the hill to victory – preferably beating a favoured English challenger in the process.

The Sundance Kid has his dreams like every other owner in the game and it is no coincidence that they revolve around Cheltenham . . . for his name will always be indelibly linked with Cheltenham during the great annual Festival meeting.

When he first got interested in betting as a school-boy, prepared to invest the last few shillings he had in his pocket on a horse he had selected to win a big race like the Aintree Grand National, he could never have entertained the dream that some day he would own his own horses. He could not possibly have foreseen that in the same year – 1991 – he would score both at Cheltenham and Aintree, winning the Coral Golden Handicap Hurdle (Final) with Danny Connors at the National Hunt Festival meeting and the Captain Morgan Aintree Handicap Chase on Grand National Day with Blitzkreig.

He had come a long way indeed from Roxboro National School to Martinstown Stud where he now lives with his attractive wife Noreen and their three children . . . . and out beyond are the Galtees and timeless Slievenamon.

6

"A Punter From As Early As I Can Remember"

"In some ways I suppose I was a punter from as early as I can remember," said J.P. McManus looking back to his primary school days in Roxboro National School in Limerick and to how he acquired the gambling bug.

"My father always kept a few young potential showjumpers and usually read a lot about horses. He also liked to have a small bet, especially on the big races. His biggest bet was £1 and his smallest bet was also £1. It rubbed off on me in that I came to love horses and also the thrill I got from collecting when my fancy won."

"One of the first bets I ever had was a few bob on Merryman II when he won the Aintree Grand National in 1960 at 13/2. I was only nine then. I also remember backing Owen Sedge with the few shillings I had in my pocket when he won the Leopardstown Chase in 1963 at 15/2 for the Tom Dreaper-Pat Taaffe combination."

His biggest problem was getting the bets on. He was not too big for his age and often had to stand outside the door of the bookie's shop and it became his practice to ask one of the regulars to place the bets for him. Later when he went to work for his father, nearly every penny he earned was spent on gambling in S.P. offices.

From Roxboro National School, J.P. went on to Sexton Street Christian Brothers School in Limerick. His education as a punter continued outside of school hours. Saturday afternoons were spent in and around bookies' shops.

Then came the day when he sat his Leaving Certificate examination (equivalent to A. Levels in Britain).

"I remember the history test was due to start at 2.30 p.m. and my problem was that I knew that after 45 or 50 minutes a Brother would come to stand at the door to ensure that no one slipped out early. I fancied a horse very much at Limerick. I managed to get out of the room before the Brother took up duty and cycled like mad to the racecourse only to arrive at Greenpark just as my fancy was passing the post – a winner."

He couldn't be blamed on that occasion for missing the bus – or the winner but it taught him the value of punctuality, which he rates very highly.

He got his Leaving Certificate – even though he had to repeat Irish, a compulsory subject – but already the gambling bug had caught him. He entertained no thought of seeking any further formal education and his "university" from this out would be the racecourse when he was not frequenting S.P. offices.

When the tax stood at 5 per cent at his local bookies, he hardly noticed. However, when it was raised to 20 per cent in the early Seventies (before reverting back to the 10 per cent that obtains today), it had a dramatic effect on J.P. "I felt the increase was too much and I couldn't afford the extra tax. So I decided that I would not bet anymore in S.P. offices. I literally stopped overnight."

He then turned his attention to on-course betting. Already he had begun attending every race meeting around the country that he could manage to hitch a lift to. In fact, he was so determined to get to the Curragh on one particular day that he eventually got there having had several hitched lifts.

"It was well worth it. I won the Jackpot of £1,200 for a £6 investment. It was my first big win and I thought I was a millionaire. It was the first great thrill of my life."

Already he was showing the judgement of the form book and the courage that would later make his name a byword. But it would be a long and expensive haul before he acquired discipline and attained maturity.

When J.P. first told his father that he was going to become a bookmaker, he could see the disappointment written on Johnny McManus's face but his father did not stand in his way, telling him: "You know there will always be a place for you in the firm if you decide to come back."

J.P. recalls: "I know now he could not have been fairer in saying that – but at that time I was convinced that I should move on."

He was 20 when he applied for, and got, a bookmaker's licence. Already he had acquired a great deal of knowledge about the game – far beyond that of many young men of his age.

He could see there was money to be made by having a pitch in the ring, although he acknowledges that it was not an easy game and in no way did it represent "money from America".

"Serious punters are well informed nowadays and they are getting cleverer by the year. Mug punters will always be a part of the scene. These, however, are not the ones that are involved in the real battles with the bookmakers or who will decide whether those of us laying the odds will have a winning or losing day. I can handle the clever punter but the mug confuses me."

He is very loath to back his own horses. Why? "I don't think I can expect to get a fair price about my own horses. Once the bookies think I am having a go, the odds they offer are quite restrictive."

He did, however, have a cut on Danny Connors at the 1991 Cheltenham Festival meeting because in this very competitive 3m 1f. handicap hurdle with 29 runners, he got the kind of odds he likes to get to his money. Danny Connors was returned at 9/1. With Mark Dwyer in the saddle he gave Jonjo O'Neill his first Festival winner as a trainer.

When J.P. McManus first started as an on-course bookmaker he was down the line i.e. not in one of the prime positions on the rails, where the big money is laid and frequently major bets are made 'on the nod' by those who have credit accounts.

He is unstinting in his praise of the contribution made

by Sean Graham as a fearless layer on the rails and of his innovative approach in the S.P. chain of offices he established. He acknowledges how much he learned from Sean and adds that it was a tragedy for the bookmaking profession and for Irish racing, which he sponsored so generously, that he died so young from a terminal illness. "It's good to see his twin sons, Sean and Brian keeping their father's flag flying in the ring today."

Amazingly enough, it wasn't until he moved to a position on the rails that many racegoers became aware that he was wearing two hats. In the Seventies he was far better known as a fearless punter than as a bookmaker. This was the decade in fact that catapulted him into the public eye and when he first really came to the notice of the media.

Down Limerick way they reckon that one of his first big coups was executed not in the sphere of horse racing but on Ireland's National Game of hurling. Outside of racing, nothing excites him more than a good hurling match, though he watches other sports on television, including soccer, tennis and American football.

Back in 1973, he was Chairman of the South Liberties club in Limerick – holding the position for three years – and that was the year when the club provided Eamonn Grimes, Joe McKenna and Pat Hartigan to the County hurling team.

All three are long-standing friends of J.P.'s and Eamonn Grimes was to captain Limerick to Munster and All-Ireland honours, the county's first titles in 33 years.

With his keen knowledge of the game, J.P. knew this was an exceptional Limerick side. They had been desperately unlucky not to defeat Tipperary in the 1971 Munster Final in Killarney. However, they were now seasoned and experienced like a chaser that is ready for the Gold Cup at Cheltenham and J.P. felt that they had that vital extra yard of speed in attack that can make all the difference.

He backed Limerick to win out in Munster even though they had to face Tipperary in the Provincial decider in Thurles. And he backed them to go all the way to win the All-Ireland Final and, of course, he was getting the right odds to his money as Kilkenny had been so impressive when defeating Cork in the 1972 All-Ireland that few afi-cionados would bet on Limerick to dethrone them.

Fate also stepped in on the side of J.P. and Eamonn Grimes and his fearless men in Green and White.

In the countdown to the first Sunday in September, Kilkenny were decimated by injuries and were only a pale shadow of the team of all the talents that had trounced Wexford in the Leinster Final that same season and which would prove the outstanding side in the country by win-ning the 1974 and 1975 All-Ireland Finals, getting their revenge on Limerick in 1974.

Anyway, while he doesn't like to reveal what he won in total in bets during the 1973 hurling season, there is little doubt that J.P. McManus banked a substantial amount.

Subsequently, he adopted the South Liberties colours of green and gold as his own racing colours which showed his affinity to the club and to the place hurling held in his heart.

Meanwhile in this decade, the stories circulating in rac-ing circles about his tilts at the ring, especially when he hit Cheltenham and Royal Ascot, had already made him a leg-end – in his twenties. His boyish features earned him the nomenclature "The Kid" from his fellow bookmakers when he first took out a licence and when he got down from his pitch to punt on a fancy of his, they would exclaim: "The Kid's having a go."

Then Hugh McIlvanney in *The Observer* wrote a feature article about him one Sunday in which he named him "The Sundance Kid" – and from that moment he was on a pedestal apart as Ireland's most famous high roller.

He could now no longer be taken for granted. The sur-vivor in him meant that he never went under, despite shat-tering setbacks that would have broken the spirit of many a punter double his age.

He had the happy knack of putting the setbacks of yes-terday to the back of his mind and was invariably thinking forward to tomorrow.

He lived by the dictum that once you had the ammuni-tion, your guns could keep firing. What had to be avoided at all costs was wasting that ammunition and ending up in hock to the bookies.

The following comments are etched in my mind from my first meeting with J.P. in the mid-Seventies.

"I am not in the game for medals or glory. There is no future in picking losers. I don't want to be remembered as 'The King of the Ring'. I want to stay in existence as a punter, ahead of the field. You ask me am I making it pay? Let me say I am still alive."

That was said to me in 1976 during the week of the Rose of Tralee Festival, nearly sixteen years before our long luncheon in Martinstown Stud in January 1992. J.P. had come a long way in the intervening period.

There was a six-man mobile Jazz Band playing "When the Saints Go Marching In" outside the Mount Brandon Hotel while at a table in the lounge area "The Sundance Kid" was playing backgammon.

The racing, not the Festival merry-go-round, had drawn him to the Kerry Capital and at his right elbow, holding as it were a watching brief, sat his friend and colleague, Jimmy Hayes of Fethard, son of one of the most respected members of the bookmaking fraternity, Dick Hayes, a gentleman to his finger-tips.

Jimmy Hayes was a brilliant student of the form book. He was "Butch" to J.P.'s "Sundance" – an inseparable pair this duo who liked nothing better than to go gunning after the bookies but they did not want to go down in a blaze of glory, in the betting sense, as Newman and Redford did in the classic Western.

Jimmy Hayes eschewed the limelight where J.P. found he couldn't escape it. While one part of "The Kid" was a very private person, there was another that didn't mind being centre stage.

You don't read any profiles of Jimmy Hayes – The Quiet Man from Fethard. He never makes it to the social columns and hasn't been discovered it seems by those columnists who are so avidly read by the Dublin 4 set. Jimmy, I guess, would prefer to have it that way and won't encourage any of them to seek him out.

In the big punting days of the Seventies, it was clear that Jimmy Hayes' reading of the form book often worked to the distinct advantage of J.P. McManus, indeed, to both of them when they got the right odds to their money about horses that they fancied but the bookies did not see as potential winners. They didn't always get it right, of course, but even the best professionals in the world cannot call it correctly 100% of the time.

Jimmy Hayes was a great believer in the maxim that you "gotta know when to fold" when things are not going right with you on a particular day. For the professional hitting a sticky patch, the most essential lesson of all was to cut down on your betting so that you would survive to fight another day.

In the final analysis everything for Jimmy went back to the form book. It was the Bible.

During that 1976 Tralee Festival meeting I recall continuing my conversation with Jimmy Hayes on the second day after he had breakfasted in his room. The room was littered with form books and the racing pages of the morning papers.

What factors, I asked, influenced him in reading the form book?

"You can only study form in relation to knowing the men who own and train the horses," he replied. "You must try and judge what race a horse is being laid out to win, how he is being brought along to reach a peak of fitness. You must also be able to pinpoint the horses from non-gambling stables that are being aimed at the bigger stake-money."

What advice had he for the ordinary punter attending race meetings?

"I think the best bets can be found in conditions races rather than in handicaps," he went on. "You may find a horse that would be giving 14lbs to another if it were a handicap. You know then you have something to bet on, granted of course, the distance and the going is in its favour."

He personally favoured betting in National Hunt races more than the Flat. "All right, a chaser may fall, but against that a horse may have time to recover from one or two mistakes if he has the edge in ability, whereas on the Flat a bad start or interference is certain defeat."

J.P. McManus, who has now dropped into the room to join us, elaborates on Jimmy Hayes' commandments on reading the form book. "You must be able to weigh up the race, take the conditions into consideration and, most importantly, are you getting value for money?"

"You must be able to go to a meeting and not bet at all if you think the odds are unfavourable to you. You may go intending to bet on a particular horse, then something puts you off or it could simply be that you don't get the price you want."

"Remember that betting professionally is not betting for fun," he summed up. "I am not in the business simply for the thrill of having a go. If I don't keep ahead of the field, then it's all meaningless. The business is about picking winners at the right odds."

It was the utter fearlessness of "The Sundance Kid" and his ability to bounce back when major gambles came unstuck that put such an intense and constant spotlight on J.P. in the Seventies, that reached far beyond the inner circle of racing regulars. There was, for example, the philosophical, almost cool nonchalance with which he dismissed a bad 1976 Cheltenham meeting, especially the failure of Brown Lad to win the Gold Cup. "We have had worse meetings than that," he would say of it later with a boyish grin, adding, however, "but Ascot was kind to us." He didn't elaborate on how much the word "kind" meant in readies.

On his own admission he was a punter more than a bookmaker in the Seventies. "The odds determine for me when to bet and when to make a book," he explained.

"You think a horse will win and when you go to the meeting you find that he is at a more generous price than you expected. He could be 4/6 when you expected him to be 1/2 and 1/2 when you thought he would start at 1/3 and even at these restricted odds he could represent value. On the other hand 25/1 can be a bad price, depending on the quality of the race."

Generally, however, J.P. and Jimmy Hayes do not like betting odds-on or going blindly for favourites. "There

would be no bookies if there were no odds-on chances,"
said J.P. "If I fancy a horse sufficiently, I will not be
deterred by the fact that he is not favourite in the market,
though you will, of course, look for genuine reasons as to
why a horse may drift. Racecourse rumour, however, can
be very misleading. It can even help certain people to get a
'price' if they circulate a false report about a horse."

J.P. has always preferred backing a horse with proven
ability rather than, say, a two year old never out before that
is reported by the "watchers" to be a veritable flying
machine or "a pigeon-catcher" on the home gallops.

He is firm too in his conviction that in the final analysis
ability counts for everything but at the same time it doesn't
matter how much ability a horse has if it cannot act on the
prevailing going. "The way I see it is that a top of the
ground specialist will invariably be beaten in hock-deep
going and, therefore, those punters who take a short price
on such a runner on the basis of what they consider to be
'inspired' information are absolutely mad. Their own personal judgement in an instance like that should tell them to
keep their money in their pocket."

"Racing is a great leveller," observes J.P. "The day you
think you have mastered the game, you will be made to
pay for it the following day.

"What you must seek to do is build up a bank of experience
that allows you to reduce and eliminate as far as possible the
factors that make for foolish betting. In a word, you act to
strict ground rules always and you endeavour to become an
investor rather than a pure addictive gambler."

"Butch" and "The Sundance" were both 25 when I first met
them in the Seventies. Since then they have added a depth of
maturity and experience to the storehouse of knowledge of
the game and the machinations of betting which they have
long had.

In their forties they are a far, far more formidable duo.

J.P. has never lost sight of the fact that he came from ordinary beginnings himself and, as the Irish like to put it, he is
not in the least 'stuck up'. There is also the very valuable
work he does for charitable causes, nothing finer than the
funds he raised for the buying of Cat Scan equipment for the

Limerick Regional Hospital.

He organised a two day Golf Classic at Limerick Golf Club. It was proof in itself of the contacts that he had made in the sporting arena on a worldwide basis that he could bring so many big names together on the same day.

Robert Sangster and his wife Susan jetted in specially for the occasion. Johnny Jones, the famous Kentucky stud owner, also jetted in and others who played included Chris de Burgh, John Magnier and Mick O'Toole.

The golfing pros included Christy O'Connor Jnr., Des Smyth, Eamon Darcy, Philip Walton, Gordon Brown and Roger Chapman.

Apart from Limerick Regional Hospital, others to benefit were various charities in the Limerick area, including the handicapped and the Hospice for the Dying.

As his fortunes improved in the Seventies, he became a racehorse owner. He didn't have to wait too long before that broad smile of his was to be seen in the winners enclosure.

He acquired Cill Dara, the mare he was reported in the media at the time as reputedly having "backed to win a small fortune" when she won the 1975 Irish Cesarewitch. He bought her at the Newmarket December sales for 20,000 guineas, a figure he comfortably recouped in bets when she won for him at Naas in July, 1976.

Cill Dara was left in training with Con Collins, the Curragh trainer. Again ridden by Christy Roche, who produced her confidently in the straight, the five year old, carrying 9st 6lbs this time (compared with 8st 9lbs the previous year) completed the double in 1977.

The bookies, who had been caught napping in 1976, took absolutely no chances with the mare. They were willing to offer 8/1 and more against any horse bar the favourite who started at 5/2 to beat her 28 rivals.

A "huge gamble" was landed, according to *The Irish Field*, when J.P. McManus won the race again two years later with the six year old Jack Of Trumps, trained by Edward O'Grady and ridden by Christy Roche. The winner went off at 7/4 despite the fact that there was good market support also for Potato Merchant and Twinburn. Although wandering about in the straight, Jack Of Trumps got home by three quarters of a length from Potato Merchant thanks to the strong handling of Christy Roche.

National Hunt racing, however, was J.P.'s first love from the outset. He has no hesitation in saying that he still prefers racing over the jumps to the finest Flat racing anywhere in the world.

If he was stirred by doing battle with the bookies at the Cheltenham Festival meeting each year, he also had the ambition from the moment he ventured into ownership to win a few of the big races there.

He experienced very costly failures on occasions but yet he had the thrill of winning events that other owners would give their right hand to emulate.

As with his punting, he showed amazing resilience as an owner to come smiling through all vicissitudes.

One has only to instance the way Laura's Beau, running on ground that was patently unsuitable for him, was pulled up in the Fulke Walwyn Kim Muir Challenge Cup at the 1992 Cheltenham Festival meeting. He came out on the Saturday and on soft going that gave full play to his stamina he won the £23,000 Ansells National at Uttoxeter, and this, incidentally, represented a first training success in Britain for former outstanding National Hunt rider, Frank Berry.

7

J.P. Wearing the Mantle of an Owner

There are many owners who would die happy after leading in just one winner at Cheltenham in their lives.

J.P. McManus, as we have already seen, has known the joy of that experience not just once but three times with Mister Donovan (1982), Bit Of A Skit (1983) and Danny Connors (1991). He has also led in Blitzkrieg, a convincing winner at Ascot in the Victor Chandler Chase and at Liverpool in the Captain Morgan Chase. He got a special thrill when his chaser, Laura's Beau, trained by former brilliant National Hunt jockey, Frank Berry, finished third behind Party Politics and Romany King in the 1992 Aintree Grand National.

Wearing the mantle of an owner, J.P. has known his ups and downs — just as he has known them as a punter.

But he is totally philosophical about it and contends that only a fool would think that you can enter the field of ownership without experiencing setbacks.

If your first love is National Hunt racing and you set as your ultimate target the winning of a race at Cheltenham, then you must be prepared for a lot of heartaches, though the odd person will strike it lucky at the first time of asking — as a jockey may win with his first ride, just as young Jason Titley did at the '92 Festival meeting.

The National Hunt Chase for long proved a hoodoo event for J.P. McManus both as an owner and punter. It was not until Bit Of A Skite justified favouritism in 1983 that the hoodoo was finally broken.

No one knows the pitfalls of this lottery of a race better than Ted Walsh, the eleven times former Irish amateur champion jockey, now a successful trainer and very popular and knowledgeable RTE personality in the racing sphere.

"Normally there is a very big field and with 28 fences to be negotiated over a four mile trip it is nearly 4/1 against a clear round — without even thinking of winning", said Ted.

Why then do the big gamblers plough in on this race with their heads down when the odds are so stacked against them?

"Racing men believe that if you get a good horse for this race, then you are on the proverbial good thing despite the obvious hazards. It's confined to horses that have never won a race before the start of that season and the majority of the field would normally comprise a moderate bunch of one-paced individuals.

"Quare Times, ridden to victory in 1954 by 'Bunny' Cox for Vincent O'Brien, was a case in point and you recall that this one went on to win the Aintree Grand National the following year. In 1986 Omerta was just right for the job and all he needed was ordinary luck in running as he won for Homer Scott", said Ted.

At the same time, however, some tremendous Irish gambles on this event became unstuck. In 1977, Mount Prague, which Ted Walsh himself rode for trainer Mick O'Toole, was the medium of one of the biggest ever Irish gambles at the Festival meeting. He started at 11/8 favourite in a field of 21 and was in mid-division on the inside when he fell at the 18th fence.

"When the gambling men get to Cheltenham something happens," said Ted "Their blood is up and they just plough in. They can go blindly and even be on something at ridiculously short odds that they would never accept on their home ground".

J.P. McManus came back sun-tanned from his honeymoon in Miami to the 1978 Festival meeting. He quickly ended all speculation on the vital question as to which race had been chosen for Jack Of Trumps. When he announced that it had been decided in consultation with Edward O'Grady to run the gelding in the National Hunt Chase, he thought to himself "Jack Of Trumps should win barring accidents."

Considering what he was to accomplish subsequently, Jack Of Trumps certainly looked tailormade to outclass the opposition in this race.

Before the end of 1978 with a glittering future apparently before him, he was voted Ireland's leading chaser of that year by the members of the Irish Racing Writers Association, who nominated him for the Irish Mist Champion Chaser Award (it took the form of a specially-commissioned oil painting of the winning chaser, executed by leading equestrian artist, Janice Linden).

"Jack of Trumps, even at five years, has already the look of a future Cheltenham Gold Cup winner", wrote Brian Fetherstonhaugh in the *Evening Press* that same autumn, noting at the same time that he was a horse with "tremendous class, having the speed to win on the Flat, and the stamina to take the John Jameson Cup at Punchestown".

Indeed, some observers were talking in terms of an "Arkle-type potential", so impressive did Jack of Trumps look when giving 18lbs and a six lengths beating to Shining Flame in winning that event. In justifying odds-on favouritism in the Embassy Premier Qualifier at Punchestown in the hands of Niall ("Boots") Madden, he beat Chinrullah by ten lengths without even being extended and he produced one of the finest performances of his career when defeating Night Nurse by six lengths in the Hermitage Chase at Newbury.

He would run Silver Buck (winner of Gold Cup) to 1½ lengths in the King George VI Chase at Kempton Park in 1980, another performance of real merit. But by this time he had developed a tendency to jump to the left and it had to be accepted that the primary targets he would be aimed at would have to be on left handed tracks.

He was well backed, ante-post, for the 1979 Gold Cup

87

but was withdrawn lame a few days before the race. With Jonjo O'Neill in the saddle, he was brought down when in contention in the 1980 Gold Cup which was to go to Master Smudge on the subsequent unfortunate disqualification of the eight lengths winner, Tied Cottage.

The following year Jack of Trumps was made ante-post favourite for the Gold Cup after finishing third behind Anaglog's Daughter in the Foxrock Cup at Leopardstown over a distance that was short of his best.

This time Jack of Trumps jumped the fences safely but as Edward O'Grady put it afterwards "he was never firing on all cylinders".

He was in a position to challenge coming to the last but faltered on the run-in as Little Owl and Jim Wilson beat Night Nurse by one-and-a-half lengths in a pulsating battle to the line.

But all that was to lay in the future as on the eve of the 1978 National Hunt Chase, J.P. was hoping for victory for Jack Of Trumps.

The David Jack gelding was backed down to 8/11 favourite. To this day many people believe that J.P. McManus could have had as much as £40,000 on the horse. But he told me that he didn't bet on him — "as I felt the odds were too short".

Jack of Trumps fell at the 17th and that same year the victor was the 10/1 shot, Gay Tie ridden by John Fowler for Mick O'Toole.

In 1979 J.P. had Deep Gale in the race, trained by Edward O'Grady and ridden by Niall Madden. "I had backed Master Smudge earlier in the day when he won the Sun Alliance Chase at 20/1. I put all I had intended putting on Deep Gale plus the winnings from Master Smudge."

Deep Gale went off at 11/10 favourite in a field of 25. It was a tremendous betting race as Pillar Brae, ridden by Ted Walsh was the medium of a spectacular gamble from 10/1 to 9/2. Deep Gale fell at the 19th when closing on the leaders while Pillar Brae went at the 8th. Niall Madden told me afterwards that he was motoring like a winner when he fell. In fact, he believed that he was so superior to the opposition that if he could have caught Deep Gale and remounted, he would have won. Still that's racing."

Despite his preference for National Hunt racing, "The Sundance Kid" would gladly seize any opportunities presented on the Flat. Indeed, he was as much a scourge to the bookies at Royal Ascot, Goodwood, Doncaster, Epsom and York among other meetings, as he was on the "Killing Grounds" of Cheltenham and Liverpool.

Much of the losses of Cheltenham were recovered with interest when supporting the top runners from the Vincent O'Brien stable. The Master of Ballydoyle enjoyed a fantastic season in 1977 with The Minstrel taking the Epsom Derby, the Irish Sweeps Derby, the King George Vl and Queen Elizabeth Stakes while Godswalk, Solinus and Jaazeiro were winners at Royal Ascot. It was also the year of Try My Best and of Alleged who, in the colours of Robert Sangster, won the Prix de L'Arc de Triomphe and would repeat the success the following year for the Vincent O'Brien-Lester Piggott combination.

At the time, there were varying estimates of the size of the "tank" J.P. had on Try My Best in the Dewhurst Stakes. The two year old duly obliged at 4/6 favourite but J.P. has never revealed how much he took out of the ring.

Suffice it to say that he was well back in business and those who thought after Cheltenham that he might be taking a one-way ticket to the Solomon Islands, had not reckoned with his "bottle".

J.P. put the hammer blows of the defeats of Jack of Trumps and Deep Gale behind him and was ready to "go to war" with a vengeance on the O'Grady trained Mister Donovan in the 1982 Sun Alliance Novices Hurdle. When that horse ridden by T.J. Ryan won the Sun Alliance Novices Hurdle it represented J.P.'s first Festival win as an owner. "I did not have a very good first day but did not mind too much, as I felt I would get it all back and more on the first race on the Wednesday. I expected we might get 12/1 to 14/1 to our money but word got out about Mister Donovan's ability and I had to take far less than those odds".

Suffice it to say that Mister Donovan started at 9/2.

Gaining a definite advantage on the bit three out, he held off the challenge of Spider's Well with Bob Champion in the saddle by one and a half lengths.

J.P.'s shrewd eye for a potential winning chaser was shown again in the manner in which he acquired Bit Of A Skite. After running in hunter-chases without success in 1981, Bit Of A Skite won three point to points in Ireland in the spring of 1982 before joining Ron Atkins' stable in England. He ran twice in novice hurdles for the Surrey trainer, being placed on both occasions and then he was bought by J.P., who moved him to Edward O'Grady's stable. He showed his first worthwhile chasing form for his new trainer when fifth to Pearlstone at Leopardstown in February '83.

The great irony of "The Kid's" tremendous tilts at the National Hunt Chase and the failed gambles on horses like Deep Gale, was that when he finally won it with Bit Of A Skite, trained by Edward O'Grady and ridden by Frank Codd in 1983, he didn't have a penny on, even though the winner started 5/1 favourite in a field of 29.

The reason for this was that a fortnight before the race one of Bit Of A Skite's feet became so badly infected that the blacksmith had to cut a large V-shaped hole in the front of his hoof. For eleven days the horse had to do all his work in Joan Moore's equine pool and on the morning of the race itself the hole was plugged for cosmetic purposes with Polyfilla.

"We just could not back him," said J.P. quite cheerfully as he savoured the moment of triumph in the winners enclosure. "Anyway, who cares now"?

"Certainly not Frank Codd," wrote John Oaksey in the *Daily Telegraph*. "He had a lovely trouble-free run throughout, came down the hill with both hands full and then easily beat off the challenge of Oliver Sherwood on Cranford Ginger."

By one of those unique coincidences, Frank Codd's name was misspelt on the racecard with a 'G' instead of a 'C' and one prominent Irish punter who knew nothing about the foot injury and had his "tank" on at 5/1 was heard to remark "how could we get beaten with divine assistance on our side"?

Bit Of A Skite incurred a 14lbs penalty for the Jameson Irish Grand National on Monday, April 4th 1983. J.P. knew that he was still "thrown in" with only 9st 7lbs and represented something to bet on. However, his big worry and that of trainer Edward O'Grady was that the foot that had given so much trouble before Cheltenham was still not right.

The swimming programme that had led to the Festival triumph was now repeated in the count-down to Fairyhouse and, indeed, his only appearance on the gallops was "a ten furlongs spin to clear his wind", as Edward O'Grady put it.

J.P., despite the risks he knew he was taking on the gammy leg, hit the ring in a fashion that the big English bookies had escaped at Cheltenham. Bit Of A Skite, which started at 7/1, was always going well except for one near-fatal error in the driving sleet and won by six lengths from Beech King after a copybook ride by Tommy Ryan. The rider said afterwards that the gelding was blinded going into the fence after the stand and galloped straight into it. Ryan was shot out of the saddle and was left dangling around the horse's neck. "I don't know how I got back" said Ryan who was cool and collected enough to give his mount every chance to recover and did not make a forward move until the top of the hill. The English challenger, Royal Judgement, which started 4/1 favourite, could only finish ninth.

Half an hour after the race, Bit Of A Skite was found to be lame. It represented a tremendous feat of training by O'Grady to get him to the start and capable of winning such a test of stamina following his exertions at the Festival meeting.

Thus in his twelfth year as a trainer Edward O'Grady won the Irish Grand National for the first time — a race his father won twice with Hamstar (1948) and Icy Calm (1951).

Edward O'Grady would go on to achieve the magnificent "bag" of eleven training successes at the Cheltenham Festival Meeting (up to 1992).

Amazing as it may seem, while J.P. has become an

integral part of the Liverpool scene in recent years, his gambling exploits there have not caught the imagination of the public or the media in the same way as his tilts at the ring at Cheltenham. Sure enough he has commanded headlines, like the one in the *Liverpool Echo* in 1981: "HERE COMES THE KID — FOR SHOWDOWN WITH THE BOOKIES."

"There will be no Panama hats, no Havana cigars and no champagne corks popping when J.P. McManus drifts into town for his annual pilgrimage to Liverpool," wrote Mike Torpey. "It's the low profile approach by the man they call 'The Kid', the deadliest punter of them all and the one bookmakers fear like the plague."

Two years later "The Sundance Kid" showed once again what a "plague" he could be to the English bookmakers.

It was strongly rumoured that he masterminded an off-course betting coup on a horse at Down Royal in February 1983. There was no racing that day in England and the Extel service giving shows of betting and commentaries from the Northern Ireland track was carried by the betting chains. It meant that credit and shop punters in the U.K., were allowed to bet on the meeting. Bets were spread around many offices in Britain on an unraced six year old in the two mile Bumper called Bit Of The Action. He was trained by Edward O'Grady for his uncle P.P. Hogan, the former top amateur rider and "King" of the point to point circuit in Ireland.

But the big English bookies hadn't as yet taken the precaution of having a "blower" service to Down Royal.

Referring back to the legendary P.P. Hogan, who owned Bit Of The Action, he is regarded as one of the shrewdest judges of a horse anywhere in the world and that judgment of a potential champion at the yearling sales has worked more than once to the benefit of Robert Sangster who has never hidden his admiration for P.P.'s uncanny eye. (Though as P.P. himself related to me in his home in Rathcannon, he has really only one good eye now. The story has it that when an eye was grafted on to balance this one, P.P. was at the sales one day with Robert Sangster and was heard to make the immortal comment: "The fellow that had this eye before me must have had a great eye for the women but certainly not for horses!").

J.P. has always maintained and he reiterated it to me at Martinstown House, "the best stroke is the one that no one knows anything about".

Methinks he will always seek to be ahead of the posse... and he is not the kind of man to be without ideas when it comes to plotting a stroke.

No matter how long you spend in the company of J.P., no matter how far-reaching the conversation, in the end it always gets back to Cheltenham.

Why is Cheltenham so special? Why does he put it on a plane apart? "Because it is about class in every sense of the word. It is about quality. Nothing can take the place of quality. You get the best horses from Britain locked in contention against the best from Ireland and nowadays also the best that France can send over, like The Fellow, beaten in a photo finish in the 1991 Gold Cup and again in '92.

"The champions come out for the Cheltenham Festival meeting. You don't see bad horses winning at Cheltenham. People aren't inclined to send them anyway unless they feel they can compete at this level. So when you have a bet there, you know you are applying your experience of the game, your judgement and your know-how to the task of deciding between the comparative merits of horses you have seen in the flesh or watched closely on television. When it works out correctly and you win, then it gives all the greater satisfaction.

"At Cheltenham you get a very strong ring, perhaps the strongest you get anywhere in National Hunt racing. It's very appealing to bet there because you can have a serious wager without the bookies running scared. Again, let me repeat — if you do your homework correctly and select the right horses, then you will be rewarded."

He talks of the graveyard that Cheltenham can become for the unwary and the head-strong. "It's different in the sense that the Festival meeting generates a tremendous atmosphere all its own. You can get mentally worn out over the three days. What amazes me always is, that you get normally very cool characters doing everything right the first day and half-way through the second and still blowing everything from that stage on — either through a failure of stamina or breaking their own ground rules on betting. Nowhere in the world is discipline required more than at Cheltenham".

And he puts his finger firmly on what lies in store for the misty-eyed punter heading for the quicksands of sentiment, especially those looking at everything through green-tinted spectacles. That aspect of Cheltenham is summed up by a born survivor cryptically thus: "Sentiment plays no part whatsoever in my make-up when I go down to the ring to have a bet. Sentiment can be very expensive. I don't care if it is an English-trained or Irish-trained runner. I will back what I think is best, going on my own judgement. If it happens to be an Irish-trained winner, that is a bonus. If I lose, I have only myself to blame."

He's loath to bet ante-post on the major Cheltenham events. "I will have to know the state of the ground before I really begin to make up my mind," he will tell you. "I find that the punters generally do better when the ground is soft. When it's fast at the Festival meeting, extra caution should always be exercised. The records prove that".

The same gang does not assemble at the Queen's Hotel in Cheltenham as used to be the case in the seventies when J.P. McManus and other leading personalities in the invading 'army' from Ireland made it their headquarters.

You would see them at late breakfast in the morning when they had come in from watching the early work-outs on the course, browsing through the racing pages over their bacon and eggs, tea or coffee and toast — Mick O'Toole and Dessie Hughes, Jack Doyle, the legendary bloodstock agent and J.P. McManus, Ted Walsh and John Mulhern. Edward O'Grady also stayed at the Queen's in that era.

The atmosphere was redolent with knowledge — and talk of how this one had gone that morning at exercise in the shadow of Cleeve Hill and the word was out that perhaps something else wasn't sparking! There was a depth of erudition in everything they had to say and all the time the patter was interspersed with banter and repartee.

That in a way was the golden age — a glittering era which leaves the writer with a sense of nostalgia for times past as Scott Fitzgerald wrote of the Jazz Age and somehow you felt that in later recessionary times it would be impossible to recapture its magic.

It was the era when big poker games, played through the night could be seen in the lounge area of the Queen's Hotel. Big money changed hands in these 'schools' involving Irish and English players who played the circuit. It was a case of on to Liverpool from Cheltenham for the Aintree Grand National meeting and then to the Festival meetings in Ireland, right down to the Listowel meeting. Some missed out on the races completely, sleeping through the day to be refreshed for more all-night action at the card tables.

Rather than play poker in that era, J.P. McManus could be seen in backgammon games for stakes the size of which we could never learn. Always, one was drawn to the circle of onlookers around him as he switched the pieces with the smooth, easy, lightning touch of an assured master.

To-day the glory of the Queen's as we knew it in the seventies and early eighties is no more, though it still attracts a racing set during the Festival week and the conversation can still be good at breakfast time as they pore over the pages of the *Sporting Life* and the *Racing Post*.

The high-profile characters including J.P. have moved out to other less crowded centres in the Cotswolds, where the gambles and strokes are planned in a quieter more relaxed atmosphere.

But in one way "The Sundance Kid" has not changed and will never change.

He is still as fearless and courageous a gambler as ever... and more dangerous now when he goes in with guns blazing, because he chooses his targets with greater care and his survival instinct has become diamond hard.

PART FOUR

TERRY ROGERS
*"All Men Are The Same Under
And Over The Turf"*

8

Why a Killing on Santa Claus Went Wrong

Terry Rogers in the days when on his own admission he was "a fearless gambler" went for what would have been his biggest killing of all on Santa Claus in the 1964 Epsom Derby.

Terry, who knew a potential champion when he saw one, either in horse racing, dog racing, coursing, boxing or poker, recognised Santa Claus's ability in the National Stakes at the Curragh in 1963. "I noted how he had to swerve around the horses in front of him and yet beat the Royal Ascot winner, Mesopotamia by eight lengths. The acceleration he displayed that day was electrifying. I got down from my bookmaker's stand on the rails and followed him into the winner's enclosure. The horses that came second and third were blowing hard. It seemed to have taken nothing out of Santa Claus, who looked as if he had enjoyed himself immensely.

"So overwhelmed had I been with the smoothness and effortless ease of Santa Claus's performance that I there and then congratulated his trainer, Mickey Rogers and cheekily remarked: 'The Epsom Derby, no doubt, Mr Rogers?' He replied: 'Yes, hopefully'. Then I ventured, even more cheekily: 'Will he get the mile and a half?' He laughed and said: 'That will not be a factor'.

"Before I could say anything else, I was pushed aside by the racing journalists who quickly encircled Mickey Rogers. I went back to have another look at Santa Claus.

His proud bearing had my thoughts racing as to the future — and the undoubted potential of a true champion in that frame. As he was led away with his long stride, a picture had already burned itself into my brain and I was visualising the field swinging around Tattenham Corner and then at the climax of the 1964 Derby, Santa Claus producing an explosive burst of finishing speed and winning with an authority that would be unquestioned.

"'Well, Terry what do you think?' That was the question I found myself being asked repeatedly even before I left the Curragh that evening and again on my return to Dublin. My reply was: 'Roll on Epsom. We have today seen next year's Derby winner'.

"Every time I had a 'touch' after that throughout the winter months I backed Santa Claus at all available ante-post odds from 10/1 down to 7/1. At the conclusion of the National Coursing meeting in Clonmel, I backed him again, taking 6/1 and then 5/1 from a bookmaker who was offering under the going rate. I deliberately took the 5/1 from my friend because I always seemed to win from him. I was digging out all the pishogues and the good vibes I could get.

"After Cheltenham '64 I decided I wanted to buy a new car. I was given a test drive in a Jensen C.V.8 sports car. The demonstrator with me remarked at one stage — 'give her the full pedal', which I did. The acceleration was so good that all I could say was: 'Wow she goes like Santa Claus'. Not being a racing man, he enquired what I meant. I explained about the colt and told him: 'When you ask this horse to go, he shows instant acceleration. Your car does the same'."

Terry Rogers wanted to buy the car on the spot. This proved impossible as he was told he would have to place his order through the agent in Dublin. This he did.

"Cheltenham '64 was Arkle's first Gold Cup, the occasion of the never-to-be-forgotten 'Irish roar' as he powered away from Mill House up the hill. I had a nice touch on him. I picked out a site for a house in Killiney's Avondale Road. So between my commitments on a new home and a new car, my bank account was lighter by

£20,000. I decided it was time to call a halt to putting any more money on Santa Claus. There was enough coming off him anyway.

"Then my luck turned and everything went wrong with the gamble on Santa Claus."

Came the day of the 1964 Royal Whip at the Curragh. Ragusa, who the previous year after finishing third to Relko in the Epsom Derby had won the Irish Sweeps Derby, the English St. Leger and the King George VI and Queen Elizabeth Stakes for the 'Darkie' Prendergast-Garnie Bougoure combination, was long odds-on. Terry Rogers was on his usual stand in the ring, laying doubles.

"I estimated that Ragusa would start at 1/10. Bill Cutler, my mentor and business partner in 1962 in the betting chain we had in the Birmingham area, was in Ireland on a break. Before he left Birmingham for Dublin that same morning, I asked him to place £3,000 on Ragusa for me. He asked me did I know anything? I said 'No'. But I planned to bet forecast Ragusa to win and other horses to be placed second to him. I also intended to put up special doubles, Ragusa to win the Royal Whip and horses in the following race.

"Ragusa was unbackable in Ireland as the on-course levy was 5 per cent on stake and winnings and at that time it was 15 per cent in the S.P. offices. That was why I asked Bill Cutler to put the £3,000 on for me in Birmingham as there was no tax on betting in Britain in 1964.

"I laid Cassim on request to win the race, also win or come second to Ragusa. Then just before the off Bill Cutler rushes up to my stand and proceeds to tell me about the bets he had phoned from the Curragh to Joe Coral, Wilf Gilbert, Hills and Ladbrokes and others. 'You're in for 50 per cent of what I have got on', he told me cool as a breeze.

"I protested that I didn't want anything more on the favourite outside of the business I had asked him to execute for me that morning. I was satisfied that I was covered for any bets I would take on the race. 'But Ragusa is a certainty', said Bill. 'Who said so?', I asked him. 'Everyone, including yourself', he responded.

"I pointed out to him that, while on his form of the

previous season, Ragusa was a lay-down, I had concluded that the colt momentarily showed weakness in his previous outing at Naas and I had only put on the £3,000 to cover the forecasts and doubles.

"His reply was — 'take down that rubbish and ask the odds and get him returned at a better price'. I took down the forecasts and doubles, tried to ask 1/8 with about three minutes left before the off. My heart was not in it. I had a premonition — 'this is going to be wrong no matter what I do'. And that is the way it turned out. Ragusa ran a bad race, finishing only third of four. Cassim won at 100/6. Every possible way I could lose on the race, I did.

"On calculating my liabilities, I found I was going to come up short. To get the money to meet my commitments I sold most of my ante-post bets on Santa Claus. I did this to the bookmakers I had backed him with, only retaining one voucher (£200 at 10/1). It was the same as being forced to sell gilt-edged share options. Incidentally, I had no intention of mortgaging my house, which coincidentally was named 'Arkle', because my wins on Arkle paid for it."

Santa Claus duly won the Derby in the hands of 'Scobie' Breasley. What really galls Terry Rogers, however, is that if he had been able to retain his ante-post dockets, he would have played up his winnings on the colt in the Irish Sweeps Derby. The colt again showed explosive acceleration in completing the Classic double, ridden this time by Willie Burke instead of 'Scobie' Breasley.

Incidentally, Terry Rogers is adamant that if Breasley had let Santa Claus down earlier at Epsom, the colt would have won as easily as at the Curragh. He came late, very late and yet his scintillating turn of foot carried him to a length victory over Indiana. Breasley's reply to those critics who did not spare him for cutting it so fine was that he had said to Mickey Rogers when he was engaged to ride Santa Claus and the fee agreed — "I will win the Derby for you if the colt is as good as you say." Then he added: "And I did."

Willie Burke, after his success at the Curragh, was given the ride on Santa Claus in the King George VI and Queen Elizabeth Stakes. In a field of four he was never going well on the very firm ground. Bill Pyers stole a march on him on the four year old, Nasram II and on turning into the short Ascot straight, Burke knew he was too far behind and did not ask the big question of Santa Claus.

"But there was always the Prix de l'Arc de Triomphe in October," recalls Terry Rogers. "Keen judges were split between Ragusa and Santa Claus. The French had no doubt they had the winner in their own Prix Du Jockey Club victor of that season, Le Fabuleux. I laid that colt at 3/1. The French gave Santa Claus little or no chance after his defeat by Nasram II in the King George.

"Bookmakers in Ireland could take what they liked out of Ragusa and Santa Claus. Santa Claus was no better than 3/1. I proceeded to lay both these colts knowing I could easily lay off in Paris. On Saturday evening I flew to Paris and on Arc day I monopolised the biggest window I could find on the Pari-Mutuel. I took at least ten minutes to lay my bets — ten tickets at a time for win and place. The Frenchman behind the window in perfect English asked me to pass him over all the money and he would do the needful. I told him — 'You will get it in my time; I don't want YOU or me to make a mistake. There is too much at stake here'. Those in the queue behind me were protesting and I guess cursing in perfect French.

"I bet just over 26,000 francs to win and 30,000 a place on Santa Claus with the French Tote. At one stage he was showing 36/1 a win and, as far as I recall, wound up starting at around 22/1. He paid just over 3/1 a place. I also had bets with English bookmakers, Hills and Ladbrokes at full Pari-Mutuel odds before I flew from Heathrow to Paris. I reckon I had £2,000 on for a win and £1,000 for a place.

"Jimmy Lindley had the mount on Santa Claus. He gave the colt a perfect ride. He timed his challenge to perfection. Santa Claus was flying when he came to the road across the track, filled with sawdust. As I read the race, he lost his action momentarily at that point. Lindley settled him and asked him to do it again. Santa Claus was really motoring at the death but just did not make it, as Prince Royal II triumphed by three-parts of a length and among the horses behind him were Nasram II, Ragusa, Le Fableux, White Label (winner of the Grand Prix), Barbieril (French St. Leger) and Belle Sicambre (French Oaks).

"I collected my place money, five tickets at a time. I stayed in Paris for a few days, got the money home via England and paid ten per cent commission to change it into sterling. With the winnings I bought the building in Talbot Street in Dublin that was to become the headquarters of my S.P. betting operation in Ireland and, in addition, I was able to purchase more offices in Birmingham with Bill Cutler."

Before 1964 was out Terry Rogers had purchased a Fiat 8 for £650, keeping the Jensen as a second car, though he did not drive it much.

As we dined one evening towards the end of March '92, Terry, looking back in cold retrospect on the eventful 1964 season, added this postscript: "I believe now that the Jensen was unlucky. All right dismiss it if you like but I am one of those who believes that something may be lucky for you or it may not.

"But then again if you look at it another way, I must admit that it was entirely my own fault in the case of Ragusa in the Royal Whip. I should never have asked Bill Cutler to have that £3,000 on for me in England. You see Bill always maintained that I was the best judge of a horse or dog he ever saw. I should have remembered too that once he saw a horse go 1/5 or lower in the betting, he could not for the life of him see it getting beat. He presumed that when I asked him to have £3,000 for me on Ragusa it was past the post. Anyway, it remains one of the great might-have-beens of my gambling days and I can still wake up in a cold sweat when I reflect on having to sell those precious ante-post vouchers on Santa Claus. You know it was like selling gold dust."

The year before – that is 1963 – Terry Rogers went for a £30,000 coup at the Galway Festival meeting in order to take up the option he had on 30 acres of land (with full planning permission for 8 houses to the acre) in Dublin's prestigious Foxrock area. On the Tuesday in the very first race of the day, he had six monkeys off Paddy Meehan on

Sedandun (a half-brother to 1963 English 2,000 Guineas winner, Only For Life), trained by the late Paddy Norris.

Sedandun, ridden by Tony Redmond, duly obliged and Terry "rolled" all his winnings on to Galway Hurdle challenger, Some Slipper, also trained by Paddy Norris and ridden by Tony Redmond, at odds of 10/1 and 8/1, making it to all intents a double.

"Some Slipper came down the hill looking all over the winner but he got caught and beaten by Ben Hannon on the 'Bunny' Cox-trained Snow Trix. I was jinxed."

Yes, jinxed when it came to the really spectacular gambles coming off on horses that certainly on the face of it had the ability to win major races but for Terry Rogers, Lady Fortune wasn't smiling on him.

The day in mid-November, 1979 that he saw Daring Run win his second successive bumper in the hands of Ted Walsh at Limerick Junction (now Tipperary racecourse) by a scintillating eight lengths, he marked him down as a future winner of the Champion Hurdle (Daring Run had earlier won by six lengths on his debut at Navan, being backed down from 5/1 to 5/2 favourite in a field of 25).

Terry had actually backed Wonderful Lily in the Limerick Junction race but, as he recalled himself: "I knew five furlongs out that I had lost my money.

"When Daring Run came in that day I made it my business to be on hand to have a good look at him and also to greet Andy Doyle from Wexford, whose wife's colours would be carried by the gelding in the 1981 Champion Hurdle – the day that was already the big target in my mind. Andy, incidentally, had been one of those who had done the commission for the late Tommy O'Brien when his horse, Moss Bank was desperately unlucky not to win the 1961 Champion Hurdle.

"I said to Andy: 'I am convinced you have the 1981 Champion Hurdle winner in Daring Run. It will make up for Moss Bank'."

Terry Rogers started backing Andy Doyle's hurdler when he was 50/1 and was still backing him when he was down to 8/1 (the gelding was beaten a neck in the Supreme Novice Hurdle at the Cheltenham Festival meeting in 1980). He stood to win £250,000 had the six year old triumphed in the 1981 Champion Hurdle. The ante-post vouchers that Terry held certainly looked gilt-edged when Daring Run beat Pollardstown easily in the Erin Foods Champion Hurdle at Leopardstown in February, even though Pollardstown was conceding six pounds.

The one danger looked to be Sea Pigeon, the reigning champion but he was eleven years old and no hurdler had won the race at that age since Hatton's Grace completed the three-timer in 1951. Still Terry had a saver on Sea Pigeon as well.

Rogers was adamant that there was only one way to win with Daring Run and that was to let him cut out the work himself and go for his race from three or four out. He saw it as mistaken tactics to hold him up and reserve him for a winning run going to the last flight.

Stan Mellor used Meladon as a pacemaker for Pollardstown, who led into the straight but Ted Walsh drove Daring Run up to him approaching the last and the Irish challenger landed with a narrow advantage but Sea Pigeon's speed proved the decisive factor as he won by 1½ lengths. Daring Run cracked in the last fifty yards and actually Pollardstown rallied to snatch second place from him by a neck.

Terry recalls ruefully: "I had pleaded with Daring Run's trainer, Peter McCreery that the tactics for the Champion Hurdle should be those that proved so successful when he was given his head and I stressed: 'Let him go on three furlongs out and keep him at it and he will steal a march just like Navan and the Junction and they will never catch him'."

The final irony for Terry Rogers was to see Pollardstown start a warm order to win the Templegate Hurdle at Liverpool but Daring Run (getting only 3lbs.), with Ted Walsh again in the saddle and riding him as Terry had asked Peter McCreery to have him ridden, beat him easily by three lengths. A strict reading of that form left Terry in no doubt that Daring Run had the beating of Sea Pigeon in the Champion Hurdle.

Not everyone will accept Terry Rogers' reasoning on that

point, as Daring Run had won when held up for a late challenge, but he was never a man to hide his opinions — irrespective of how many feathers he ruffled in the process.

It's really as a bookmaker, who was prepared to make a book on anything within reason, that his friends think warmly of Terry Rogers — and spin legends about him — rather than as a punter.

For thirty years he was an integral part of the racecourse scene. It was impossible to imagine Galway Races without Terry Rogers. Or the Curragh on Derby Day. Even if you made your way to Laytown races, run on the sands beside the seashore in mid-August, you would find him there. Terry's doubles and trebles were famous and the odds very attractive to the small punter.

Something died in the Irish ring when Terry Rogers at 60 decided in 1988 to call it a day.

I mean something of the unique colour and atmosphere that Terry brought to it. He found that his knees were beginning to give out on him as a result of the hip dislocation he had suffered in a car crash when driving to Galway in 1971. It was painful to stand on his pitch for three hours and he realised it was time to call it a day.

Terry always maintained that on-course bookmakers can stay too long at the fair, so to speak. "I suppose it's only natural as you move into your sixties that you can lose some of the sharpness of your reflexes. In my own case my son was not interested in following me into the business of making a book at the races, so there was no alternative but to dispose of my seniorities (pitches)."

At the Curragh on Derby Day or on the occasion of the running of one of the other Classics, the contrast between the approach of Terry Rogers and David Power could not be as sharp — and yet in its very contrast, it showed what made the Irish ring so unique and appealing. David, scion of a famous bookmaking family — his grandfather, Dick and his father, Paddy being renowned layers in their time — bending his head quietly to take a whispered bet of '£3,000 to £2,000' on the nod (on occasions he would just put up the price of the "jolly" or favourite) and Terry, priding himself in 'The Red Menace' tag in the days when

107

he was not thinning on top but carried a flaming shock of red hair, calling the odds in machine-gun fashion and at the same time keeping up a non-stop patter that delighted the inevitable throng that surrounded his stand or pitch.

He prided himself in giving a full comprehensive betting service – from singles to doubles and trebles, to forecasts, how far a horse would win, also betting two chances, win or come second to another horse, mostly the favourite, occasionally a rank outsider.

This meant, of course, that if, as in the days when Vincent O'Brien was carrying all before him, there were runners that looked unbeatable on the book and, therefore, little or no business was being done, Terry was ALWAYS doing business. He was the forerunner of the era when it became popular to bet without the favourite and maybe to bet "without two". In a word, he was a man before his time in setting new parameters for betting.

Not that Terry couldn't lay a big bet either. Yes, he certainly could. Indeed, he took some of the biggest bets laid in the Irish ring and at the same time maintained his reputation of being the essence of promptness when it came to paying out (his motto, as he put it himself, was : "Prompt payments and no civility!").

Barney Curley is the first to vouch for Terry's total integrity when it comes to meeting his commitments to the punter.

There was the day at Leopardstown – February 15, 1964 to be exact – when Rogers was at the receiving end of a major gamble on a market "springer", namely Brogeen Gorm, trained by Tommy Burns in the opening race on the card, a maiden hurdle. The owner, Ian Murray, the Terry Ramsden of his day, backed the horse with Terry to win £26,500 in two separate bets, the first realising £16,500 the second £10,000 and by today's values we would be talking about a sum of almost £250,000 in total. He took thirty-three monkeys off Terry for himself and then going in again for connections and friends had another twenty monkeys. The horse came down to 100/9 though he was returned at 50/1 on the Tote. The irony of it was, from Terry's viewpoint, that Brogeen Gorm only got home by a short head from the 33/1 chance Dry Paint, which he owned in partnership with Bill Cutler. Terry and Bill had gone for an S.P. "touch" on Dry Paint.

Terry Rogers made it his business that same evening to go down to the Mail Boat in Dun Laoghaire and post his cheque to Ian Murray to ensure that it would arrive in his home in Glasgow first thing on Monday morning.

The last bet he laid to someone acting for Robert Sangster was £22,500 to £10,000 at the Phoenix Park on a hotpot from the Vincent O'Brien stable which came in a winner. "I must have taken about eight bets in all from commission agents acting for Sangster and every one of them was a winner," he recalled.

In the United States too he made his mark. He laid a bet of £100,000 to £9,000 on Dewey Tomko during the running of the Irish International Poker Tournament in Las Vegas in December, 1985 (the bet was laid in dollars but at the time the dollar was almost showing parity with the Irish punt).

No, Terry never flinched from the heat in the kitchen as a bookmaker and revelled in the cut and thrust of the business – at the highest level.

Terry Rogers in his capacity as commission agent-cum-bookmaker tried in October and November of 1983 to execute one of the most astounding commissions in the whole history of gambling. This too should have a place in the *Guinness Book of Records*.

It happened in the lead-up to the 1984 American Presidential Election when Ronald Reagan was seeking a second term in the White House.

Larry Flynt, publisher of *Hustler* magazine – the man who was shot in the abdomen by a sniper during the adjournment of his trial in Georgia, where he faced charges of publishing obscenity, and ended up in a gold-plated wheelchair, paralysed from the waist down – was having a poker session one evening in September, 1983 in his Beverley Hills mansion in California. The participants included a few of the big-name professional poker players. Flynt had taken part in May of that year in the World Hold 'Em Championship in Las Vegas, backing himself to win 10 million dollars and he was actually tournament leader at the end of the second day.

He now posed the question to his guests: 'What chance do you think I would have of becoming President of the United States?'

The initial reaction was that Flynt was simply saying this out of devilment in order to stir up a friendly argument. Someone ventured that in a three-horse race, he would be rated a 10/1 chance and this was said out of deference to Larry, the guy who had made the 10/1 quote signalling at the same time to his friends in John McCririck tic-tac fashion "a million to one".

Flynt said he would take the 10/1, though Terry Rogers personally told me that if he had been present and was pressed to tell the truth, he would have been compelled to say that Larry's chances of making it were the same as "me throwing a stone at the moon and hitting it."

However, Flynt, who had graduated from a log cabin in Ohio to a pink private jet and a nine-magazine empire, announced: "I am willing to back myself to win 20 million dollars that I will make it to the White House as President."

The people present would have dearly loved to have laid him but they knew that Federal law prevented them from doing so, certainly in California. "You will have to try somewhere else," Flynt was told. These people were afraid that Larry might write about it in a magazine.

His magazine publishing empire put him in the multi-millionaire category and he could easily put down the money to set out to win 20 million dollars.

One of those in the group in Beverley Hills that evening flew back to Las Vegas acting as Flynt's agent and enquired was it possible to get the bet on there. Of course, even if it had been possible it would have been deemed illegal under the American Constitution, as no candidate in a Presidential Election could be seen to get involved in the kind of betting operation on himself that Flynt had now hit upon. It is also illegal to bet on elections in Nevada.

So the only option was to place the bet in Europe.

Benny Binion had heard the gossip in the Cardroom in Binion's Hotel and Casino about what had evolved from the poker session in Beverley Hills and said that the only man who could do the commission was his very good friend, "the Irishman, Terry Rogers."

"How are we to know we will get paid?" asked Larry Flynt's agent.

"If he says he will get the commission on, I will personally guarantee him for the 20 million dollars," said Benny Binion.

Such was Benny's faith in the total integrity of Terry Rogers.

Shortly afterwards Rogers was summoned to the United States. No information was given to him during the trans-Atlantic call. He was simply told: "Your presence is required urgently in Las Vegas. It can't be discussed on the phone."

"I took the first available plane to Las Vegas, where I met Larry Flynt's agent," he recalled. "After being filled in on the details of the commission, I enquired: 'Where do I get the cash?'

'Don't worry about the money. It WILL be available,' I was told.

"My reaction was that I would have to back Larry Flynt to win 30 million dollars, indicating at the same time to Flynt's agent that as sure as night followed day, I would get knocked for at least one-third of the sum.

"I also made it clear that I would do the very best I could. I would not take less than 100/1. 'If I don't get some value, I am not prepared to execute the commission,' I said. But then I added: 'I think I should have no problem getting better than 100/1'."

Instead of coming home to Dublin, Terry Rogers flew direct to London and immediately set about trying to get the money on. First of all, he rang the "Big Four" betting chains in Britain – Ladbrokes, Hills, Corals and Mecca. Nobody wanted to know. Terry Probert, then Head of the Future Book Department of Mecca, when asked what odds he would quote to real money (Terry pointing out to him at the same time "Flynt's millions-to-one") responded: "If a B cowboy movie actor can become President of the United States, then there is nothing to prevent the

111

publisher of a pornographic magazine from making it to the White House as President also. We are not interested – even at 100/1."

"Esals, however, laid Flynt to lose them 3 million dollars," said Terry Rogers. "Barney Eastwood laid him to lose a million dollars and Alfie McClean laid him also to lose a million dollars, both giving odds of 200/1. Sean Graham and Malachy Skelly laid him to lose smaller amounts, not exceeding to lose 100,000 dollars, also at 200/1. I laid him to lose one million dollars myself at 200/1.

"By the time I was finished getting Larry's money down, I had only backed him to win 11½ million dollars. It took me over two months to get the money on.

"Plenty of bookmakers I approached tried to back Flynt for me at odds of 200/1 but when they rang any of the 'Big Four' they failed to get a quote. So they laid me themselves to small amounts, that is between 2,000 dollars and 40,000 dollars. From each of these genuine bookmakers I knew I would get paid as they were laying what was in their capacity to pay – without pressure.

"The first week in December '83 I arrived in Las Vegas intending to go down to Beverley Hills with Flynt's associate the next day. But Larry was arrested and within a few days was sentenced to fifteen months in jail on a charge of contempt of court. He withdrew from the Presidential race in January '84.

"Esals did not send the receipt for the commission I did with them until after Larry had withdrawn. They went out of business in the summer of '84."

President Reagan was duly re-elected for a second term in the White House.

The final word on that amazing story lies with Terry Rogers, who revealed to me that Larry Flynt had planned to come to Ireland in 1983 to play in the Eccentric Club International Poker Championship in the Killiney Castle Hotel. When he was informed, however, that his two armed guards would not be allowed to bring in their weapons he cancelled the scheduled trip.

He enquired through an intermediary of Terry Rogers

whether the Irish police who would be protecting him would carry guns. He was told that ordinary gardai in Ireland didn't carry weapons, though the Special Branch did.

"I would love to go to Ireland but, sorry, 'No Way'," came his final response. "I don't think the reflexes of your police would be good enough. My men would not mess about if they suspected that I was being threatened."

When you have been shot by a sniper and end up in a wheelchair, I guess you get kinda touchy about personal security – very touchy!

Terry Rogers touched the pulse of things in his own character when he confided to me that the sheer showmanship which he displayed in making a book on the rails, the non-stop patter he engaged in with the punting fraternity obviously stemmed from a love of acting in his blood that was never fulfilled on stage.

"I realise now that I would have loved to have been an actor if I had not followed my father into the bookmaking profession," he explained. "But in my young days there were none of the opportunities to train to be an actor that there are today. I mean there was no Academy like that run by the late Brendan Smith. It seemed the natural thing to do to go to work when I dropped out of school.

"I suppose I always had the gift of the gab and I wasn't averse to catching the attention of people in public. I know I left an impression wherever I went, no matter what the company and, amazing as it may seem now, I was just being myself and doing what came natural to me."

His critics would say that he could be loud without ever being vulgar. Certainly his booming voice could fill a room when he was in full flow or be heard a distance at the races.

Yet the man who has invariably been so at ease in the company of gamblers, whether those who follow the horses or the dogs or who live for poker or shooting craps, has a side to him that seems totally foreign and contradictory to this same world. One of his favourite authors happens to be Dostoevsky and books he returns to again and again are *The Idiot, Crime and Punishment* and *The*

Gambler while he has read Victor Hugos *Les Miserables* not just once but a number of times.

And the true Dubliner in him identifies readily with Joxer and Captain Boyle in Sean O'Casey's wonderful and timeless classic of the broken ones, *Juno and the Paycock*, as he identifies with the plays of John B. Keane — none more so, strangely enough, than *No More In Dust*, which was written around the theme of a young girl from the Kingdom of Kerry marrying a bookmaker from Dublin.

"You know," he confessed, "I button-holed John B. one day and asked him if, as people were constantly saying to me, it was true that the girl in the play was based on my wife (formerly Marie Broderick from Listowel, J.B. Keane's town) and John B. responded with a laugh that everyone seemed to think his plays were about themselves but the characters were usually broader than just one individual person. And on reflection I think he was right in that."

The contradictions in Terry extend to the way he will fight tooth and nail over the small print in an agreement if the other person wants a written contract and how upset he can become if he thinks he has been 'done' to the inherent generosity of his nature when it comes to helping lame ducks and raising money for the charitable causes so dear to his heart. Because his wife, Marie who was so close to him and understood him so well, died of cancer in 1977, he actually gave an ice-making machine to St. Luke's Hospital where Marie died — a spontaneous gesture born out of his desire to be of assistance to the helpless.

As he put it to me himself: "When visiting St. Luke's I had seen visitors bringing in ice for the patients. It seemed incredible to me that the Hospital had no ice-making machine, so I immediately ordered one."

And the Eccentric Club of which he is President ("you have got to be eccentric," he replied with a smile when asked what were the qualifications to join the club), ran poker tournaments that always had a charitable base to them. One day I accompanied Terry to Seville Place to see the outstanding work being accomplished by the Sisters of Charity in providing meals for needy folk in Dublin and knew that the generous cheques he handed over were

114

advancing that good work.

In 1979 he was responsible for raising the first funds for St. Vincent's (Psychiatric and Geriatric) Hospital, Richmond Road, Fairview (he actually gave to the hospital the fees which he received from RTE Radio for a programme on magic he appeared on with Tony Sadar). Incidentally, the Radio programme brought such a response that the Hospital doubled its fund-raising target.

He also raised funds through poker tournaments for the Church of the Visitation Fairview Roof Restoration and Decoration Fund and also for the Sallynoggin Old Folks Association.

And recently he has been backing the commendable efforts of those involved in Hospice Care for the dying in Listowel.

Who else but Terry Rogers could think of running off the Irish Poker Championship on Good Friday and not allowing any alcohol to be served on the premises — or not permitting the first card to be dealt until after 3.30 p.m. "when Our Lord has been taken down from the Cross".

Who else but Terry Rogers would remind you that St. Dismas, the penitent thief who died on the Cross beside Christ, was known in the States as "The Hoodlum Saint".

Remind you too that Dismas was the Patron Saint of Gamblers. "He was probably caught making an illegal book and paid the ultimate price," said Terry, laughing spontaneously at the thought. "I like to think also that he was the first of the true gamblers because he went all in on his hand when he asked the Lord to forgive him and to remember him when he came into his kingdom and was assured that he would enter paradise that same day. Whereas the other thief, Gestas, would not repent."

Who else but Terry Rogers could be so contradictory in his dress. I have seen him in Las Vegas when he has sported colourful Chinese wedding shirts and a baseball cap (though on one occasion he wore a formal suit and a bowler hat for a publicity shot) when the norm was to sport a Texan hat while back in Dublin you could find him on occasions in a conservative pin-striped suit that would have made you conclude, if you didn't know the man, that he had just stepped out from a city brokerage.

Yet he has walked with kings and rubbed shoulders with captains of industry and has known Cabinet Ministers on first-name terms and never lost the common touch. "All men are the same, under and over the turf," he is fond of declaiming.

And he adds to that: "All rogues go racing, but not necessarily all people who go racing are rogues."

He was born to be a bookmaker and a gambler. His father, Ignatius Terence Rogers or Terry Senr. (Terry himself is Terence Ignatius) hailed from Elphin, County Roscommon. He began the family bookmaking business as an "illegal" S.P. bookmaker in 1909. Then too as an athlete he competed under an assumed name with the famous Dublin character, "Masher" Gatley, in the big Powderhall professional track handicaps in Scotland (he would have been warned off competing in amateur athletics at home in Ireland if he had been caught) and did quite well in winning his heats and reaching the semi-finals in a few events, though he didn't win out ("he went for the dough, not the glow," recalled Terry).

He made a book on amateur athletics at Jones's Road, where Croke Park, the headquarters of the Gaelic Athletic Association, now stands.

"All the big bookmakers of the day, including 'Banana' Scott, Dick Duggan and others bet on athletics according to what I was told by my father," said Terry.

As a kid Terry used to go to race meetings with his father. Terry Senr. commenced making a book in 1909, the year the King of England's horse Minoru (bred at Tully, County Kildare by Col. Hall Walker) won the Epsom Derby by two lengths at 4/1 and it seemed that the punters were on the Royal challenger to a man with their bets, just as Lovely Cottage was all the rage for the 1946 Grand National and cleaned out the bookies. "Many of the bookies couldn't meet their liabilities on Minoru but my father was able to pay out," said Terry.

Terry Senr. started as an on-course bookmaker in 1914 and the first meeting he stood at was at Limerick races on St. Stephen's Day that same year.

Terry wouldn't describe his father as the greatest or cleverest bookmaker in the world. "He had an office in Hawkins Street and it was his custom to time the customers' bets by Flynn's clock across the road, where the Fleet Bar is now. It was all right until he discovered that a few of the regulars had hit on an amazing winning streak. The staff out of the old *Freemans Journal* had put the clock back a few minutes one day and were actually placing bets after they had seen the results coming in on 'the tissue'."

"The sting is not new," remarked Terry.

Because he wasn't a big success at the game himself, Terry's father tried to dampen any enthusiasm his son showed to become a bookmaker. But it was no use. Terry was hooked on it from an early age and there was going to be no other life for him.

Terry, who was born in the Dublin suburb of Blackrock, from which Pat Eddery also hailed, laboured from his school-days in Dun Laoghaire under the handicap that he suffered from a form of dyslexia — and still is today (it consoles him to think that Michelangelo was also dyslexic).

"I could read figures upside down and back to front but never in the normal way. Just imagine it, the figure 395 would be there in front of me but I couldn't see it the same as other students. I would see the numerals moving on the paper, changing position before my eyes and one minute I would see 935 and the next 953.

"The nightmare of doing the English paper in the Pre-Intermediate Certificate examination at Easter still haunts me to this day. I am convinced I should have got honours, in fact did more than enough to attain the required level but ended up with no marks. Because of my complaint I must, on reflection, have written all the answers down in reverse mirror style."

He left school at the age of 15 in total frustration because he felt deeply wounded at the fact that he hadn't got the reward he knew he should have got for the knowledge he had acquired in his studies for the Easter exam.

He refused to go back to school. When questioned about it in later life he would respond by asking: "Where would all the College graduates be if there were not the school drop-outs to employ them?" ("I actually pinched that line from a show on radio called 'Anything Goes' and the credit must go to a Mr. Brennan, a prominent radio actor.")

He was still sharp as a razor, however and mental arithmetic problems came easy to him. Indeed, if he inherited one facet of this character from his father, it was his genius with figures pertaining to bookmaking and his knowledge of odds and all kinds of multiple bets from doubles and trebles to Yankees and Canadians and Goliaths.

Bets could be slung at him from all sides at a race meeting or at a dog track and the young Terry Rogers would be able to tell the clerk what a particular runner was 'taking out' while the man was still struggling to calculate the exact figure.

Even as a schoolboy he displayed the innovative spirit that would blossom fully when he followed in his father's footsteps and became a bookmaker.

During the Second World War he dealt in pigeons, rabbits and eggs. He would buy pigeons at 1s/9d in Dun Laoghaire and sell them for 3s/6d to Jascourts in Dublin–this firm bought fowl for shipment to England. He also bought rabbits down the country and had little difficulty in disposing of them in Dun Laoghaire and Dublin as roasted or boiled rabbit could be found on many a family table where the Sunday joint is the norm nowadays.

"The eggs I would sell to Welshmen on board the Mail Boat before it left Dun Laoghaire or I would go round from door to door selling them," Terry Rogers recalled.

In the Emergency days, the Republic of Ireland had its local security force akin to Dad's Army in Britain. Terry's father was attached to it, prepared to do his bit for his country. Every Wednesday night there was a dance in the local hall in Dun Laoghaire. There was no bar and no catering. "I used to buy lemonade for 2d and sell them for 6d. A 300 per cent profit wasn't bad!"

He first made a book at a coursing meeting in Kilcullen on New Year's Day, 1946. He had gone there with his own dog, Proud Bog, a runner in one of the stakes. "I got such a bad price about him that I decided to stand myself and call

118

the odds on the other courses."

So at 17½ years of age Terry Rogers Jnr. had entered the profession for which he was tailor-made as events would prove.

He took out a licence in 1947 and the first place he formally made a book was at the now-defunct Naas dog track. Though he would have his ups and downs, it is true to say that no one became better known in the Irish ring as Terry Rogers did in his prime.

Six years in England became his third level education in being hardened into the rudiments of the bookmaking profession. At the same time he would return home at week-ends to give a helping hand to his father on the racecourse. "In time I earned enough to start up as a bookmaker myself."

He was established in his own right as a bookmaker with a national — and indeed international — reputation when his father suffered a stroke in 1968. He admits that he got "the gift of the gab" from his mother Lily who was a native of Dun Laoghaire.

Initially, he was better known laying the odds at dog meetings and coursing meetings than on the racecourse. He bet at dog tracks that have long since disappeared — like the flapper track at Chapelizod and now-defunct Clones while he had a regular pitch at Dundalk, which still survives.

Terry was recognised by racing people as the best judge of a photo finish result. Yet, he will remember August, 1957, as "Black August".

"I lost the money I had accumulated over six years of hard work – both as a bookmaker and gambling myself on photo finishes – all on one race. In fact, I had to borrow £600 from Bill Quinlan to pay the bookmakers as I had invested £13,000 on the loser in that particular photo finish. When the picture was shown to the judge by the operators of the mobile photo finish camera unit, the result went against me by a head. I was skint to all intents and purposes.

"The only currency I had was a collection of silver coins which I had been collecting for years. With these as my 'tank' I went to the dogs in Clones the very next evening. Betting was small and very cagily, I won just under £30. I was back on the road again.

"Bill Quinlan was paid back his £600 at Limerick races on St. Stephen's Day, 1957.

"Reflecting back on that night in Clones, I must say that I always think – and speak – well of Clones people and of the dog track there. It was kind and they were kind to me.

"The year 1958 I might describe as an up-and-down-and-up year. I was going well with the money I won backing Ballymoss, especially when he triumphed in the Prix de l'Arc de Triomphe. Then I opposed him in the Washington DC International Stakes at Laurel Park.

"I had put Bill Quinlan on notice that if Ballymoss won the American race I would be calling for another loan. Bill was in Dublin on the day of the race and we listened to the commentary together in the Clarence Hotel.

"The sharp track and the American jockey got 'Scobie' Breasley and Ballymoss in a pocket for a run until it was too late.'

Terry was back with a vengeance by the end of 1958 – on the road to success and to becoming one of the most colourful and at the same time dynamic bookers in the Irish ring.

He was never to know the position again where he would be skint and have to turn to a collection of silver coins to 'get out', so to speak.

Among the punters, he was known as a bookmaker of total integrity, whatever about his idiosyncrasies or his penchant for blowing his top if someone got under his skin.

As his reputation grew, so did everyone instantly recognise that face at dog tracks and racecourses around Ireland. He brought colour and he brought something different — that sense of interplay between the punter and the bookie that creates an atmosphere you never get at racecourses abroad where there is only the pari-mutuel (tote) operation and at tracks like Acqueduct and Belmont Park in New York you will see them looking at the board, betting only in numbers and getting to the parade ring to

120

J.P. (The Sundance Kid) McManus (above) on his pitch on the rails at Leopardstown and his friend and colleague Jimmy Hayes, the form book expert, dubbed "Butch" when the duo first hit the bookies with a vengeance in the Seventies.

J.P. McManus shows his expertise at Backgammon in a game over coffee with the author, Raymond Smith in his Martinstown House home in Kilmallock, County Limerick.

J.P. (top left) pictured against the background of his home at the Martinstown Stud and (top right) in his study replete with racing and bloodstock publications and (above) playing golf in a Pro-Am Classic by the Lakes of Killarney with John Magnier and Dermot Desmond.

J. P. McManus (above) and his wife Noreen, savour another moment of triumph at Cheltenham, as they proudly hold the trophy won by Danny Connors in taking the 1991 Coral Golden Handicap Hurdle Final and (below) with Jonjo O'Neill who trained Danny Connors to bring off a cleverly-executed coup at remunerative odds, while Laura's Beau (left) is pictured winning the 1992 Ansells National at Uttoxter.

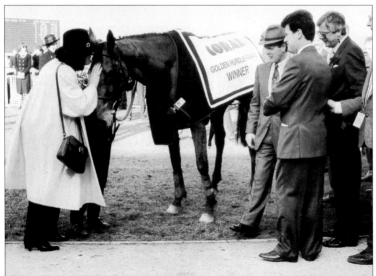

John Magnier the boss of Coolmore, who spearheaded 'The Syndicate' in the golden Seventies with his father-in-law, Vincent O'Brien and Robert Sangster who is pictured (right) with his wife Susan, at the Keeneland July Yearling Sales.

THE KEENELAND BATTLE FRONT . . . Vincent O'Brien and son Charles study the catalogue at the July Yearling Sales and (right) Sheikh Mohammed with trusted adviser, Michael Osborne at his elbow as the big decisions are taken on what yearlings to purchase.

John Mulhern . . . there is flair about everything he does, even in the way he smokes his cigar.

John Mulhern pictured with his father-in-law, former Taoiseach (Prime Minister) Charles J. Haughey at Leopardstown on the day Flashing Steel won a novice hurdle for "The Boss" and (below), realising another Cheltenham Festival ambition as he receives the trainer's trophy after Galmoy's triumph in the 1987 Waterford Crystal Stayers Hurdle.

THE INCOMPARABLES – Caroline Norris's study of the peerless Lester Piggott in conversation with the Master of Ballydoyle in the weighroom at the Curragh on a day in May '92. The great Piggott-O'Brien partnership was renewed when Lester came out of retirement in 1990 and had a fabulous four-timer for Vincent at the Curragh.

FROM CHELTENHAM TO THE CARIBBEAN – Mick O'Toole with winning owner, Mrs. Anne-Marie McGowan and Lord Plummer after Davy Lad had won the 1977 Cheltenham Gold Cup and (left) with Steve Cauthen on the Sandy Lane golf course in Barbados.

look at the horses is completely foreign to them.

In 1950 he was sufficiently ahead to be able to commute to Britain where he worked for top layer Bill Cutler, who got him two dog race meeting pitches at Cradley Heath and Tamworth in partnership..

"We first met at the 1949 Waterloo Cup," Terry recalled. "Over the three days of the meeting the flag only went against my judgement in three courses; in fact the dog I backed in those particular courses actually led and got the first turn but the lead was wiped out by the subsequent work of the one that had been led. Naturally, Bill Cutler was impressed, very impressed and suggested that I might purchase a dog for him, which I did and this same greyhound won him a lot of money, breaking seven track records. Our friendship developed and we were to become very close friends as well as partners."

That friendship survived everything — even the "Ragusa Affair" and Terry having to sell the bulk of his ante-post vouchers on Santa Claus.

In 1961 Terry saw the opportunity stemming from the legislation that legalised betting shops in Britain. "We established a chain of 52 shops throughout the Midlands called Cutler Prescott. We sold out to Ladbrokes in 1972 for £750,000. By today's values they would be worth £20 million."

Such was his adventurous spirit as a bookmaker that Terry Rogers made betting on the proverbial two flies going up a wall seem nothing untoward. He was one of the first bookmakers in Ireland to quote the odds on political issues. Incidentally, he believes that betting on General Elections should not be allowed.

On his own admission to me, Terry laid one of the most amazing bets of all and I feel it deserves another place in the *Guinness Book of Records*.

His mother was on her way to judge a dog show in Salthill, Galway when the car in which she was a passenger was involved in an accident near Oranmore. Another car came out a side road and Lily was tossed through the windscreen and survived.

When the civil case eventually came up for hearing,

121

Terry Rogers just couldn't resist the temptation of laying bets with the barristers on how much his mother would be awarded.

There was only one winner – a barrister, who later became a judge. "A very good judge, a very good judge indeed," laughed Terry.

It was his penchant when accident claims were being heard by a judge and jury in the High Court in Galway to make a book on what damages would be awarded above and under certain levels.

He might set the ambit at under £8,000 or above £10,000 or again under £12,000 or above £14,000.

The barristers representing the insurance companies or those for the claimants loved the "action" it created at the luncheon breaks in the hearings. Terry became quite expert at reading the minds of the juries especially when it came to high-profile cases that had aroused a lot of local interest.

"All right I know you may say it was the ultimate in crazy bets," said Terry with that spontaneous laugh of his. "But we had a lot of fun. Fortunately for me, I never did it in the courtroom itself. I know I would have been put away for contempt of court and shown no mercy by any self-respecting judge."

He was not so lucky when he quoted the "Shamrock Line" on the World Hold 'Em Poker Championship in Las Vegas in 1986, and ended up being detained for eight hours.

But that is a story in itself...

9

When Terry Rogers was Arrested in Las Vegas

Terry Rogers will never forget the day when he was arrested in the Card Room of Binion's Horseshoe Hotel and Casino in downtown Las Vegas during the first break of play on the third day of the 1986 World Hold 'Em Poker Championship.

Three agents of the Nevada State Gaming Control Board, acting on an anonymous telephone call to the effect that illegal sports betting was taking place on the World Series of Poker, swooped on the Card Room and Terry Rogers ended up being held for eight hours in Clark County Detention Centre before being eventually released on his own recognisance.

Now the Horseshoe Casino did not hold a Sports Book licence at that time and, therefore, would not have been entitled to officially run a book or quote odds on the World Series of Poker.

An agent was sent down, on the basis of a tip-off, to investigate. He had no difficulty in finding where the action was. It was at a table inside the roped-off area (confined to players and media representatives) at which Terry Rogers was sitting and there were armed security guards in attendance to ensure that no unauthorised persons got into the area.

The action was not hidden or disguised. In fact, it was quite open to the players in the Card Room area, who were inquiring during the break what way Terry Rogers' "Shamrock Line" rated their particular chances and the remaining contenders generally. "My prices were being bandied about to all and sundry," recalled Terry.

The "Shamrock Line" was used by the professionals to hedge or take or lay bets. Terry's short list of prices for the 1986 World Hold 'Em Championship was published in the magazine *Poker Player* and picked up by the Press Association. It still gives Terry immense satisfaction that he quoted Berry Johnston from Oklahoma the 20/1 favourite and he duly won the title that same year.

The agent surveyed the scene and reported back but there was no one in a senior position at the Gaming Control Board's headquarters to take a quick decision. The result was that two more agents came to The Horseshoe.

"The agents showed their identity cards to the security guards who had no option but to let them through," said Terry Rogers, taking up the story. "The three agents surrounded my table, producing their IDs at the same time. Just before the agents swooped an Irish player, who had just been knocked out of the tournament, had asked me for a bet. I said 'you have it – but write it out'. As it was being handed to me one of the agents declared: 'Let nobody move.' Naturally no one did!

"The chief security guard went away to alert Jack Binion, who was quickly on the scene. He was asked if he was aware of what was going on in the Cardroom area. He replied 'yes,' but added: 'It's harmless.' The agent's response to that was: 'We will decide that.'

"The agents then asked if they could have some place where they could conduct interviews. Jack Binion told them that The Horseshoe had its own interrogation room and they could readily use that.

"All those sitting at the table were ordered to proceed to the interrogation room. One of the players in the tournament, 'Bones' Berland, who had only been sitting at the table waiting for play to resume, screamed in fright, 'I am not with them, I am in the tournament.' This was instantly confirmed by me and Jack Binion re-confirmed it. 'Bones' was let go and I only hope that the fright he got on that occasion had nothing too with the heart attack that killed him about eighteen months later."

Terry Rogers was handed a card listing his rights printed on it. Then the senior agent recited them from another card and asked: "Do you understand?" Terry replied: "Yes."

Terry followed up quickly by declaring that he was giving up his right to remain silent. "I would like to know what I am being charged with and also what offence I have committed?" The agent replied that he did not know for sure but one of the charges would be "conspiracy" (in the States this covers a multitude and represents a classic 'out' for holding a suspect).

Terry then asked would it help if he explained his activities. The response came – "You have the right to remain silent."

To this Terry responded: "I have done no wrong, so I see no need for me to remain silent. If I find out what I am being charged with, I will get an attorney but not until then."

He was then stripped of his possessions and money (he had over 25,000 dollars in cash). One of the agents remarked: "I only earn that in a year and he is treating it like loose change."

The climax came when a car pulled up outside The Horseshoe. "I was handcuffed with my hands behind my back and taken away to the Clark County Detention Centre, that is the local jail. Then the police took over and it was a case of further interrogation and we had to go through all the formalities of finger-printing and I also had to have a mug shot taken of me," recalled Terry.

It was the same in the case of three others who had also been held in the swoop on the Cardroom of the Casino.

But it was the arrest of Terry Rogers that was news – very big news.

The impact it made was such, in fact, that CBS news in its west coast area bulletins relegated President Reagan to second spot that evening while making Terry's detention the lead item. The news-reader began: "Terry Rogers, the Irish bookmaker was arrested for gambling at making a book on the World Series of Poker in Las Vegas today . . ."

He continued against the background of still shots of Las

125

Vegas and of the downtown area where the World Series of Poker was still in progress. The cameras beamed in on tournament players who had readily agreed to be interviewed, among them men who had known Terry for a number of years and had come to regard him as "one of our own."

Everyone interviewed expressed shock, disgust and indignation at the action of the Gaming Control Board. There was spontaneous praise for Terry for holding the Irish Eccentric International No Limit Hold 'Em Championship in Las Vegas and of the tens of thousands of dollars that had been raised for the mentally under-privileged of the State of Nevada by helping Opportunity Village, the favourite charity of Mike Callaghan, a former State Governor and owner of the *Las Vegas Sun* newspaper.

Of course, the fact that a very colourful Irish character was to all intents and purposes "locked up" made headlines in all the local papers and captured the imaginations of all the residents of Las Vegas and Nevada State generally.

The local papers prefer a good gambling story any day to happenings on Capitol Hill in Washington and just as CBS did it in the case of their television news bulletins, the print media put President Reagan down-page as Terry screamed out from Page One in bold black type.

Rogers erupts into a great belly-laugh at the thought that he had up-staged the President of the world's mightiest power.

The bottom line was that Terry was DIFFERENT in the eyes of all those rooting for him in Las Vegas and beyond its immediate boundaries. He answered to all the non-conformist actions that they expected of your typical Irishman, who kicks the traces and let the devil take the hindmost.

Later as Terry was being released from detention, one of the policemen remarked to him wryly: "You got a 'walk thru' man. You've certainly got some 'juice' in this town."

Translated for those not acquainted with the Las Vegas vernacular, it meant that Terry didn't have to seek independent bail but was allowed out on his own recognisances and the fact that he had 'juice' meant that he packed

126

a punch with people of influence, people who could call the shots.

On arriving at the Clark County Detention Centre, Rogers found that right down to the taking of his fingerprints, the process that had to be gone through took hours to complete.

He noticed from his holding cell a bunch of girls in all their finery, earrings and heavy make-up being brought in – "handcuffed with their hands in front, as against the fact that we had been handcuffed with our hands behind our backs."

Obviously there had been a successful raid on some joint. They were taken away to a different part of the building.

Looking back on it six years later, Terry admitted that he quite enjoyed the experience – "as we were treated very well and a holding cell is far different from an ordinary prison cell. I mean, you are in a fairly big area, and you certainly don't get the feeling that you are being consigned to solitary confinement."

The outcome of the Nevada State Gaming Control Board's "bust" for illegal bookmaking was that Terry Rogers argued through his attorney that the business was only done with players who played in the World Hold 'Em Poker Championship – inside the tournament area.

The Poker Players Association of America had asked him to price the players, in order that they could hedge among other players. He obliged and his list of prices was printed with the shamrock logo – thus the "Shamrock Line" – to denote it was the Irish line, that is Terry's handicap line.

Terry further argued that it was no different from being in a no-limit game of poker. If he had been convicted all no-limit card games would have to close in the State of Nevada.

His attorney was Oscar Goodman, who had been recommended by Benny Binion and who was the top attorney specialising in charges and cases of this kind.

All charges were dropped including that of conspiracy, provided there was no counter suit for illegal detention.

When Terry Rogers was being handed all his possessions back, including his money, Will Hart, the Senior Agent of the Nevada Gaming Control Board Enforcement Division remarked to him, as he gave him his card: "If you ever get into trouble in this town again, don't hesitate to call me."

Whenever Terry goes to the United States now, he carries Hart's card with him.

One of those who came forward and spoke for Terry Rogers was Mike Callaghan, who, as we have already seen, was a former State Governor. In June, 1987 a Seminar of Gaming Attorneys was held in Dromoland Castle and a top representative of the Nevada Gaming Control Board said at a luncheon in the presence of Mike Callaghan, who had flown in from the States, and Terry Rogers, who delivered a paper that Terry's arrest in Las Vegas was a mistake and that it should never have happened. "I sincerely hope it doesn't happen again," said Mike Callaghan amidst applause from the Las Vegas delegates present.

The epilogue to Terry's brush with the agents of the Nevada State Control Board was that he was granted the title of Rt. Hon. Col. Terry Rogers, Kentucky Colonel by William G. Wilkinson shortly after he became Governor of the State of Kentucky. It is the highest honour that can be bestowed by the Commonwealth of Kentucky. Terry had the parchment confirming this framed. It occupies a position of honour in his flat in Dublin's north-side.

Terry had been visiting Las Vegas – that city of "glitz and glitter" forged out of the Nevada Desert – since 1970 when he travelled there to purchase equipment for his Amusement Arcade in Salthill, Galway. It was then that he first rubbed shoulders with Benny Binion, who was to play a key role in the development of the World Poker Championship, carried on today by his son, Jack.

However, it was really from 1980 that Terry Rogers became an integral part of the Las Vegas scene each May during the World Series of Poker. That evolved from his initiative in inaugurating the Irish Poker Championship, each competitor paying £500 to compete and an extra £50 for the charities which the Eccentric Club, of which Terry was President, supported.

When Colette Doherty emerged as the first ever Irish champion, Terry was the driving force in ensuring that it didn't end there. He ensured that she put down the $10,000 from her winnings to compete in the World Hold 'Em Championship itself. The fact that "the girl with brown eyes" from the Emerald Isle had the gumption to enter brought more worldwide attention than ever before to the Las Vegas event and the credit went to Terry Rogers.

Even though she did not get beyond the first table on the first day in Las Vegas in 1980, Colette Doherty had blazed the trail for Ireland. Others would follow. Donnacha O'Dea, son of Denis O'Dea, the film actor and Siobhan McKenna, one of Ireland's finest actresses, made it to the last table more than once and established himself as capable of more than holding his own with the best. Noel Furlong followed and as Irish champion also made it to the final table, taking sixth place in the world.

Terry Rogers has been credited by Bobby Baldwin, President of the Mirage Resort Hotel in Las Vegas and by Eric Drache, the former Co-ordinator of the World Series of Poker with being the greatest single factor after Benny Binion with spreading poker on an international basis.

Terry brought top professionals from America to Dublin for a major tournament in the Killiney Castle Hotel in September, 1983 that was acclaimed the most ambitious venture ever staged outside the United States. It put the game on a new footing internationally.

Four world champions, "Amarillo Slim" Preston (1972), "Puggy" Pearson (1973), Stu "The Kid" Ungar (1980 and '81) and Tom McEvoy (1983) competed, also Perry Green, The Man From Alaska and leading pros from Britain. McEvoy emerged the winner.

The previous year Bobby Baldwin, the 1978 world champion had come to Dublin to take part in the Eccentric Club's International Tournament and this was won by Derek Webb, one of the top British players, who had competed in Las Vegas. Terry Rogers took runner-up place.

Terry became a consultant to hotels in setting up international tournaments. He helped advise in the organisation of tournaments in the Royal Swaziland Hotel in Swaziland in Southern Africa, in the Concorde Hotel in Aruba in the Nederland Antilles off South America and in Caesar's Hotel in Lake Tahoe.

He was on first name terms with everyone who was anybody in the world of poker. To the English competitors he was 'Tel', to the security guards in Binion's he was "Mr. Raw-gers" and to the Irish participants he was simple "Terry", mentor and motivator.

To the Japanese tourists watching him as he fed the squirrels in Colorado's Grand Canyon on cookies and rolos, he was the very epitome of the eccentric Irishman and they HAD to be photographed with him.

Yes, flamboyant Terry Rogers was unquestionably unique in the eyes of those who made it annually to the World Series of Poker. In a word, he had become a fixture every bit as much as Johnny Moss, "Puggy" Pearson, Doyle "Texas Dolly" Brunson and the incomparable Jack (Treetop) Straus.

You have got to understand and appreciate how it all began, the wealth of tradition behind it, to realise why Terry's arrival each year meant so much to the real pros and why they set up such a spontaneous outcry when they learned that he had been detained for something they regarded as ludicrous in this hard-bitten world.

Men drive into Las Vegas in smooth cadillacs now where in the Old West they rode into dusty prairie towns seeking action. The Stetson is retained as the Texan symbol – the symbol of a nostalgic world that a certain breed of men will not let die. You live a lot of the passion and cama-raderie that was the Old West in Binion's during the days of the World Series of Poker.

It provides the setting for old friends who may not see each other for the rest of the year. As Jack Straus explained it to me, in the Old West you had the trappers and prospectors who lived in the hills and others who were on the move all the time, some maybe living with the Indians. Every few years they would rendezvouz and have what might be described as a 'festival'. There would be all kinds of games and sports – and card sessions also. It was out of this idea of the 'rendezvouz' that the World Series of Poker eventually evolved.

They come then to Las Vegas in April, leaving towards the end of May, men who play the circuits outside this city that never sleeps and who are top of the pile maybe in their own areas; really good players who would mop up most others in a long day's poker journey into night. They come too, men who make their wealth out of oil and cattle in Texas and who want for none of the luxuries of life – men who may have so much that they can hardly count their wealth.

The finest no limit Hold 'Em players were to be found in Texas before non-Texans learned the game. Among the oil-rich millionaires you can discover amateurs who have outstanding skill at the game and who are prepared to back their belief in themselves with money. What they seek is action – the kind of action that money cannot buy but their wealth allows them to put down the 10,000 dollars required to compete in the "Big One". Of course, they will have played in private head-to-head matches against the professionals back in Texas for stakes far, far higher than 10,000 dollars. In Binion's Horseshoe Casino in May, however, they find the setting and the atmosphere that brings out the qualities you expect to see in true champions.

They come too the "home town champions" and the "weekend wonders" – as they dub them in Las Vegas – guys who have made a name for themselves in their own localities and now want to see if they can beat the world.

"They all come to Las Vegas eventually," was how "Puggy" Pearson, world champion in 1973 put it. "And they find out what they want to know, maybe at a cost in money and pride, but they have to know it, otherwise they would not come."

They may strike it lucky in the World Hold 'Em Championship and get beyond the first table on the first day and may even make it to the second day – and many of them are encouraged by the thought that 1979 saw Californian public relations consultant, Hal Fowler become the first amateur to win this prestigious event, besting a field of 54 players to edge out Bobby (The Wizard) Hoff for first-place money of 270,000 dollars (i.e. 50% of the pool, the balance

131

being divided up between the players down to the No. 6).

Encouraged too by the knowledge that in 1980 Stuart (Stu) Ungar – The Kid from New York – beat Doyle Brunson in a shoot-out at high noon to become World Champion, taking first prize money of 365,000 dollars. He was then only 26 and had been at odds of 50/1 before the Championship.

"The Kid is going to be a really great player," Doyle Brunson predicted. "He is like a young jungle animal when you think you have him cornered. His instincts tell him what to do and he seems to come up with the right move – instinctively."

And Brunson was right. The Kid retained his title in 1981, this time beating Perry Green, the Man from Alaska in the final confrontation.

Usually the amateurs and less experienced professionals wither in the fierce fires and under the intense pressures that develop as the field is drastically reduced.

Las Vegas in May then is a world of high rollers, some of them not content to employ their skill solely at poker – where they can turn the odds in their favour, especially against players less skilled than themselves – will bet on anything from horses to American football, baseball and basketball, and golf matches. And they will toss away small fortunes won at the card table in casino games of chance.

Like Perry Green, the runner-up for the World Hold 'Em crown in 1981 who confided to me that he won 250,000 in one year playing poker and then lost 200,000 dollars of that total shooting craps. "I like shooting craps," he said with no sense of regret.

The crap table is his way of finding diversion. "If poker was my sole means of livelihood, it would not be fun losing 200,000 dollars at the crap table," he admitted. But Perry, who took over the family fur trade business from his father, doesn't have to worry about money.

Jack Straus from San Antonio, Texas was 500,000 dollars richer after winning the 1982 World Hold 'Em title. But inside eight days he blew the lot betting on golf matches, in which he participated, and on taking the odds on other

132

sports events (most of it at golf).

One day he had asked me to join Stu Ungar, Doyle Brunson and himself in a fourball for 10,000 dollars a head. That would only be for 'openers' as there would be additional side-bets on birdies and eagles and whose ball was nearest the hole at every par-three after we had hit from the tee and right down the line to betting on how near you might get to the flag when blasting out of a bunker – and who would sink the last four-footers to six-footers if it came down to that on the 18th green and everything rested on a few crucial putts. Naturally I declined, for even if I had that kind of money I knew I would freeze playing for such high stakes with men who showed the fighting qualities of jungle animals when they looked defeat in the face.

Jack Straus, incidentally, saw courage as an all-important ingredient in the make-up of the true professional gambler, be it at poker or horse-racing or, indeed, in any form of sports betting. "You cannot hope to get anywhere without it."

Yet he added this very important proviso – before you go into any serious gambling situation (and that would hold true, of course, for a punter going into the ring, say at Cheltenham during the Festival meeting or at Royal Ascot), you must ask yourself the question: Can I afford to play for high stakes?

You cannot play or compete at such a level if you are concerned about your bankroll.

In Las Vegas you touch the very pulse of the world of born gamblers and the philosophy that moves them. For these men life itself is a gamble. Doyle Brunson, author of the classic 600-page work, *How I Made A Million Dollars Playing Poker*, learned only four months after he got married that he had "incurable" cancer. He survived against all the odds, after major neck surgery and, on his own admission, through his wife's "great belief in prayer always."

Jack Straus, who liked to quote the immortal phrase "better a day as a lion than one hundred years as a lamb," certainly lived every minute of his life – like a lion.

Bearded Jack, known as "Treetop" by his fellow professionals – he stood 6ft. 6ins. tall – was not alone an outstanding character but a student of life who had a great feeling for people. Of all the professional poker players I met during my trips to Las Vegas, I liked him best of all and so too, I know, did Terry Rogers. It hit us very badly when we learned of his untimely and sudden passing before he had reached his 60th birthday.

They tell a story about him which gives a greater insight into the sensitivity of his character and the motto by which he lived than anything I could hope to portray in this chapter.

The Taxman had decided to make an assessment, and, remember, that Uncle Sam, apart from expecting the professional poker player to pay his share in taxes from his earnings, can bill his subjects for a cut from the winnings when someone hits the Jackpot at one of the Las Vegas slot machines.

The bill Jack Straus received was a mammoth one of one million dollars or more – emerging no doubt from some computer in Washington that made absolutely no allowance for losses incurred. Even a poker player as great as Jack Straus could lose sometimes!

Jack decided to appeal. While he was waiting his turn to be called, he could not help listening to the case of a man who was endeavouring to save his house because he had failed to meet his liabilities of about 50,000 dollars.

His wife and kids, he complained, had walked out on him because of the mounting pressures after the tax bill arrived. The little guy, like a beaten dog, broke down and sobbed: "If you take my house from me, my wife is less likely to come back and bring the kids with her. Please leave me my home," he begged.

From the back of the room, Jack Straus piped up at that moment – "Stick the 50,000 dollars on my tab. It won't make that much difference!"

Jack was always there each May to welcome Terry Rogers with open arms, as if he was a grizzled trapper or prospector coming in from the hills for the "rendezvouz". The same in the case of Doyle Brunson and Bobby Baldwin and Stu Ungar and Perry Green and all the others. And most of all from Benny Binion before he passed on.

134

They loved Terry for the style and non-stop reparatee he brought to the green-baize table when he competed in the Preliminary World Hold 'Em Championship in 1981.

They loved him for his judgement when he gave them "a line" – the Shamrock Line – on the "Big One" itself, the World Hold 'Em Championship and for his courage in getting involved in the betting action himself. He spotted the genius of Stu Ungar and made a killing on him by backing him at 50/1 to win the 1980 crown and at 25/1 to retain it the following year. "I knew after watching him for just a few hours that he was special," said Terry.

They loved him most of all for opening up new horizons worldwide for the game of poker. In their eyes he was a character out-and-out.

All that lay a decade ahead when Terry Rogers first hit Las Vegas in 1970 – to buy gaming machines. And poker was the furthest thing from his mind.

An invitation to dinner came from Benny Binion, who told him that while he was from Texas himself, his grandparents came from Ireland "around the time of the Famine."

"Any squirrel on tonight?" Benny mischievously queried the waiter, as Terry nearly collapsed over his menu. "Not this evening, Sir," the waiter shot back, not batting an eyelid. The "special" comprised stone crabs and prime rib of beef, New York cut. "That's fine," said Benny, telling the waiter at the same time to add "ranch dressing" with Terry's salad. And, yes, bring a carafe of Burgundy.

Terry acquainted Benny with his bookmaking operations back in Ireland. Benny in turn regaled Terry with stories of Texas and Montana and his early days as a bootlegger. "He was obviously enjoying himself hugely trying to shock me," recalled Terry.

He also impressed Terry by telling him he had been under observation from the time he hit Las Vegas. "He knew where I was staying, what room I was in and how many times I had been in The Horseshoe the previous two days."

The friendship developed from that evening and stood the test of time. And Terry got to see the Perry Como show (after failing a number of times to book reservations, there was such a demand), Benny simply advising him to ignore the seemingly endless queue and head instead for the guest line – "I'll fix it." He said it was not the only thing he fixed!

Each time Terry returned to Las Vegas after that – over six trips in all up to 1978 – he missed out on meeting Benny Binion. And each time he was told that Benny was at his ranch in Montana. The only way he could be certain of contacting him was during the World Series of Poker in May.

So it happened in 1978 when Terry Rogers was privileged to see Bobby (The Owl) Baldwin from Tulsa, Oklahoma, one of the "College Boys", battle out the final table with Crandall Addington and become World Champion at the age of 25.

"I was completely thrilled with the whole affair," said Terry. There and then he became convinced that "the game was designed for the elan and panache of the Irish" and that representatives from Ireland would in time make their mark on the World Hold 'Em Championship. He decided on the spot also that he would bring an Irish champion to play in the World Championship.

It evolved from there – Colette Doherty's debut in 1980 and all that followed.

The journalists covering the World Series of Poker like myself wanted "a line" or odds on the different contestants and increasingly, as a greater and greater world spotlight turned on the annual May event, Terry Rogers found himself supplying this service.

On the eve of the 1980 World Hold 'Em Championship, I asked Terry to give me his list. He gladly obliged, adding that he would check out at the same time what Jackie Gaughan, a local odds-maker and owner of the El Cortez Hotel and Casino was quoting.

Terry takes it up: "I rang the El Cortez and was informed that Mr. Gaughan was not in the hotel but a new line would be available the next morning at 9 a.m. I recall I had made Doyle Brunson favourite with Gabe Kaplan and Dicky Carson and with Johnny Moss, World Champion in

1970 (voted by his peers), and '71 at 33/1.

"Next morning Jackie Gaughan walked into the sombrero Room restaurant in Binion's while I was having breakfast and gave me his list. My prices were slightly higher with one exception – he was quoting Johnny Moss at 100/1. 'That price you are quoting about Johnny Moss is a mistake,' I said to Jackie, showing him my own odds of 33/1. He just shrugged his shoulders and remarked: "That's the line.'

"I only had 50 dollars in cash in my pocket, so I handed it to Jackie and said '100/1 to 50 dollars,' adding 'you can now change the line as I regard 100/1 about a player of Moss's ability as utterly ridiculous.' Again he shrugged his shoulders: "The line's the line.'

"Then all hell broke loose. Pat Callahan, an Irish-American professional poker player was first in to take the 100/1. Others followed.

"Before he had finished his cup of coffee, Jackie Gaughan had laid Johnny Moss to lose 1,000,000 dollars. Word of the bets being struck reached out from the Sombrero Room into the Casino proper and a number of people headed off down to the El Cortez where Jackie ran his betting business – and more bets were struck. Before Jackie could get down to ticket and record the action a further 750,000 dollars liabilities had been incurred.

"Johnny Moss was down very low at that stage with one per cent of the chips and then came back, so much so that he jumped to a point where he was tournament leader in the money placings and could well have won the title for the fourth time. Then his luck ran out when he got Doyle Brunson all in, only to see his house of queens beaten by Doyle's four nines. He then lost out to Stu Ungar for all that he had left in chips. Doyle and Stu fought out the final, which The Kid won.

"But I am convinced that if he had won the big pot against Doyle Brunson, he would have taken complete control of the game and become odds-on favourite to win out. However, fortune smiled on the brave Jackie Gaughan of Irish-American stock.

"My most cherished memory of the 1980 World Series

will always be of the kingly courage of Jackie Gaughan, who did not shut up shop when the betting men put down their money on Johnny Moss. That was what I call making a book and standing by the line and not running scared when the first REAL money came for your 100/1 outsider. His total liabilities were just under 2 million dollars. It was the bravest thing I ever saw in betting."

Between the winning bets he had on Stu Ungar when The Kid retained his World Championship crown in 1981 and his own winnings in private poker games, Terry Rogers deposited 100,000 dollars in "The Cage" in Binion's and paid for two entries from Ireland to the 1982 World Hold 'Em Championship. When he returned in '82 his "Shamrock Line" had Jack Straus one of the co-favourites at 16/1, along with Bobby Baldwin, David "Chip" Reese and Doyle Brunson.

It's history now how when it came down to the wire at the last table on the last day it developed into a head-to-head between Jack Straus and Dewey Tomko from Florida. Dewey looked home and dry for the 500,000 first prize when after "the flop" had been dealt he had a pair of fours and still had the edge after fourth street. Jack Straus needed a ten now for the title. The odds against him getting that were 14/1. The dealer burnt the top card before dealing fifth street. He turned over the ten of clubs. Jack Straus was World Champion.

Terry Rogers little knew it – but he was only four years away from being arrested as he shared with Jack Straus his moment of ultimate triumph.

By 1986 the "Shamrock Line" was the official line for the World Hold 'Em Poker Championship and, in fact, was being used in every poker publication. Terry paid his 10,000 dollars to play in the "Big One" and got knocked out in the first hand.

Having participated in the tournament meant that Terry was entitled to stay in the tournament area.

Three hours after play ceased on the first day he distributed his "Shamrock Line" to players who had been involved. The next morning he was inundated with bets. He had to get help. He accepted the offers. The third morn-

138

ing he had a table put at his disposal inside the playing area.

That table became the focus when the three agents from the Nevada State Gaming Control Board made their swoop and Terry's world was changed for eight amazing hours.

The last word on that extraordinary episode in an extraordinarily colourful career lies with Terry: "I was a guest at the Frank Sinatra Show in the Golden Nugget Cabaret Room the night after they released me. Two of the people who had been arrested with me were also guests. Frank was in tremendous form that same night. One of my companions could not help remarking: 'Some contrast. Yesterday the Clark County Detention Centre, tonight front-row seats at Sinatra'."

Terry had come a long way from the day nearly forty years earlier when he took out a bookmaker's licence.

He saw the arrival on the scene of some of the greatest gamblers and also had a pitch in the ring through some of the most exciting times in Irish racing history – the era of P.J. ('Darkie') Prendergast, the trainer he dubs the greatest when it came to bringing off a "job" ("if I wanted a man to plan a robbery, I would send for 'Darkie'," was how Terry put it); then the rise up the ladder of Vincent O'Brien, the 'King' first of the jumps scene both at Cheltenham and Aintree and then, turning his attention solely to the Flat, winning the Epsom Derby six times, apart from all his other brilliant achievements; Paddy Sleator – "there will never be his equal"; Georgie Wells – "among the best I felt to get a horse ready for a coup"; Mickey Rogers – "he always aimed for big targets and it was a tremendous achievement of his to win the Epsom Derby twice in six years with Hard Ridden (1959) and Santa Claus (1964)."

He heard all about the trail-blazers in the bookmaking profession from his father – men like 'Banana' Scott and 'Happy' Harry Evans and Dick Duggan. And he saw in action in the ring men who won unstinted respect for the way they operated as bookmakers – Paddy Power, father of David, Jim Rice, 'a great bookmaker", Patsy McAlinden, another of the fearless Northern Ireland bookies who left a lasting legacy.

During the Second World War the petrol rationing meant that the circumstances in which one could drive a car were very strictly regulated.

But it didn't stop the bookies getting to the races, even at the most out-of-the-way Provincial track. "If they couldn't get there by turf-burning trains, let's say they discovered that there was a funeral down the country of a near and dear relative and the petrol coupons would be manufactured out of thin air to allow a car to be pressed into service and four or five bookmakers would pile into it to give a fitting 'farewell' to the granny or grandfather or first cousin," Terry recalled.

There were powerful combinations that the bookies feared like that between Joe McGrath and Michael Collins, father of Curragh trainer, Con Collins. Also the partnership between trainer Hubert Hartigan and Joe Canty.

Terry Rogers on the domestic front did not confine his gambling to laying the odds on all kinds of sports activities.

He gambled too on buying shares in the tickets drawn in the Irish Sweepstake on the horses he judged could be in the first three. Naturally he would be in for a substantial return to his investment if he could hit the winner and maybe the second horse as well, if not the third also. Generally speaking, people were quite happy to sell a share; that way it meant you were guaranteed something at the five-figure to ten-figure level should your horse run badly and end up out of a place. "I paid for a lot of my expansion in the Sixties by buying shares in winning horses," said Terry.

But one year – 1972 – it all went wrong for him when Steel Pulse, trained by 'Scobie' Breasley and ridden by Bill Williamson won the Irish Sweeps Derby at 10/1 in a field of fourteen with Scottish Rule second and Ballymore third.

"I had bought shares in the Sweeps tickets on practically every other runner in the race that I considered had a reasonable chance," recalled Terry. "And then at the racecourse itself, the last bet I laid on Steel Pulse was £5,000 to £500. In all I lost £24,000 on that Derby."

Terry Rogers too got involved in gambling on shares.

140

You might ask "why?" when his forte was his astute judgement of a potential champion in the racing game or at the dog track or a coursing meeting, even in the boxing ring, and, as we have seen, at poker.

But again it can be put down to the risk-taking element in his make-up. He wouldn't be happy if he wasn't going for a killing of some kind as a gambler or quoting a line as a bookmaker. It was in his blood from the cradle.

He has had his ups and downs at the shares – more downs than ups.

As some shrewd professional punters will avoid betting in handicaps like the plague, so wise investors in shares will keep out of oil and gas.

But Terry Rogers made some very hefty investments in oil shares. He admitted to Damien Kiberd of the *Sunday Business Post* that his worst ever investment in an oil share was on Bula Resources. "I was a long term investor in Bula. For many years I was the biggest private investor in the firm. I bought 460,000 of them at 50p each. Early on I had 670,000 purchased at an average of 8p or 9p each. I sold the lot for 2½p each. Twenty-six grand. That's all I got for them."

Before Bula he went for a killing on Tara, buying a quantity of them in Canada at ten shillings each and selling out at £14 ("I only got paid a quarter of what I set out to acquire and, therefore, made far less than I should"). He went into Irish Distillers in the week before the October '87 crash ("I bought and sold in the same account and lost nine or ten grand"). "Unfortunately too I was a name (that is part of a syndicate) in Lloyds and this has cost me considerably in 1991-92. I tried to get out in 1988," he said.

"I was jinxed all along," he added ruefully.

His successes: "I made money over the years on Aran. I won't deny that. But twice I failed to get into the share when I should have done so. I did well too out of Northgate. I'm not really bothered about stocks and shares now, though I have a few Silvermines and Aran left."

Overall, he admits, he did not make the REAL money from his investments in stocks and shares that he should have made.

But it makes no difference in the final analysis. Terry Rogers will be remembered not for his ventures into the stock market but as a bookmaker first and foremost who gave the small punter a better chance of winning and as one who always paid promptly.

Any regrets? "One way or another I wouldn't have changed a thing," he laughs.

You see, Terry is one man who can say with Frank Sinatra – "I Did It My Way".

A fitting epitaph for his tombstone – if he should decide to write one.

PART FIVE

PADDY SLEATOR
The Master of Grangecon

10

Those Blitz Campaign Days with Arthur Thomas

In his heyday as the Master of Grangecon there was no one the bookies, both in Ireland and England, feared more than Paddy Sleator.

He was a master of the betting coup. There had always been a good leavening of big punters among his patrons and he considered it an essential part of his business to be able to tell them when to "put the money down".

Few episodes in the history of National Hunt racing match the strike rate he achieved when he teamed up with Warwick trainer, Arthur Thomas in the early sixties and the blitz campaign they waged over a four-year period saw the winners flow with a regularity that was unparalleled in its consistency. Little Scottish Memories, who got nearly as fulsome a press in his day as Arkle did in later years, won in all 23 races while operating out of Warwick. Paddy Sleator has confided to friends that he never trained a more consistent horse than this one. And, naturally he had a special affection for Scottish Memories.

Although the public image of Sleator was of a man who made a fortune from gambling, he rarely bet more than £200 on a stable "good thing" and his normal investment was more likely to be £100. But, of course, there were owners with horses in the stable that loved to have a real tilt at the ring and when the ring was hit, the bookies certainly felt it.

Someone who knew him well remarked to me that it

was always best and most profitable to get the word from Paddy on the Wednesday preceding a Saturday tilt at the ring rather than on the eve or morning of the race itself. In the actual final count-down to the projected gamble, Sleator's enthusiasm would be softened by whispers concerning fancied runners from other stables and he would look for a hundred reasons why his own one could get beat.

"As often as not I would wind up cutting my own intended £100 bet to a pony or even a tenner," was how he put it to Louis Gunning. Louis, the former deeply-respected Racing Correspondent of the *Irish Press*, came to greatly admire the Master of Grangecon from a close study of his achievements over a thirty years' span. And he concluded that he was "without peer among National Hunt personalities in his cool judgement of a horse's ability and in his critical assessment of form".

The bookies learned to take no chances whatsoever with any Sleator runner they sensed was "on the job". Immediately those doing the commission for the stable went into action around the ring, boards were quickly wiped clean and a horse could go from odds-against to odds-on in a twinkling. Conversely, you might get one that seemed on the face of it to stand out as a gilt-edged proposition but when there was no "inspired" money forthcoming, it would drift right out of the reckoning.

Over a span of half a century Paddy Sleator was always among the leaders of his profession, a breaker of moulds and a maker of them in that his very success saw rules introduced to clip his wings. And yet when he challenged those who set those same rules by reaching out to new horizons, it ultimately rebounded to the benefit of trainers who had been jealous of him and, indeed, to Irish racing as a whole.

There is no better illustration of this than the momentous decision he took to concentrate all his best jumpers in England and, as Louis Gunning noted, "in retrospect it probably did more for the good health of Irish National Hunt racing than any action at official or unofficial level".

In opting for the course he chose to take, Paddy Sleator was staging a one-man rebellion against the limitations and constrictions imposed by the programme planners on all classes of jumpers — from the maidens and novices right through to the "has-beens", old horses past their best but still lodged on handicap marks which related to their peak performances in their younger days. He was deeply perturbed also at the low level of prize money which pertained in Ireland in that period and the powers-that-be must have known that many stables could not have survived unless they brought off successful gambles.

Just as Vincent O'Brien had shown with Hatton's Grace and Knock Hard, Paddy Sleator proved that a horse of real ability could reveal the talent to win both in the National Hunt arena and on the Flat. He landed an unprecedented hat-trick of victories in the Irish Cesarewitch with the bumper horse Sword Flash, Havasnack and the subsequent 1960 Champion Hurdle winner, Another Flash.

It resulted in a rule being introduced precluding bumpers winners from Flat handicaps unless they made themselves eligible by running three times under Turf Club rules. So Paddy Sleator's expertise in exploiting the talent at his disposal within the framework of the rules as they had existed, rebounded against him and his patrons and caused another restructuring of the face of Irish racing.

His response was not to pull up his roots and leave Ireland entirely but to seek greater opportunities for the best material in his Grangecon yard. The direct outcome was the establishment of the Sleator-Thomas partnership.

Quite a number of Sleator's patrons were English and, therefore, they could understand the logic behind his move and, furthermore, they would be able to follow their horses with greater facility while getting an enhanced return for their investments (apart altogether from the increased betting opportunities).

Everything seemed to fit into place perfectly in the jig-saw. Arthur Thomas had a second yard available at his Warwick establishment and superb all-weather gallops.

The horses sent over from Grangecon to be based there would appear on the racecards as "trained Arthur

Thomas" but, of course, Sleator himself would be the brains behind the whole operation. He would even go so far as to supply stable and work staff and the horses would invariably be ridden by riders he trusted.

Much of the campaign planning was done from an "operations room" set up in a flat in Ballsbridge owned by Paddy Sleator's friend, Ted Curtin. Looking at a map of Britain, Sleator could see that Warwick was ideally situated as a command centre for fanning out to all the important jumping courses in England and Scotland. It was also close enough to Birmingham airport to enable the "Field Marshal" to travel to and fro without any great inconvenience and he could be readily on the spot for the "real action" at the English racecourse of his choice any weekend.

"It is doubtful," Louis Gunning recalls, "if English trainers had any idea of the full force of the blitz to which they were going to be subjected when Clipador became the first winner for the Sleator-Thomas partnership at Wincanton in 1961. Between that and 1966, when the partnership ended, the winners came off the Warwick assembly line almost conveyor-belt style. And what names there were among them: Harwell, Black Ice, Another Flash, Rupununi, Extra Stout, Albinella, What a Boy and Scottish Memories.

"Yet again the price of success for the mastermind of Grangecon was bitter-sweet. Jealousy was now engendered in local trainers who saw Thomas merely as the man-of-straw and his Irish partner as the man who was sweeping up too much of their stakes money. By a very elastic interpretation of a rule relating to payments to an amateur, Thomas had his licence refused and bland assurances to Paddy Sleator from official level that he might be able to make an accommodation with some other English trainer proved to be mere window-dressing."

The authorities in Ireland could not but have taken cognisance of the fact that National Hunt racing in the country had been poorer for the absence over a stretch of four seasons of the star jumpers from Grangecon.

Action followed. "There was as a result a more liberal

147

spread of opportunities made available for maiden and novice jumpers," recalled Louis Gunning, "and more importantly the gap between stakes money levels on English and Irish courses was narrowed. Paddy Sleator's English patrons would find it more rewarding to have horses with him at Grangecon now."

While much has been written about Paddy Sleator's "English adventure", not many are aware that during the ban on racing imposed as a result of the foot-and-mouth disease outbreak in England in 1968, the Grangecon trainer took a batch of seven horses to be stabled at a jumping course at Cagnes-Sur-Mer near Nice. Between them they won £12,000 in stakes money in seven weeks and five of them — kept out of claiming races until the last week — were entered and sold handsomely afterwards.

Fate decreed that Paddy Sleator would become a trainer — as a result of contracting a bout of rheumatic fever when he was nine.

The family doctor barred him from bicycle riding, a normal medium for letting off steam by boys of that age. Recommended instead was the more leisurely activity of jogging and trotting a pony up and down the hills which radiate the picturesque area of Grangecon in County Wicklow.

Thus was born a love of horses in young Paddy Sleator, soon reflected in his graduation to gymkhanas. By the time he had become a teenager it was so ingrained in his blood that he progressed to hunting and point-to-pointing and from there to an embryo champion amateur rider.

Before he reached his twentieth birthday he was the proud owner of his first racehorse. He was a somewhat decrepid old horse called Slaney Boy and he cost just £12. That was the price Dublin breeder, Richard Ball was to pay for the dam of the great Ballymoss many years later. Paddy trained Slaney Boy himself and rode him to win a steeplechase over the old Boyerstown Hunt course near Navan.

Already it was obvious that he had that touch of genius in his make-up that Vincent O'Brien would reveal from the day he set up as a public trainer in his own right in 1943 and the following year sent out Drybob to dead-heat for the Irish Cambridgeshire and won the Irish Cesarewitch the same season with Good Days. Frank Vickerman netted £5,000 from the double (it would have been £10,000 but for the dead-heat in the first leg of the Autumn Double) and Vincent himself got the nest-egg of £1,000 that would make all the difference to him as an 'unknown' trainer of 27. It was out of his £5,000 winnings that Frank Vickerman bought Cottage Rake in due course and this fine chaser in winning the first of three successive Gold Cups in 1948 started the cycle that would see Vincent O'Brien become 'king' of Cheltenham for a decade.

It was in 1929 that Paddy Sleator arrived in Grangecon and took out a trainer's licence the same year. Dublin publican and racehorse owner, Thomas O'Reilly recognised the potential in young Sleator and sent him a young horse named West Wicklow — and thereby hangs a tale.

Bred in Kells, County Meath and a son of a moderate stallion called Tangiers, West Wicklow was not a big or a very imposing horse. He was eventually entered for a bumper at the Leopardstown April meeting and Paddy Sleator himself had the leg up. The horse won at 20/1 and in so doing beat Tidley Bates, owned by Daniel ('Dom') Leahy.

Leahy had gone for a real old-fashioned "touch" on Tidley Bates, which went off a very warm favourite.

An objection for crossing was lodged against West Wicklow. It failed. Later it was sought to have West Wicklow disqualified on the grounds that he was trained in a stable which housed an "illegal" horse. Someone had discovered that Slaney Boy, before arriving in Grangecon, competed in flapper events.

Paddy Sleator survived that disqualification bid also. The final irony was that Dom Leahy purchased West Wicklow for a reputed 2,000 guineas — a lot of money in those days — and got the losses on Tidley Bates back when 'Wicklow' won the English Cesarewitch in 1929 when he was trained by Captain Hogg and ridden by Gordon Richards' brother, Cliff.

149

"The exercise was probably of inestimable value to the young rider-trainer in educating him in the niceties of argumentation with the Stewards," recalled Louis Gunning. "In the years of brilliant success which followed, there were clashes galore between him and officialdom. I remember many of them and can say with some conviction that on a round-by-round basis, Paddy Sleator emerged as a clear winner on points. Behind his impressive features dwelt a razor-sharp mind which but for that boyhood bout of rheumatic fever could well have taken him to the top of many alternative professions.

"He went so quickly to the top as an amateur rider over hurdles and fences as well as on the Flat that the Stewards decided to restrict him from riding in any but amateur riders' races. His case formed the basis of the present day rules regarding the types of races in which amateurs may ride and the number of races in which they may ride against professionals. In the year (1934) in which the ban was imposed he won the Galway Plate with Reviewer. His fondness for this great mid-summer steeplechase and his exceptional skill in 'laying one out' for it was exemplified by his record of eight training successes starting with Silent Plate, which Tim Molony rode to victory in 1948 and continuing with Amber Point (1954 and '55), Knight Errant (1957), Sparkling Flame (1960), Royal Day (1967 and 1969) and O'Leary (1976)."

Apart from Tim Molony, other renowned jump jockeys associated with the Sleator-trained Plate winners were Paddy Farrell, Bobby Beasley and Bobby Coonan.

In 1957 Sleator brought off the coveted Galway double, winning the Hurdle with Mrs Paddy Meehan's Tymon Castle and the Plate with Mrs Ann Biddle's Knight Errant, who also won the Hurdle in 1958.

'Peerless Punchestown', with a world of tradition behind it, appealed to him in a very special way and he loved to win at that Spring meeting. On April 28, 1953 he had the distinction of turning out the winners of four races including the Kildare Hunt Cup, the Punchestown Cup and the Prince of Wales' Plate and the following day he won the Conyngham Cup with Surprise Packet. The next

150

year he saddled another four big race winners at the same meeting.

Amazingly enough, he never won the Irish Grand National but that was the only worthwhile Irish chase to elude him. Other notable feats by the Master of Grangecon included a memorable raid on the three-day July meeting at Killarney in 1959 when with six horses he won eight races.

In an assessment of Sleator's strike rate in the fifties and early sixties, Michael O'Farrell, Racing Correspondent of the *Irish Times* noted in an article in the *Irish Racing Annual* that in 1956 he trained the winners of 32 National Hunt races and 29 Flat races and two years later be became champion trainer for the value of races won. "However, from 1955 to 1961 inclusive he was top trainer judged by the highest number of winners turned out, a feat not quite equalled by his old buddy in arms Paddy Prendergast, leading trainer in the same category from 1949 to 1954.

"Sleator's 74 winners in 1958 was the highest number achieved by any trainer in Ireland or England that year and it was in this period also that he brought off his hat-trick of victories in the Irish Cesarewitch with Sword Flash, Havasnack and Another Flash."

As a master of the coup, Sleator believed that it was useless for a trainer "going to the well" unless he was prepared to utilise the talents of jockeys that he knew could "do the job" for him. If you employed less than the best, then it was a case of digging your own graveyard with the bookmaking fraternity.

It was no mere coincidence then that one of the greatest of National Hunt riders was associated with Paddy Sleator in the hour of signal triumphs and rode some of the best-known horses from the stable. Bobby Beasley was on Another Flash when he won the Champion Hurdle in 1960 from Albergo and Saffron Tartan, finishing third on the same horse in 1962 behind Anzio and second in 1964 to Magic Court when a ten-year-old.

He was christened Henry Robert, being a son of Henry Herbert Beasley while his grandfather, Mr Harry Beasley rode in thirteen Grand Nationals, was second in three and won on Come Away in 1891. Old Harry rode a winner at Punchestown when 68 years old and his brother Tom, Bobby's great-uncle, won the National three times.

Bobby Beasley rode as an amateur at the age of 16 and in 1953 he turned professional. It was fitting that he should keep up the family tradition by winning the Aintree Grand National in 1961 on the Fred Rimell-trained Nicolaus Silver while he won the Gold Cup in 1959 on the Danny Morgan-trained Roddy Owen.

When Beasley eventually left Paddy Sleator, Bobby Coonan took over. Bobby hailed from Ballymore Eustace near Grangecon and his partnership with Sleator saw Coonan, who was to develop into a rider of outstanding reliability and coolness, win seven Irish N.H. Jockeys Championships and he rode the winner of virtually every big National Hunt race in the country.

He was on Sweet Dreams for the Kevin Bell stable when the eight year old won the Irish Grand National in 1969 for Mrs Paddy Meehan; he won the Wessel Cable Champion Hurdle on the Kevin Prendergast-trained Prominent King in 1978, scored on 100/6 chance King Vulgan in the Harold Clarke Leopardstown Handicap Chase in 1970 and was associated with three of Paddy Sleator's Galway Plate winners, Royal Day (1967 and '69) and O'Leary (1976).

Michael O'Farrell contends that Paddy Sleator had no equal in the art of placing a horse to the best advantage and that is why the bookies came to dread him.

"He constantly poured over the pages of the *Calendar*, studying articles and conditions as a professor of mathematics might tease out some fascinating problem," recalled Michael O'Farrell. "This meticulous attention to detail was to stand him in good stead in his preparation for his extraordinarily successful four-year stint with his horses in England.

"He was never particularly keen to send horses to Cheltenham or for other top National Hunt races in England, though he did have some successes at the Festival meeting. He also sent horses to win the Mackeson Gold Cup, the Rhymney Breweries Chase and the Friary Meux Hurdle."

Terry Rogers (top) preparing for the start of the Irish Poker Championship and causing a stir as he dons a black bowler hat at the poker table in Las Vegas and (below) at his pitch in the Phoenix Park during his colourful days as a leading rails bookie. Chatting to him is Sonny Molloy.

The late Jack (Treetop) Straus from San Antonio, Texas, who lived by the motto "better a day as a lion than one hundred years as a lamb", savours the unforgettable moment when he won the 1982 World Hold 'Em Poker Championship from Dewey Tomko.

Straus receives the warm congratulations of his close friend, Terry Rogers and tells him laughingly: "I'll be coming to your international tournament in Dublin now as world champion and not as a Texas bum."

Former dual world champions, Doyle "Texas Dolly" Brunson (at Straus's left shoulder) and the slim Stu "The Kid" Ungar (at Dewey Tomko's right shoulder) are there to acclaim 'Treetop', their golfing companion for mind-boggling stakes.

Phil Bull, the man who invented Timeform and also a highly-successful punter and Alex Bird, the man most feared by the British bookmakers in the period after the Second World War for his ability to show a profit on his investments each year and (below) Bird in front of his sixteenth-century moated manor before taking his Rolls-Royce Silver Cloud to the races.

Jeff Smurfit (top left), who lived constantly on the high wire of life; Patrick Gallagher (top right), who gambled £750,000 in buying a quarter share in Try My Best hoping he would win the English 2000 Guineas and Epsom Derby; Tim O'Toole (bottom left), who was only satisfied if aiming for the moon and 'Mincemeat Joe' Griffin, (bottom right), whose life was a film script in itself.

Tommy "The Coalminer" O'Brien (right), who blazed a trail in the Sixties as a gambler who won and lost awesome sums by today's money values.

Miss Dorothy Paget (at right) used to bet in telephone numbers. It was nothing to her to put £10,000 on one of her horses when that sum represented a veritable fortune by today's money values.

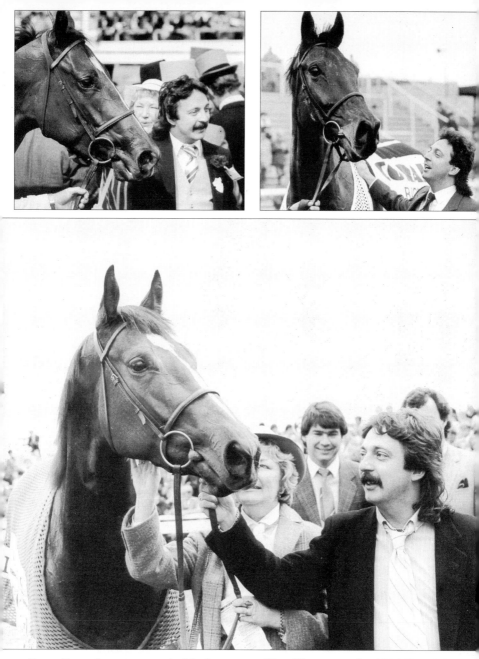

Terry Ramsden was reputed to have won £1 million over the 1984 Royal Ascot Coronation Stakes success of Katies (top left) and (top right) celebrating another killing when Motivator won the 1986 Coral Golden Handicap Hurdle Final, while (below) he savours Katies triumph in the 1984 Irish 1000 Guineas, having brought off a major coup at 20/1. He ended up, however, losing £57 million to the bookies in three years.

Paddy Sleator (below), the Master of Grangecon, pictured on the training grounds in 1977 with the inevitable cigarette and holder and (top left) Paddy 'Darkie' Prendergast and (top right) Jimmy Fitzgerald, the Man from the Horse and Jockey, who has rocked the ring at Cheltenham with some spectacular gambles.

Once in the seventies Michael O'Farrell asked Sleator why he would not send one of his better winners on the domestic front to Cheltenham. "Why should I?", he countered. "Aren't the prizes good enough at home without travelling them across the water."

"Paddy Sleator was not one to make swans out of geese and while he placed his charges to win the maximum number of smaller races open to them, he was not very adventurous," was the opinion expressed by Michael O'Farrell, while acknowledging that the prize money had been very much improved in Ireland by the time Sleator's "English campaign" with Arthur Thomas came to an end in 1966.

"On the other hand," Michael O'Farrell went on, "Paddy Sleator occasionally had a horse so good and an owner so insistent that he had no option but to go for the big time — as with Another Flash."

John J. Byrne's hurdler became the third Irish-trained horse to win the big race, following the steps of Distel (1946) and triple winner, Hatton's Grace (1949-'51).

Sleator's other Cheltenham Festival winners included Sparkling Flame (1961 Spa Hurdle), Scottish Memories (1965 Cathcart Cup), Havago (1965 Gloucestershire Hurdle) and Ballywilliam Boy (1970 Gloucestershire Hurdle).

Racing journalist, Tom MacGinty, admired by everyone in the sport for his knowledge and integrity, had this point to make: "If Paddy Sleator was conservative in the programmes he mapped out for his horses, I am sure he saved his patrons a lot of needless expense. He never did get enough credit, I felt, for some of the horses he sent on to English stables.

"I think particularly of Doorknocker. A difficult horse to train, he was seven before he won his maiden hurdle but was so well schooled that he won the 1956 Champion Hurdle only a few months after he had joined Willie Hall in Britain."

Overall, however, Sleator's achievements on the international plane in the National Hunt sphere could in no way be compared with those of Vincent O'Brien. My

153

own personal view is that the Master of Grangecon cannot, therefore be rated ahead of the Master of Ballydoyle, even though I realise that his many admirers will be only too willing to debate the issue with me.

There was a stage in his career when Vincent O'Brien, on his own admission, had to "gamble to survive" and he made the bookies reel time and again both in Ireland and England with some of the most spectacular coups in racing history. However, in time when he acquired millionaire owners and turned his attention completely to the Flat he did not see the need to gamble anymore.

However, Paddy Sleator's was *always* seen as a gambling stable. And when he made the point to Michael O'Farrell that he saw no great need to send his horses across the water to challenge for major prizes in Britain, he was no doubt conscious of the fact that, apart from the improved prize-money to be won for his patrons on the domestic front they would also make a "killing" in the ring each time he told them that they could bet with confidence.

Vincent O'Brien was always aiming BIG. No target was too high on which to cast his sights. The late Paddy Norris, who was his Travelling Head Man for years, told me over dinner one evening that he might suggest to Vincent early in the year that such a horse might win a maiden in the spring and the response would come: "No, I have this one in mind for the Gloucestershire Hurdle in twelve months time". It might even be a target two years on.

He was prepared to wait and wait and wait — to achieve his international ambitions.

To my mind then, it was a pity that Sleator with his immense talent as a trainer was not prepared to cast his net on a much higher plane for the sake of winning more major races for this country. There is no doubt whatsoever that he had the ability to do so.

I have to quote here also the example set by Jim Bolger, who fears no one when it comes to getting involved in competition at the highest level and confesses that it is this type of competition that really turns him on.

It has to be said, however, that Paddy Sleator, carrying not an ounce of spare flesh and cutting a figure of sartorial excellence with those finely-cut suits topped with a trilby and looking so cool and in control with the inevitable cigarette in that long holder of his, created a charisma around his name that was to endure beyond retirement. And that in itself is a measure of the impact of his mastery of his profession.

Grangecon in the "Garden County" became synonymous with his name. Whenever I go there, I immediately feel that I am in country made for the training of horses. Twelve years after Paddy Sleator had won the Champion Hurdle with Another Flash, Francis Flood, who had emerged from the Sleator school, sent Glencarrig Lady over to Cheltenham from his Grangecon base to win the Gold Cup in the hands of Frank Berry.

Before turning to training Francis Flood had been a top-flight jockey, winning a stream of amateur titles. Today his son, Francis Junr., still only in his twenties, has established a big reputation for himself among the amateur riders and shared the 1990-'91 Amateurs' crown with Tony Martin (both on 17 winners). He won the 1989 Guiness Galway Hurdle on the locally-trained I'm Confident at 33/1.

In 1991 Victor Bowens, who had been a pupil of a pupil of The Master, as he was with Francis Flood for about a year and a half before becoming established as a trainer in his own right in the Grangecon area, enjoyed the biggest triumph of his career to date when he sent out Firions Law to win the Digital Galway Plate by an impressive three lengths in a field of twenty-one, withstanding a strong English challenge in the process.

That success came exactly fifteen years after Paddy Sleator had won the race for the eighth time with O'Leary.

So the Grangecon link with the Galway Plate was being maintained and the tradition set by Paddy Sleator was being carried on in a manner of which The Master could be proud.

Paddy Sleator celebrated his 80th birthday in February, 1989.

His daughter, Diane Nagle of the highly-successful Barronstown Stud, itself in Grangecon, thinks that it was very fitting that the occasion should have brought together quite a number of Paddy's close pals, including Jack Doyle, P.P. Hogan, Jack (Boiler) White, Ted Curtin, Michael Purcell and Micheal Fitzgibbon of Thurles. Shirley Beasley was also there.

I can imagine the yarns that were spun that evening as the boys opened up and I feel that if one could have got a tape-recorder going, it would have provided the material for a radio documentary that would have been a sure-fire winner.

Yes, a pity I didn't make it...

PART SIX

JOHN MULHERN
*Owner and Trainer, Raconteur
and Polo Player*

11

Flair About Everything He Does

Flamboyant John Mulhern from Celbridge, County Kildare added to the legends of how the Irish celebrate in victory at Cheltenham after his horse Friendly Alliance had won the Grand Annual Challenge Handicap Chase on the opening day of the 1981 Festival meeting.

First he tried to charter a small plane to fly with a group of friends to Manchester to take in the game between United and Nottingham Forest. When that did not prove possible, he hopped into a chauffeur-driven limousine with his friends (the car was waiting outside the racecourse), got to Old Trafford in time to watch the game and the party was back in Cheltenham the same evening — before I myself had finished dinner.

Then the celebrations began in style in the Queen's Hotel. The imposing Grand Annual Challenge Trophy was placed in the centre of a table reserved in the dining room. Champagne corks popped and a cheer went up as John's friends lifted their glasses to the 11/2 success of Friendly Alliance, trained by Fred Winter and ridden to a 15-lengths victory by John Francome. "There's no better day for an Irish horse to win at the Cheltenham Festival meeting than St. Patrick's Day," he exclaimed as an Aer Lingus hostess pinned shamrock on his coat.

John Mulhern was the man seen in the memorable opening shots of the BBC documentary on the Irish at

159

Cheltenham, screened on the Sunday night before the '81 Festival meeting. He views Cheltenham as the Olympics of National Hunt racing and he fulfilled a lifetime's ambition when Friendly Alliance won for him at the Festival meeting.

In 1984 Mulhern pulled off a master stroke by buying Mac's Friendly from the Paddy Mullins stable of Goresbridge, County Kilkenny on the morning of the National Hunt Chase and had the satisfaction of not alone seeing the gelding emerge a very easy winner by five lengths from "Mouse" Morris's representative, Red Shah but land a spectacular gamble down to 11/4 in the process.

Mac's Friendly went into the record book "trained Paddy Mullins" and was ridden to victory by his son, Willie, now training successfully in his own right, as is Tony, of course. It was Willie, in fact, who had purchased Mac's Friendly the previous December for his father's stable.

Nothing would have given John Mulhern greater satisfaction than to show the flair to buy on the very morning of the race itself the winner of an event that has so frequently proved a "punter's graveyard" for the Irish, in particular.

But then there is flair about everything he does — from the way he smokes his outsize cigars after dinner to the manner in which he asks the waiter to bring "two Remys" rather than simply calling for two brandies.

Owner and trainer, company managing director, raconteur and polo player, John Mulhern appreciates the good things of life today because he knew times as a student when he thought nothing of putting his books and instruments into pawn in order to get the "readies" to invest in some "good thing" from Paddy Sleator's stable.

He is at his most entertaining when he looks back on his days as a veterinary student in Dublin — days that coincided with Sleator taking the decision to concentrate all his best jumpers in England.

John Mulhern was quick to observe the betting opportunities presented to keen students of the form book by the Sleator-Thomas partnership, even to impoverished students who would certainly have to use their wits to try and get a "tank" together to really have a go any time they thought the odds were in their favour.

"I was crazy about horses in those days," he recalls. "And as far as I was concerned, there were two trainers that really mattered — Tom Dreaper and Paddy Sleator. That was, of course, because my first love was National Hunt racing and these two trained only hurdlers and chasers.

"When Paddy Sleator decided to station horses with Arthur Thomas, it was definitely the day for anyone who was wide awake to sit up and take notice. It had to be daylight robbery. And with no danger of arrest!

"I was studying as a veterinary student at U.C.D. at the time. We found that it became necessary now and then to put one's books and instruments 'in hock' in order to get the resources to invest in these horses. But in our youthful enthusiasm we never had any doubt in their ability to oblige.

"When one reflects that they were ridden by Bobby Beasley, who at the time in Ireland and England had no peer as a National Hunt jockey in my book, then one's investment was as secure as it could possibly be when the initials on the horse's paddock sheet should have been 'P.S.' instead of 'A.T.'."

There came a day — April 18, 1961 to be exact — when John Mulhern, student and investor in the fortunes of the Sleator-Thomas runners in England, travelled over to the now-defunct Woore meeting, an official National Hunt meeting in those days. The purpose of the trip was to back a horse called Donvada. Owned by Peter Barrett, it was running in the Novice Hurdle and had won earlier at Bangor-on-Dee.

"When I arrived at the course I met the late Johnny Lehane, who said to me: 'Do you think Donvada will win?' I replied: 'He must be a certainty, Johnny'.

"I was taken completely aback when he made the simple statement of fact: 'Caduval is the greatest certainty ever to run in a novice hurdle'.

"I could hardly believe what my ears were conveying to

161

my thought processes. All the pre-race plans for a nice 'touch' had been thrown completely out of gear!

"Caduval, trained by a Mr Lubecki, had recorded a hat-trick of wins on his way to Woore. He was to be ridden by Lauri Morgan that day. The name will mean nothing to the younger generation of racing followers, I know, but Lauri was an Australian Olympic three-day event rider and used to ride Colledge Master, which I have always rated the supreme hunter chaser of all time.

"The ground was bottomless that day at Woore. Donvada was very small and Fighting Don's progeny were not entirely happy on that kind of going. However, Donvada opened favourite over Caduval.

"By looking for £3,000 to £2,000 a number of times in the certainty that it would not be taken — in fact, it nearly caused a few heart attacks among faint-hearted bookmakers in the Woore ring! — we very quickly convinced them that the really 'inspired' money was for Donvada. Caduval drifted and became better value for money.

"It was then that we hit the ring with all the resources on hand and Caduval finished up at 11/8.

"God bless you Johnny Lehane and may the Lord have mercy on your soul.

"To put it in a nutshell, Caduval won by five lengths in the proverbial canter.

"I remember only the journey by taxi back to Manchester Airport with a crestfallen Bobby Beasley, fearful of the reception from Mr Sleator when he arrived in Dublin. As a matter of interest, Caduval went chasing and won the Broadway Chase at Cheltenham and undoubtedly was a horse of some real potential.

In John Mulhern's case, some of the best yarns he spins not surprisingly revolve around the Cheltenham Festival meeting.

"In 1961, the year that Saffron Tartan won the Gold Cup in the hands of Fred Winter from Pas Seul and Mandarin, we had gone over specially to back a horse in the first race on the final day," he recalled. "The race was known in those days as the Spa Hurdle — a three mile conditions event, replaced first by the George Dullen Hurdle and now the Waterford Crystal Stayers Hurdle.

"Paddy Sleator had entered — and fancied four months before the race — a horse called Sparkling Flame. But on the day his confidence had waned slightly and Duke of York, ridden by Mr D. Scott, suddenly became all the rage in the ring. But personally I had no doubt that Sparkling Flame was not only value for money but different class than the opposition. The brilliance of Bobby Beasley from the last flight won the day. Duke of York was second.

"Having bet £550 to £200 quite a number of times and having just flown in for the day, I had the onerous task of collecting the goodies. The bets had been laid in cash all around the ring. So anyone who knew me would have witnessed the extraordinary sight of one John Mulhern handing up the winning dockets one by one and stuffing the bundles of notes into an Aer Lingus overnight bag. Before the horses had moved out from the parade ring for the next race, I had left the meeting and was already en route to a lecture in Earlsfort Terrace, counting the readies into neat bundles in the taxi as I winged my way from Prestbury Park."

Student days in Dublin in the early sixties for John and his pals were days when an old 10 shilling note could go a long way and you could live in the lap of luxury if you were able to command a fiver. There was a great sense of camaraderie between them, those in the money one day helping out those who they knew they could trust to see them right on a day when their own funds would be very low or even non-existent. Parties at the week-ends, poker sessions into the early hours and always the racing, of course; they certainly knew how to live and if Joyce had been around with them, he would have got material to write a sequel to *Ulysses*.

The zest for life and living and the personality that made him shine out in a bevy of real characters stayed with John Mulhern from those veterinary student days in Dublin — the Dublin of the Red Bank and the Dolphin and Jammets, of Brendan Behan and Patrick Kavanagh in all their glory. Today he will give in a tip what would have kept him going for maybe a month in the early sixties.

Now he is Managing Director of Clayton Love Distribution Ltd., which has the lucrative Findus Frozen Foods franchise for Ireland. This means that the company distributes McCain oven-ready chips, which John Mulhern described to me as the answer to the harassed housewife's prayers as they dispelled any danger of the kitchen being set on fire!

But racing followers naturally think of him first and foremost as a trainer and one capable of making the bookies squirm when going for a "touch". He was a permit holder for two years before he got a full licence in the late '70s. "I have more horses than the Queen has soldiers," he said to me laconically over dinner in the early '80s.

A true-blue Dubliner, he was born with a love of racing in every vein of his body. His grandfather was Manager of Boss Croker's interests in Ireland while his uncles Tom and Max were officials of the Turf Club for many years.

The best steeplechaser he ever saw was Royal Approach (by King's Approach out of Flotation), trained by Tom Dreaper for Lord Bicester. "I believe he was better even than Arkle," he asserts.

And the most impressive Flat horse in his view was the 1971 Epsom Derby winner and King George VI and Queen Elizabeth Stakes winner Mill Reef — confirming his greatness, in the opinion of John Mulhern, by winning the Prix de l'Arc de Triomphe the same year.

He rates Lester Piggott the greatest Flat jockey of all time — greater even than the legendary Fred Archer. He saw no one to compare with Piggott when it came to getting a horse running in front — and winning.

Over the sticks the jockeys he really enthused about were Tommy Carberry, Tommy Carmody, Jonjo O'Neill, Frank Berry, Adrian Maguire and John Francome. This sextet he put ahead of all others of the crop of riders of recent times.

He rated John Francome "the finest horseman" of English National Hunt jockeys. He admired the sheer professionalism of Frank Berry when he was in his prime as a jockey and added that when Tommy Carberry was

164

really 'turned on', there was no one to match him.

He related the story of being in hospital after a car crash and sending a message to Tommy Carberry to the effect that — "You will just have to win this one for me, Tommy, if the hospital bills are going to be met" and, sure enough, Carberry got his mount up in a driving finish from the last a win a hurdle race at Mallow against all the odds.

Racing starts for him each year on November 1st and really tails off on April 1st. True, he may have runners on the Flat but he would never get the same kick out of winning a big event on the Flat as would be the case if he won at Leopardstown's Christmas meeting, the Fairyhouse Spring meeting , the Punchestown meeting or at Cheltenham.

When small fields in two year old races bring only a handful of spectators to some of the summer meetings, John Mulhern has been known to derive a lot of enjoyment from playing polo.

The Phoenix Park is home of the All-Ireland Polo Club (no disunion there!), where it has been played for well over a century.

Indeed, in 1906, as John Mulhern informed me over dinner one evening in Jury's Hotel, 20,000 spectators were present to watch a contest on one Sunday afternoon. Shades of times past — a decade before the Easter Rising...

He scoffs at suggestions that it is an elitist game for West-British types. He is the last man you would suspect of trying to keep alive vestiges of colonial days. Those who have played polo with him have included a tyre remould expert, a quantity surveyor and a sheep farmer.

The All-Ireland Club is the oldest polo club in Europe. Horse Show week in August is the week, according to John Mulhern, when you see the best polo in Dublin. "Then you see polo as it should be played, a throw-back to the days when the greatest team to represent Britain was comprised of Irishmen."

My knowledge of polo, unlike my knowledge of gaelic games, horse racing, dog racing, golf, rugby, soccer and even cricket, is nil. And so as we reached the last of the bottle of Volnay and the cheese-board was brought, John

Mulhern explained that a chukka of polo takes 7½ minutes — chukka being a bout of play, with four chukkas in a match. And if you were to be part of a great chukka, I got the impression that it must be akin to the feeling Lester Piggott got when he won the Epsom Derby on Sir Ivor, Nijinsky and The Minstrel.

Sadly, I'll never know at first hand what the feeling is really like and can only take John Mulhern's word for it.

Why not golf for relaxation with some of the Curragh trainers, I asked him innocently? "It takes between 3½ hours and four hours to play a fourball. I have not four hours to give to anything," he replied.

He is not a man bound by the calendar or the dictates of a clockwork regime when it comes to taking holidays. "If I had one 'on ice', I just would not go away to the sun in winter," he said.

I suspected that if you gave him two tickets to fly Concorde for a holiday in Barbados while the Leopardstown Christmas meeting was on, he would almost certainly decline, though he would accept them afterwards (even then he squirms at the thought that he might find himself sun-bathing beside a Newmarket trainer, who would not arouse his enthusiasm for a tête-a-tête on training tactics; however, he would gladly forget the sun and seek the shade for a long lazy afternoon's conversation about riding tactics if John Francome happened to pass by and say 'hello').

Having acquired Friendly Alliance late in 1977 – after being very impressed watching him winning his bumper first time out from a field of fifteen at Fairyhouse – John Mulhern came to realise that there were very few 2¼-mile chases in Ireland. It was this very fact that prompted him to send him to Fred Winter who had as his first jockey the best horseman in England in John Francome. He also trained near enough to Cheltenham. "I had concluded that Friendly Alliance would not have a long horse-box trip to get to the Festival meeting. You see there was only one goal as far as I was concerned — the Festival meeting in March '81," recalled John Mulhern.

"As a preliminary to that bid, he went to Cheltenham at

166

the end of September, 1980. He won the George Stevens Handicap Chase over 2 miles with 12 stone on December 6 of the same year. Tommy Carmody had the mount and he was a very easy winner.

"His next victory was on March 17, 1981. It had been a long haul from the evening I rang Charlie McCartan Snr. from the Hibernian Hotel in October '77 — but it was worth it all..."

Tommy Carmody, after spending three seasons in England with the powerful Dickinson stable, during which time he won the King George VI Chase three years running on Gay Spartan (1978) and Silver Buck (1979 and 1980) while finishing runner-up twice in the English N.H. Jockeys' Championship and third on the other occasion, decided to return to Ireland in the summer of 1981 to ride as a freelance. The English public, incidentally, really woke up to his full capabilities — already recognised in Ireland — when he brought the Peter McCreery-trained Hilly Way with a magnificent jump over the last to beat Menehal by 2½-lengths in the Queen Mother Champion Chase at the 1978 Cheltenham Festival meeting. The same day in the previous race, the Sun Alliance Novices Hurdle, he came with a decisive run on the inside on odds-on favourite, Mr Kildare and, jumping the last in wonderful style, stormed clear up the hill to win by two lengths.

John Mulhern, always an admirer of Carmody's talent, struck up a very successful partnership with the Limerick-born rider, who was first spotted riding in a pony-race in Kildare by trainer, Liam Browne and was asked to join the stable as an apprentice. Tommy accepted — and never looked back.

The partnership was successful two years running at the Cheltenham Festival meeting when Galmoy took the Stayers Hurdle in 1986 and '87 and there were some notable triumphs also on the home front. In 1992 Carmody retired prematurely on medical advice. His last ride was for John Mulhern on Airy Mountain in a novice chase at Naas on January 25, 1992; the horse fell heavily at the 11th fence, suffering fatal injuries and leaving his jockey with a badly-damaged left shoulder, which still after five months

167

treatment had not fully recovered and Carmody had no option but to face the inevitable.

In January, 1988 John Mulhern had commanded headlines in the national media in Ireland when he married Charles J. Haughey's very popular and personable daughter, Eimear in a secret wedding ceremony. Again there was a real touch of flair in the way he arranged the wedding ceremony and the evening that followed. he went to Leopardstown races giving the impression that it was going to be just another afternoon at the track. Friends were told casually to join him for a drink afterwards. You can imagine their surprise when they discovered that it was the day that one of Ireland's most eligible bachelors had fallen, as it were at Becher's Brook!

Yes, as Dex Nix wrote in the *Sunday Press*, the very man who had once boasted that if he wrote his autobiography, it would be called "The Horses I Knew And the Woman I Came Across" would have to change the title or scrap the idea of the book altogether.

The fact that Charles Haughey was then leader of Fianna Fail (he had held the position of Taoiseach or Prime Minister more than once since December, 1979, and before his retirement in 1992) inspired the headline writers to describe John Mulhern as "The Man Who Married The Boss's Daughter".

But, of course, John Mulhern and Eimear Haughey shared a similar passion for horses. Eimear runs the very successful Abbeville Stud and in 1987 raised more than £400,000 from the sale of fourteen yearlings, much of it at the Cartier Million Sale.

I remember once asking John Mulhern why he had decided that his red silk racing colours should have a distinctive white question mark emblazoned on them. He gave me a glance through a cool smoke ring from his Havana cigar that conveyed clearly to me that there should have been no need to ask.

The bookies, who had suffered from his tilts at the ring, certainly didn't need any explanation.

When the money went down the question mark became irrelevant . . .

PART SEVEN

MICK O'TOOLE
A Taste for the Big-Time

12

"The Bacon and Eggs Come Dearer on the Curragh"

It was morning time on the Curragh and some of his owners had joined Mick O'Toole for breakfast after watching the horses on the gallops.

The day — Saturday, December 27, 1980 — Irish Sweeps Hurdle Day. Naturally the conversation turned to the prospects of Carrig Willy springing a surprise in the big race, the centre-piece of the Leopardstown Christmas meeting.

The opportunity came to have a bet with the representative present of one of the biggest bookmaking firms in Britain and Ireland and odds of 40/1 were taken on behalf of the group, breakfasting on bacon and eggs, to win a total of £64,000.

Mick confessed himself, after Carrig Willy, starting at 33/1, had held on to win by a head from Corrib Chieftain with Connaught Ranger three-quarters-of-a-length away third, that he had "just a few quid" on. And for the bookmaker's representative who took the main bet from his owner-group, he reserved the classic comment: "The bacon and eggs come dearer on the Curragh!".

It was spontaneous quips like these that endeared Mick O'Toole to the British media, who naturally gravitate to those who can readily offer the quotable quote. And no one is as quotable as Mick O'Toole when he is in the mood.

But then he is a character in every sense of the word and has been since the time he started off as a dog trainer.

171

The Dublin dog tracks in those days, with the unique and colourful Joxer-like and Covey-like individuals who frequented them, had to bring out the wit in anyone born with the gift of seeing the funny side of things. And Mick O'Toole was certainly born with that gift.

His relaxed, genial manner, his quick-fire retorts and repartee made him as popular with the English racing fraternity at Cheltenham and Royal Ascot as he was instantly recognisable as just personable "Mick" to everyone on the Metropolitan circuit at home or indeed at the smallest country meeting. It came the same to him to play golf over the Curragh course in the company of fellow trainers as at Sandy Lane in Barbados in January with Robert Sangster and other high rollers.

He fitted easily into the company wherever he happened to be in the world whether it was in Galway during the Festival meeting or in the Hyatt Regency Hotel in Lexington during the Keeneland July Yearling Sales or rubbing shoulders with the most cosmopolitan crowd imaginable on the sands at Laytown in August. He invariably brightened the scene with his presence.

Behind the seemingly carefree, almost nonchalant manner he exuded when relaxing with friends there lay a hidden flair for aiming for the "big ones" both over the jumps and on the Flat and never did this blossom so well for him than in the seventies and eighties.

His record at Cheltenham in the period from 1975-'81 was truly outstanding. He sent out the winners of nine races, though Chinrullah, which triumphed in the Queen Mother Champion Chase in 1980, was subsequently disqualified on technical grounds.

Chinrullah had taken the Arkle Challenge Trophy Chase the previous year. Likewise Davy Lad, which won the Sun Alliance Novices Hurdle in 1975, came back to score in the Gold Cup at 14/1 in 1977 and the same year Mick O'Toole had a second success when Mac's Chariot was victorious in the supreme Novices Hurdle, which Hartstown would win for the stable in 1981.

The Sun Alliance Novices Hurdle was won for the second year running with Parkhill's success in 1976 and that Festival meeting also saw Bit of a Jig take the Stayers Hurdle. One of the most difficult races of all to win fell to Mick O'Toole when Gay Tie scored in the National Hunt chase in 1978.

O'Toole's taste for the big time was not confined to the Cheltenham Festival meeting. Three months after Davy Lad had won the 1975 Sun Alliance Novices Hurdle, he was being acclaimed in the winner's enclosure at Royal Ascot following Faliraki's triumph in the Norfolk Stakes and he had had an earlier Royal Ascot winner when Balios was successful in the Ascot Stakes in 1972.

Had not Dickens Hill run up against such a brilliant colt as Troy in 1979, Mick O'Toole would assuredly have gone into the record books as one who had the distinction of achieving the Epsom Derby-Irish Derby double in addition to a Gold Cup triumph. As it was, Dickens Hill had to be content with runner-up spot in each Classic. However, there was the thrill for Mick O'Toole in seeing Dickens Hill take the Irish 2,000 Guineas while the colt also had a fine win in the Coral-Eclipse Stakes.

In addition O'Toole was voted "Flat Trainer of the Year" (1979) by the Irish Racing Writers Association and received the Sean P. Graham Award for doing most to promote Irish racing on the International Flat scene that season. Tony Murray, the rider of Dickens Hill and Madame J.P. Binet, the owner, also received Sean P. Graham awards.

It was quite a leap for Mick O'Toole from Harold's Cross greyhound track in Dublin to Epsom on Derby Day and Royal Ascot with its morning suit and top-hat brigade. Equally, preparing Dickens Hill for his tilts at an Irish Classic and two English Classics was in quite a different league entirely from getting a "dark one" ready for Edinburgh in April, 1966 — eleven years before he won with Faliraki at Royal Ascot. He was then an "unknown" small Irish trainer to the English racing public.

Jack Doyle recalled that Mick O'Toole planned his first spectacular coup in England as an S.P. job. The filly Lintola was sent over to the Scottish track and she was to be ridden by the very strong and capable lightweight, Johnny Murtagh.

173

Everything went according to plan until the start was delayed by three minutes. And by the time the starter got them away, the money spread judiciously around the offices, began to percolate back to the course. "Instead of starting at 100/7, Lintola went off at 6/1," said Jack Doyle ruefully.

The next time Mick O'Toole went for a big "touch" at Edinburgh he was beginning to be known in racing circles in Britain, though as yet not a "name" trainer.

"So you might say, we were returning to the scene of the crime," Jack Doyle explained with a smile. "We had got Lester Piggott to agree to ride. He had picked up another few mounts and looked to have at least three good things. Our suggestion to him was that he could have £100 for the ride or £100 on at the best odds we could get. He agreed to the £100 on.

"It was a lot of money in those days and while the colt Mick O'Toole was sending over wouldn't have won a race at Royal Ascot, Goodwood or York in a month of Sundays, he seemed tailormade to justify a gamble in a moderate race at Edinburgh. After agreeing to the ride, the question Lester asked me was: 'Will he win?' My reply was: 'He should — with your help'.

"It was probably the first time Lester had been there for years, which showed that normally he wouldn't be turned on at the thought of venturing so far north. We flew up from London, Mick O'Toole, Lester and myself. Lester that evening, as I look back on it, rode one of the greatest races of his career — better in its own way than the way he won the Epsom Derby later on such as Sir Ivor, Roberto and The Minstrel. But he got done in a finish of noses, through no fault of his own.

"He got done also on the other two favourites he rode. Normally Lester hadn't a lot to say but on the flight back to London, you could have cut the silence with a knife. Making it worse was the fact that as Lester came in on the third beaten hot-pot, the Scots punters let him know what they thought of him in no uncertain terms. I still wince at the memory of one of them shouting in an unmistakable accent: 'Gwan home, Lester, you're nae as good as you thought you were'."

But whatever that 'wee Scot' may have thought of Piggott after his faith in the Maestro had been shattered through losing his few bob perhaps, nothing could shake the faith of Mick O'Toole and Jack Doyle in the genius of Lester Piggott and for both of them he had to be rated 'The King' among Flat jockeys. They would think of no other when "going to the well" — whenever it was possible to engage him.

It was no mere coincidence that Lester rode Faliraki to victory for Mick O'Toole at Royal Ascot. Mick himself talked to me of Lester's "supreme mastery" and his ability to pull out that something extra that could make all the difference in a driving finish.

And seventeen years after triumphing on Faliraki for O'Toole, the amazing and seemingly ageless Piggott chalked up his 30th Classic win at the age of 56 with a superbly-executed victory on Robert Sangster's colt Rodrigo de Triano in the English 2,000 Guineas.

The scene switches now to the Queen's Hotel on Gold Cup morning, 1977.

Dessie Hughes, lean as a gunfighter and as deadly in his riding days in a High Noon shoot-out, is smoking a slim Panatella and talking to me after breakfast about his attitude to pressure — the pressure of riding a fancied runner at Cheltenham and one that is carrying a tremendous amount of Irish money. Down the table are Mick O'Toole and Jack Doyle. An occasion made for racing talk at the highest level.

I detected in Hughes that air of suppressed dynamism, yet cool poise, that I have found in the great ones in other sports also, whose sheer talent explodes when there is everything to be gained and a world to be lost on the days that really matter. It is not easy to define this quality. In their presence, however, you sense that the most intense moments of challenge fire them to produce something beyond themselves, the inspirational flourish that sees a chaser or hurdler brought into the last with a breath-taking surge, or the power-packed finish Lester Piggott mustered in winning his eighth Epsom Derby on The Minstrel in

175

1977. Or Muhammad Ali in his moments of greatest triumph, like the defeat of the seemingly unbeatable George Foreman in Kinshasha.

For instance, when Dessie Hughes rode Bit of a Jig in the Lloyd's Bank Hurdle in 1976. Mick O'Toole had said beforehand that this one was the nearest to "a good thing" at the Festival meeting.

It seemed, however, that he was going to "get done" by the Fred Winter-trained Simon's Pet at the last flight. Then Hughes set Bit of a Jig alight and the Irish cheers echoed the acclaim that lovers of the sport retain for a superb piece of riding, as he edged it by three-parts-of-a-length.

Or one may recall his balance and the power he generated as he won the great battle from the last on Monksfield over Jonjo O'Neill and Sea Pigeon in the epic 1979 Champion Hurdle.

Or again we may recall the 'Irish roar' he set up as he had his last victory as a jockey at Cheltenham when scoring a highly-impressive win on Chinrullah in the 1980 Queen Mother Champion Chase.

Now Hughes is telling me on that morning in '77 that the pressure never worries him — "not even when riding a hot favourite and the fortunes of thousands of Irish punters riding with me."

It would not upset his composure through a race. "When I get on a horse in the parade ring, I leave everything else behind me and set my mind totally on the race ahead. All my concentration is on winning."

He admitted though to being anxious, even somewhat keyed up in the count-down to the great events like the Gold Cup or Aintree Grand National. But he never got nervous. Perhaps that was part of the story too — if there was no feeling of being keyed up beforehand, the adrenalin would not flow in the veins and you could fail to turn it on when that extra something was demanded.

The Gold Cup was the big one. It was the one, he asserted, that made the greatest demands on horse and jockey.

"My life's ambition is to win the Gold Cup," said Dessie before we parted after breakfast. Before the day was out he would have realised that ambition.

Hughes loved big race riding. He loved the atmosphere of the Cheltenham Festival meeting and there was no better rider over this track. In his estimation, you would have to be very unlucky to get into trouble there. If your horse was good enough, then there should be no reason to advance a hard luck story afterwards. "But Cheltenham demands knowing."

"I had good Cheltenhams and a few exceptional years. In the final analysis, confidence is the start and finish of race riding — even more so than talent, I believe. And confidence can only be built up riding winners. I got plenty of falls during my career but happily they never affected me to the extent that I lost my confidence afterwards. Over the jumps, it has to be recorded that mentally and physically bad falls can finish a jockey. It's how he comes back after taking a bad fall and getting hurt that counts."

He counted himself lucky that for the vital years of his career as a jockey he rode for Mick O'Toole who seldom tied him down to orders. "He trusted my judgement once I was on his charge and while on occasions things did not work out as we expected, it never upset the happy relationship we enjoyed.

"The partnership I was to establish with Mick came good at Cheltenham when I got a really big break by riding Davy Lad to victory in the Sun Alliance Hurdle in 1975. That, incidentally, was Mick O'Toole's first training success at the Festival meeting. The following year was even better with Parkhill and Bit of a Jig and 1977 topped that again as I shared the Gold Cup triumph with Mick on Davy Lad and in addition I rode Mac's Chariot a winner for the stable."

In all Dessie Hughes rode eight winners at the Festival meeting in the period 1975-'80, seven of them for Mick O'Toole.

In winning the 1977 Gold Cup by six lengths on Davy Lad, Dessie Hughes came from a long way back to outstay Tied Cottage and Tommy Carberry. It was a race marred by tragedy for Fred Winter as Lanzarote, the former

177

Champion hurdler had to be destroyed. The fall of Lanzarote resulted in the bringing down of Bannow Rambler and one of the Irish professionals had laid a bet of £70,000 to £20,000 on this one to "get out".

It was a triumphant week overall for Irish stables, producing a magnificent seven winners — only one short of the 1958 record. The Festival meeting actually ended with four Irish winners on the last day, Meladon, Kilcoleman, Rusty Tears and, of course, Davy Lad.

I will remember 1977 personally as the year when the Aer Lingus dispute saw racegoers switch in their thousands to the boats and it was almost like the evacuation of Dunkirk, such was the press at the embarkation points on the Monday of Cheltenham week. I took the boat from the North Wall. So many "readies" were carried in big wads that someone cracked that if a few armed robbers had decided to have a go, then there would have been a ready script for shooting "The Great Boat Robbery".

We got so caught up watching the poker sessions that we hadn't time to think of heaving stomachs. At one point I voluntarily took on the task of serving the drinks so that the members of one school (a priest right in the centre wearing his clerical collar!) would not have their concentration broken.

I sat in to play a few hands in another school — for the proverbial buttons. But nothing to compare with that big school to end all schools that started as the boat left Dublin behind and only ended with a fantastic ace-pot as we berthed in Liverpool (it has now passed into history how one young man took the next boat back, having lost his entire "wad" for the races).

The success of Davy Lad in the Gold Cup saw Mick O'Toole bring off a nice ante-post 'touch' of £25,000 as he had a monkey (£500) on the David Jack gelding at 50/1 before Christmas with Sean Graham.

But O'Toole would have taken a very substantial six-figure sum from the bookies had Davy Lad become the first horse since Golden Miller in 1934 to complete the Gold Cup-Aintree Grand National double. The bet went down with the fall of Davy Lad at the third. "A horse fell right in front of me at the first," recalled Dessie Hughes. "It frightened him and he became too deliberate after that — and went."

Two years on from his memorable 1977 Festival meeting, Mick O'Toole was confirming his versatility as a trainer as Dickens Hill was led into the winner's enclosure at the Curragh after winning the Irish 2,000 Guineas in the hands of the late Tony Murray while the same colt took second place in the Epsom Derby and again in the Irish Sweeps Derby.

In fact, he was "Mr Versatility" himself in that his early training successes were not achieved on the racecourse but on the greyhound track and on the coursing fields. His uncle, Paddy Byrne was a noted trainer in the forties and from his kennels at Islandbridge, Dublin turned out Lilac Luck to win the Irish Greyhound Derby at Harold's Cross in 1945, having earlier — in 1942 — taken the Blue Riband of Coursing at Clonmel with Mettlesome Negro.

The O'Toole home was in Dublin's South Circular Road and young Mick learned all about the game from uncle Paddy, later gravitating to training himself. Even then he showed the penchant for challenging across-Channel, which he would carry on when he started training racehorses. He had the distinction of being the first Irish-based greyhound trainer to take the English Oaks. He won the race for Joe McKee, a Belfast bookmaker, when his charge Marjone won at Harringay in 1965.

Coursing and tracking — it all came the same to Mick. And he turned out Glideaway Dreamer, owned by Art McGooking from Antrim to win the 1963 Coursing Derby. Another big winner was The Saint (Corn Cuchullain).

As an owner, he had other fine dogs in Young Ferranti (Cesarewitch winner, 1968) and Frenchman's Cove. What was the fastest dog he ever saw on the track? "Yellow Printer was as good a tracker as I ever saw," he replied.

It was from another uncle, Willie ('The Rasher') Byrne that Mick O'Toole learned the rudiments of how to train horses — and plan a coup. Willie was a man the bookmakers came to dread. When the stable had a cut,

179

things seldom if ever went wrong. One of the biggest coups of all was the success of Marshall Ney in the 1954 Jersey Stakes and this in a way blazed the trail for Mick O'Toole's subsequent successes at Royal Ascot.

The legends surrounding 'The Rasher' Byrne's name are part and parcel of the lore of Irish racing and its plethora of unequalled characters. It was he who was supposed to have said that he never slept with his wife the night before a coup — "in case I talk in my sleep".

And again when this "dark one" with little or no form to his name had been tried "a certainty" to win a big handicap, the young lightweight jockey who had been put up to get the full benefit of his allowance, asked as he was about to leave the parade ring, what were his final instructions and the immortal comment came back from 'The Rasher': "Just ensure that he's turned the right way at the off and that will be that."

When he streaked out of the fog with the rest of the field trailing behind him, the commentator was momentarily lost for words as he hadn't considered it all that important to dwell too long memorising the colours of this "no-hoper"...

When I returned to the Curragh stables of Mick O'Toole towards the end of June, 1992, I managed to catch him before he left for Bellewstown races, where he turned out Enqelaab to justify 4/6 favouritism in the last race. He was running a tighter ship now, with around 50 horses in his charge where in the late seventies the total was never less than 90. And he had disposed of some of the land attached to the stables to the Irish National Stud, as they needed it due to the demands of the new motorway.

At 60, the ebullience I had always found in Mick O'Toole remained undimmed. And his ability to think – and act – on a number of different planes at the one time was also unchanged.

He's on the phone now telling someone about a mutual friend who has passed away suddenly that morning and he has hardly put the phone down than he has to finalise declarations with his secretary and meet a caller.

In between all this – and more – he names Dickens Hill

naturally as "the best horse I ever trained," that is on the Flat, of course. He acknowledges that the colt was very unlucky to be a three year old in the same season as Troy. Only for that, he would have savoured the satisfaction of having a dual Epsom Derby-Irish Derby winner in addition to a Cheltenham Gold Cup winner.

Did he make a killing on Dickens Hill? –There was no need for me to back him as my percentage from his successes was enough."

But he still gets immense satisfaction out of remembering the confidence he had in Davy Lad winning the 1977 Gold Cup and having that bet of £500 at 50/1 with Sean Graham.

He confided that no success gave him a greater thrill, however, than his first at the Cheltenham Festival meeting – and that was when Davy Lad won the Sun Alliance Novices Hurdle in 1975.

Likewise, he was particularly thrilled to have had two winners at the Royal Ascot meeting.

He recalls too with a special sense of satisfaction how Dr. Paddy Morrissey of Naas, Jack Doyle, the legendary bloodstock agent and himself brought off the first big Jackpot at the Cheltenham Festival meeting in 1969.

Jack Doyle takes up the story: "We were staying in Stroud in the Cotswolds. I was sharing a room with Paddy Morrissey. He was working on the form book through the night and I kept waking up and saying to him: 'Put in Merrycourt'. And in his concentration he would snap back at me: 'Go to sleep now and don't be bothering me.' I'm afraid I kept at him to such an extent that he finally decided on including Merrycourt and Josh Gifford rode it as it won at 50/1."

Jack Doyle recalled that Pauline Wallis (later Mrs. Pauline O'Donnell), who made such an impact on the greyhound racing scene on both sides of the Atlantic also had a share in the Jackpot success. The Tom Dreaper-trained Muir was the banker in the Champion Chase and also included was the Willie O'Grady-trained Kinloch Brae in the Cathcart Cup.

"In those days no announcement was made about how

many units remained as you went into the last leg of the Jackpot," said Jack Doyle. "We had no way of knowing how much we stood to win, whether we would scoop the entire pool or have to share it. We knew, however, that with that 50/1 winner, the chances were that we would take it all.

"So there we were in the ring before the last race and we decided to do some laying off to cover our outlay and get a profit on top of it.

"A lady punter somewhere in England also hit it correctly – how much she knew about the form book we never got to know – and it meant that instead of scooping the pool of over £100,000, we had to share it.

"But my insistence in the middle of the night that Paddy Morrissey put in Merrycourt meant that we got at least £10,000 each out of it. And by the values of 1969 it was a lot of money."

PART EIGHT

TERRY RAMSDEN
*Lost £57m to the Bookmakers
in Three Years*

13

"I Like the Flat, it's a Quicker Death"

Once when he was asked if he preferred the Flat to National Hunt racing, Terry Ramsden replied: "I like the Flat best, it's a quicker death".

He didn't realise then how prophetic those words would prove to be, because in three short years before the money ran out in 1987, the flamboyant cockney who was dubbed "Little Tel" or "Our Tel" by the British tabloids, lost £57 million to the bookmakers.

This, remember, is not an estimated figure. It is one that emerged from an affidavit filed by Det. Insp. Richard Cumming of the City Police detailing the betting habits of the man described at one point by the Jockey Club, with multi-million pound justification, as "a great supporter of racing".

A break-down of that staggering £57 million total — as revealed by Michael Gillard in *The Observer* Business section in February, 1992 — showed that during 1985-'86 Ramsden lost £25 million. The next year his luck changed. He only lost £24 million. In the final year the bookmakers took just £8 million from him. (His total personal expenditure in those same three years, including his betting, came to £96 million.)

But the story of the sheer magnitude of his gambling operations doesn't end there.

Back in the period between 1982 and 1984, the Customs and Excise estimated that he had gambled £77 million —

losing £20 million.

So over five years (1982-'84 and 1985-'87) his outlay on gambling went well beyond the £100 million mark and his accumulated losses reached close on £80 million. If one were to take the overall period from 1980 to 1987, it can be readily assumed that he lost over £100 million.

Little wonder that the *Racing Post* described him as "the biggest punter in the history of the turf".

I feel that it can truly be expanded to give him the tag of the heaviest gambler of all time on a global scale with the doubtful honour at the same time of being supreme among mug punters, and this despite the fact that he once netted £1.5 million on winning bets on one horse.

It was nothing to Ramsden at his peak to have £100,000 on one of his horses.

There is little doubt that he would have gone to the wall much earlier than he did as a punter but for the success he enjoyed as a financial wizard before the stock market crash of "Black Monday" in October, 1987.

He was happily accommodated by the major bookmaking chains, Ladbrokes and Hills in particular, where a true professional in the late Alex Bird's mould would experience the greatest difficulty in getting on one-tenth of what Ramsden would "invest" in an individual bet.

At his peak Terry Ramsden had 76 horses in training and was listed in a Money magazine as Britain's 57th richest individual, with a fortune estimated at £87 to £100 million.

The final irony was that, having gambled away close on £80 million in five years, he was warned off by the Stewards of the Jockey Club for a "mere" £2 million — a sum he would have viewed as "small change" in the heady days of his glittering performance in securities trading.

Ramsden generated an estimated £3 billion turnover in Japanese warrants in the period 1979-'85. The awesome scale of his operations on the international stock market can best be gauged from the fact that when Glen International crashed in October, '87, there were accumulated losses of £142.2 million and Ramsden faced personal liabilities of some £98 million on deals worth £343 million.

Ladbrokes pulled the plug on him in the racing sense when they took him to Tattersall's Committee, the Jockey Club's watch-dog Committee to which the bookies turn when someone defaults on betting liabilities.

Under the settlement formula, Ramsden had undertaken to repay in five-figure monthly instalments the debt of £2 million. When repayment proved difficult, the arrangement was renegotiated. However, he failed to meet the new payments schedule and it was then that the "warning-off" took place under the Jockey Club's rule 203, excluding him from any premises owned, licensed or controlled by the Stewards.

In effect, he was banned from all racecourses — including racecourses run by the authorities in other countries with which the Jockey Club has reciprocal arrangements — or from entering his horses in events.

Under the Gaming Act, betting debts are not legally recoverable but are debts of honour, which means that if a punter was content to be banned indefinitely from racing, he could, in theory, refuse to pay anything.

English racing writer, Jonathan Powell noted that Ramsden "lost often enough to encourage all the big bookies to want his business".

There were some influential people in racing who contended that he should not have been facilitated so easily in a 'wild' betting spree, to which the rhetorical response was made by Ron Pollard of Ladbrokes: "What is 'wild'?"

There are bookies, however, that I know who, conscious that a line should be drawn on moral grounds in protecting punters they know from plunging over the precipice — if only to save their families from the proverbial poorhouse — will call a halt to giving unlimited credit.

They don't want the charge levelled against them that they were ruthless to the point of not caring. Just as the responsible publican won't serve alcohol to a known alcoholic of his acquaintance who enters his establishment.

In the world of mega-punting, however, the world

frequented by mugs like Terry Ramsden, using money like confetti, such fine lines are rarely drawn. I'm afraid questions of conscience don't enter into it. "The bookies see them coming," to quote the time-honoured phrase of the ring and the mug punters will get all the credit they want — as long as they can keep meeting the bookmakers' monthly statements. But once the crash comes, the very same bookmakers will apply the full letter of the law to recoup what is owed to them, that is if the unfortunate punter fails to fulfil a commitment on phased payment of his debt, if unable to clear it off in one lump sum.

In fairness to the bookmakers, it has to be said that a bet, even "on the nod" is a contract — a binding contract. If I go into the ring and whisper to a reputable bookie I know and who respects my integrity that I want "a score" (£20) on a particular horse, he will take it that I have given my word to pay should the horse lose — just as I know he will pay me if the horse in question is first past the post. In such a transaction, I may not even get a docket. He may just say to his clerk "down to pal". It's a two-way business transaction. I have no place entering the ring and looking for credit if I know I can't meet my commitments. It's as simple as that.

The ultimate irony for Terry Ramsden and something that brought him into public conflict with Ladbrokes was the stopping of a cheque for £25,000 on a cash bet he had with them. Ramsden was reported at the time to have started legal proceedings in an attempt to force payment of the cheque in question, which he claimed was first issued after the horse he had backed won.

However, Ron Pollard of Ladbrokes stressed that the £25,000 was withheld in line with the instalments deal that Ramsden had entered into with the firm.

"All he has to do is to honour the agreement he reached with us," said Mr Pollard, who described as "rubbish" Ramsden's allegation that he was "owed" £25,000.

As Ramsden's racing empire was dissolved, Michael Seely reported in *The Times* of February, 1989 that five horses were disposed of at Doncaster for the "paltry" sum of 23,900 guineas, even though the quintet included Old

Hubert, winner of the Chester Cup.

The Jockey Club turned down an application from Ramsden that he be allowed to transfer the horses into the name of his wife, Lisa.

It was learned that the Jockey Club did not want to see their system circumvented, as they considered that transferring the horses into Mrs Ramsden's name would merely have been a method of getting round their rules.

An indignant Terry Ramsden wrote a bitter letter to the *Racing Post* in which he claimed that the so-called 'Sport of Kings" was run by "stuffy, uppercrust gentlemen who have had obvious delight in refusing all efforts by the largest-ever *working-class* racehorse owner to get back on a racecourse".

He went on: "Firstly, Tattersalls will not even allow me to put my side of the story concerning the Ladbrokes dispute. I, therefore, am tried, convicted and sentenced without a hearing. A sense of justice and fairness that will undoubtedly stand England in good stead!

"Secondly, the Jockey Club in its infinite wisdom has declined my wife a licence to race horses because I am disqualified.

"My wife satisfied it that she would pay her own way — she has an AAA credit rating, no debts and not so much as a point on her driving licence. But that is not enough for our 'lords and masters'. She is now to be held responsible for my legal debts."

He accused the Jockey Club of having "short memories" in relation to the £700,000 he had given to racing charities and the £300,000 he had spent in addition "sponsoring those who were being unfairly treated (lady jockeys, stable staff, etc.)" and of "a man who was trying to show his own people (the working class) that racing is a sport to participate in for all".

He concluded: "Well, the only fool here is me, because I was wrong. And my advice to the working public is this — don't bet, don't race, don't expect any treatment of fairness.

"If you can accept those terms then I wish you well, for this is a sport which makes its own rules to suit itself."

Commenting on that letter, David Pipe, the Jockey Club Public Relations Manager, said: "It is not our policy to discuss or give any details in these situations. They are a privileged matter between the disciplinary or licensing committees and the individual concerned. It is as much to protect their position as for any other reason, that we do this."

Pipe added: "If at any stage Mr Ramsden had come to the Jockey Club for advice instead of castigating us, we might have been able to help him. He had 15 days' grace after Tattersalls' posting and we would have been happy to advise him about how the horses might have been transferred, sold or even leased. It is one of the things we are here for."

Terry Ramsden's rise from humble beginnings to millionaire status, to owning his own investment company, Glen International, also a stud farm in Kentucky and another in Newmarket and homes in London, Essex, Scotland, Bermuda, Portugal and Finland was the stuff of "emergence from the log-cabin syndrome" that Americans delight in telling and retelling. But it made far more tragic his fall and all that stemmed from it — right down to a period of detention he spent in Terminal Island prison, Los Angeles before his return to Britain on charges of fraudulent trading and false accounting relating to the activities of his collapsed Glen International group.

Just before the fall, he stood on top of the world at the age of 36. He didn't mind telling the world that he hailed from the back streets of North London and from a poor family. "My grandfather, Alf, trained the England amateur boxing team for many, many years. Born out of Stepney, he was. Oh, yes. Oh, yes," was how he revealed it to Michael Hern of the *Evening Standard* around the time in May, '87 when he decided to widen his interests to become a boxing promoter, bringing one Billy Aird on board as manager of the fighters.

"Listen," he went on, "where I come from and where he (Billy Aird) comes from, growing up's hard work. So we're not frightened to work.

"Me? I'm not interested in a couple of blonde birds an' a

189

boat an' a blue sea. I'm interested in work." As the story went at the time, Ramsden thought nothing of working 90 hours week after week.

The only child of a Post Office engineer (father) and factory worker (mother), he won a scholarship to grammar school, where he excelled at maths. After working as a barman and petrol-pump worker, he arrived in the City at 16 with a lot of ambition. He put his foot on the ladder that would lead him to immense wealth as a dealer when he started as a humble insurance clerk with the stock-broking firm Hedderwick Stirling Grumbar. There he developed his fascination for — and mastery in — warrants trading and especially the giant Japanese market.

"I started in Hedderwick's back office and ended up as the firm's top business producer in the last year I was there," he would recall later.

"He wrote business like a train," said one ex-colleague. He was on his way to becoming the key London player in Japanese warrants.

After a sojourn with the Anglo-Australian broker, T.C. Coombs, he was soon totally on his own, converting the Scottish shell, Glen International into his personal trading vehicle. Coombs, at any rate, had grown concerned about his "maverick" style. In fact, he was thinking so big and aiming so high that it was impossible to control him and he was always liable to breach capital limits.

He assaulted the Japanese Stock Market with all the aggression of a General McArthur. His role in trading Japanese equity warrants would before "Black Monday", '87 make him — to use his own words — "the largest player by a long, long way in these warrants."

At one point he had seven strategic holdings in seven of the best companies in Japan and in pure assets had well in excess of £100 million. He acquired, for example, a large stake in the world's top bearing manufacturer, Minebea and played a part in a hostile takeover attempt which was to fail as the full might of the Japanese bureaucracy was mounted to delay, block and otherwise thwart his advance to his goal. If any general was persistent enough and determined enough to break through it was the cockney whizz-kid but he hadn't reckoned with the subtleties of the Japanese mind when it came to defending their own interests and they didn't have to become kamikaze pilots in the financial sense to do so. Yet, even though he failed, Ramsden can claim that he was the first Westerner to mount a hostile takeover bid for a Japanese company.

It was when he discovered the potential of Japanese warrants that Ramsden put his foot firmly on the ladder to becoming a millionaire. These are long-term options which gave the right to buy shares in a Japanese company at a certain price within a certain time. Because warrants represented a fraction of the share value with small amounts of cash, a large stake in a company could be acquired. The attraction to speculators was the potential for large movements in warrant values when there were smaller movements of the underlying shares.

But the reverse of the coin was that when stock markets fell, equity warrants fell even more dramatically.

The warrants existed in some profusion because Japanese companies, borrowing money on the international markets, attached these same warrants to the loan stocks to make them more attractive. Terry Ramsden spotted the loophole it left — the Japanese had failed to realise that the warrants could be detached from the loan stock and traded separately. By buying cheaply and shrewdly, he was able to build up his strategic holdings in various companies at a knockdown price.

The time difference between London and Tokyo meant that Ramsden worked through most nights at his Essex home. After grabbing a few short hours sleep, his chauffeur would drive him in mid-morning to his City office in a Mercedes complete with computers, print-out machine and two phones.

It was inevitable that he should want an escape from the tension of playing the market in equity warrants. And he found that escape in gambling on horses and in the ownership of horses. In a word, it was one kind of tension being replaced by another (as with the former Army bomb disposal friend of mine who after he had risked his life dismantling a bomb would find escape by having a "cut" on a horse or a dog and if he had a nail-biting win in a photo-finish, all the better).

"Racing and betting is a hobby and I do it for the crack," Ramsden said at one point when his involvement was getting ever deeper with each passing day. "But the hobby is growing and I'm not quite sure when it becomes a business," he admitted.

But then he was living by the dictum: "I never saw a haversack with wings. You can't take it with you."

Everything in the garden continued to be rosy while the stock markets held and he was making spectacular killings in speculating in Japanese equity warrants.

He was the archetypal entrepreneur, generating in the six years from 1980 £3.7 billion in business dealings. Set against that awesome figure and the profits accruing from it, his losses as a ferocious gambler even appeared containable — until the crash came.

Then too gambling, whether on business ventures or horses, was part of his very nature as he was on record as stating after he had bought the filly Katies, which won the Irish 1,000 Guineas for him in 1984: "I bought her unseen. You know I'm never really frightened to take a risk because that's what life is all about."

The £1.5 million he paid for Katies was recouped with interest when he had a substantial bet on her at 20/1 to win the Curragh Classic and that was unquestionably the most spectacular coup of his career as a punter. He hit the bookies again for six when she defeated Pebbles at the Royal Ascot meeting.

He claimed to have won a cool £1 million over that Royal Ascot success of Katies and he made headlines in the aftermath of that triumph when he said: "My name is Terry Ramsden. I'm a stockbroker from Enfield. I've got long hair and I like a bet."

For some reason best known to himself he decided to find out what her value was and offered her for sale at Goffs. He had put a reserve of £3 million on her. Most owners would have snapped up the £2.8 million that was bid — but not "Our Tel". He had her led out of the sales ring unsold. It was a costly exercise, as he had to pay a penalty of some £60,000 to the auctioneers. He shrugged it off, however, in typical fashion.

Like Noel Furlong with his Destriero-The Illiad £4 million double bid at the Cheltenham Festival meeting in 1990, Terry Ramsden went for a seven-figure killing that would have really left the bookies reeling if it had come off when he doubled his own horse Brunico in the Daily Express Triumph Hurdle and Dawn Run in the Gold Cup at the 1986 Festival meeting.

For two months beforehand he had been snapping up all available prices (Brunico started at 16/1 and Dawn Run at 15/8) and some estimates put the amount he would have won at over £5 million, though Ramsden himself simply said: "If Brunico had got there, I'd have won several million."

"Got there" meant that Brunico, staying on best of all, found the post coming just too soon when beaten half-a-length by the 40/1 shot, Solar Cloud, ridden by Peter Scudamore.

That was, of course, the first race on the Thursday. It was galling for Ramsden to watch Dawn Run and Jonjo O'Neill fight back from what seemed an impossible position after jumping the last to win the Gold Cup in a tremendous finish from Wayward Lad and Forgive 'N' Forget.

And making it more galling still was the fact that his own horse, Motivator, starting 15/2 favourite, took the Coral Golden Handicap Hurdle Final on the Wednesday by six lengths and in the process was reputed to have taken £1 million out of the ring.

What a Cheltenham it would have been for him had Brunico bridged that diminishing half-a-length in the Triumph Hurdle.

The same year his racing silks of blue and white — matching the colours of his favourite soccer club, Tottenham Hotspurs — were carried into fourth place in the Aintree Grand National by Mr Snugfit, which went off at 13/2 favourite and Ramsden had again gone for a massive killing both in single bets and in doubles and trebles.

He had £50,000 each way "on the nose" on Mr Snugfit at

8/1 and was unlucky at least that he did not win the place bet as 'Snugfit', responding to pressure from the third last, finished fastest of all and would have been third in another stride (Classified denied him third place by half-a-length).

He doubled Mr Snugfit with two horses of his own, Stearsby which won the Whitbread Best Mild Novices Chase on the Thursday at 11/4 and Brunico, third in the Glenlivet Hurdle on the Friday, starting 7/4 favourite and he also had trebles coupling all three.

"I'll probably jump over the stands," said the colourful Ramsden when asked by one newsman how he would react if Mr Snugfit won the Grand National.

In cold retrospect, however, there is little doubt that had Mr Snugfit and Brunico both won to add to the triumph of Stearsby at the 1986 Liverpool meeting, Ramsden would have given it all — and more — back to the bookies in due course. He was in that category of mug punters who are NEVER satisfied. The bigger the win, the greater the urge to aim for the moon and in the end they are taken out by the bookmakers.

No one could, however, deny that the man had flair and a penchant for commanding the headlines. Nothing funnier than the way he acquired unfashionable Walsall thus stopping a proposed merger with Birmingham. Barrie Blower of SWAG (Save Walsall Action Group) was perusing a copy of the *Sporting Life* when he chanced upon an article about Ramsden. "I want to buy a First Division club," said Ramsden in the course of that article. That gave Blower his opening to get on the "blower".

There followed a telephone conversation of classic simplicity.

Blower got straight to the point: "Do you want to buy a football club?"

"Which one?" asked Ramsden.

"Walsall."

"Where's that?"

"In the West Midlands."

"What Division are they in?"

"The Third."

"How much do they want?"

"About £400,000."

A few helicopter trips later, the deal was sealed.

After Walsall scored victories over Chesterfield, Port Vale, Charlton and Birmingham to qualify to play Watford at home in Fellows Park in the fifth round of the 1987 FA Cup, it gave Peter Hayter of *The Independent* the opening to write this very amusing intro to his preview:

What is the connection between Walsall Football Club, Stearsby (second favourite to win the Cheltenham Gold Cup) and 500 turkeys? Give up? Terry Ramsden, of course. He owns them, or at least he did until he distributed the turkeys among the club's old-age pensioner supporters at Christmas.

Now he is waiting to give the bird to Watford's own eccentric millionaire Chairman, Elton John who Ramsden calls "the other bloke".

Where did Ramsden turn to find his new manager? Barcelona? Bayern Munich? Bishop's Stortford, actually. Come on down, Tommy Coakley, star of Motherwell, Arsenal (briefly), Detroit Cougars and Malden Town, among others.

Coakley takes up the story: "I knew Terry (Ramsden) at Malden. Before he took over, we were complete no-hopers, slaughtered by everyone. He became chairman, sponsored the jerseys and we won the league and cup final.

"He wanted us to get into the Isthmian League, so he paid for floodlights — we had to have them to reach the required ground standard. I left for Bishop's Stortford because I just thought he was being unrealistic and I never heard from him for a year until just before the start of this season.

"We were at Ascot races. He said: 'What are you doing on Monday?' I said: 'Not a lot.' He said: 'How would you like to be manager of Walsall?' And that was it. We had this discussion in the helicopter on the way back to his home. It was all a bit strange."

After the crash, Ramsden had to sell Walsall for £1 million after being Chairman of the club for just seventeen months and it didn't end there, for the newspapers were also reporting that the Midland Bank was trying to repossess a house of his in south-east London's expensive Blackheath area.

The distribution of 500 turkeys among Walsall's 500 old-age pensioner supporters at Christmas was one of those magnanimous gestures that endeared Terry Ramsden to people when he was riding the crest of the wave financially. In helping charitable causes, he never forgot the fact that he came from humble beginnings himself.

There was nothing finer than the way he chartered Concorde on a supersonic charity trip in May, 1985 to raise cash for sick children. Passengers paid £800 for a return trip to Helsinki — the first time Concorde flew to the Finnish capital. After allowing for expenses, Ramsden aimed to donate £3,000 to the children's wards at Basildon Hospital, Essex. "A wonderful idea," said a hospital spokesman. "Fantastic," said a spokesman for British Airways, adding that they were thrilled "so many children would benefit from the flight".

Charities he contributed to included Bob Champion's Cancer Fund, the Heart Foundation and the NSPCC.

Ramsden was so angry when a Sunday newspaper carried claims made by three ex-minders that amounted to sex slurs on his character that he took a full-page advertisement, costing £32,000 in *The Sun* to clear his name over the allegations. His wife, Liza (23) was expecting their first child at the time and Ramsden said in the advertisement, which he wrote himself: "I do not recognise the man portrayed in the article as myself and I wish to set the record straight."

The heavy gold chain around his wrist and the long dark hair resting on his shoulders hardly gave him the image of your normal staid City type with a rolled-up umbrella.

He didn't care about turned-up noses. But the notoriety he gained when his 30-stone plus "minder" Wayne Jackson was accused of assaulting a punter at Cheltenham races was something Ramsden could have done without, though it has to be stressed that Jackson was cleared of the charge at Gloucester Crown Court.

When people asked why he needed to be accompanied

everywhere by bodyguards, he replied: "It is a regrettable step that I took with reluctance. Friends were concerned that I did not pay enough attention to security. I can't still go strolling around as if I was a broker's clerk at the Stock Exchange."

The bodyguards couldn't save him when "Black Monday", '87 brought the collapse of his fortunes.

Inside six months he was battling in the courts against a charge of fraudulently evading payment of £536,000 VAT between January, 1984 and January, 1985. After a ten-day trial at Southwark Crown Court he was acquitted.

The flamboyant lifestyle was back in all its champagne glory that same evening as he headed for the glitter of London's West End with his blonde wife, wearing a catching mini, to forget the pressure of the trial and the £250,000 in legal fees and "many millions more" in lost City business which it had cost him.

After the champagne corks had popped, he took in the premiere of a film he had financed at the Odeon in Marble Arch.

It's title? "Lost City".

That night in a way was the last big splash of the cockney tycoon. The City was lost to him now and, even though he rejoiced at the fact that the court verdict had cleared him of "this stigma", it was all cruelly downhill, with one problem after another arising for him. The Department of Trade began an inquiry into Glen International, whose accounts were long delayed.

The climax came in the autumn of 1991 when he was arrested in the United States and appeared before an assistant US attorney of the Central District of California on a warrant issued in London. British authorities confirmed that an extradition application would be pursued 'in due course'.

Held in custody at Terminal Island prison, Los Angeles since September '91 it seemed initially that he would stick to his vow to fight any attempt to extradite him but he changed his mind in February, 1992 and agreed to be returned to Britain.

At one time Ramsden had been director of no less than

197

22 companies.

When Glen International ceased trading in September, 1987 and the Serious Fraud Squad moved in, it had recorded debts of £258 million and a deficit of £124 million.

The motto by which he lived came back to haunt him: "They don't make haversacks with wings to them? You can't take it with you when you go. So I might as well enjoy it while I'm here."

He may not have realised it but he was echoing the words of "Mincemeat Joe" Griffin when he said forty years earlier — before the fall of his empire — "Money for me is for spending and for making people happy. I have made a lot of people happy..."

Ramsden did too in the good times.

PART NINE

JEFF SMURFIT
*'The Salesman' Who Lived
Life On The High Wire*

14

Played Baccarat With Sinatra In Caesar's Palace

Some knew only the legend. And the legend was to grow ever since that night in Las Vegas in a screened off area of Caesar's Palace that he played Baccarat or Punto-Banco with Frank Sinatra – "Frank had his bodyguard standing behind him and I had a well-known jeweller from Dublin," he recalled later.

Sinatra, very relaxed after his opening show, was enjoying a couple of drinks over the game – Jack Daniels Bourbon. "The stakes were reasonably substantial," was all Jeff Smurfit would venture when I asked him if it was a big game.

But legend had it that the stakes were so high that something in the region of 1,000,000 dollars had to be transferred from a Smurfit bank account in Dublin to get Jeff out of Las Vegas and that he had to borrow 1,000 dollars to pay his flight back to Ireland!

He laughed on both counts, though admitting that he had, in fact, come out a loser that same evening – but how heavily he wouldn't say.

"I did not really lose to Frank Sinatra, as some reports suggested," Jeff told me. "It would be more correct to say that I lost to the house. If I had followed Frank's luck against the house, I would have had a good night too." (In losing to the house he would have lost to Caesar's Palace and that is how the legend grew in Dublin of the seven-figure sum being transferred to the casino in question and

200

why Jeff Smurfit didn't have to pay his hotel bill when he was checking out.)

On the question of having to borrow money to get home, he explained: "My wife and I had our air tickets home like everyone else who had attended the Variety Club Convention in San Francisco. Owning a travel agency as I do, I would have had no trouble, anyway, in getting an air ticket in any part of the world," he told me.

"You see, I had just run out of ready cash, so I borrowed a thousand dollars from a friend. It was nothing. He had my cheque when we stepped off the plane in Dublin. One of the most pleasant surprises was that when I was checking out of my hotel in Las Vegas, I was informed that my stay was on the house. My bill was very substantial as I had done a lot of entertaining."

It's the tradition in Las Vegas that if you are a high roller in the big game league, then they are not too worried about "comping" you when it comes to your hotel accommodation, meals and drinks (in fact, if you were simply a pensioner arriving in a Greyhound bus for a week's vacation, there is nowhere in the world where you can eat cheaper than in Las Vegas).

Anyone who was able to sit down with Frank Sinatra and not run scared when the stakes got big was certainly one they were going to admire in this city in the desert where the action goes on right around the clock – and they would admire him all the more when they learned he was from the Emerald Isle.

Jeff Smurfit could meet any commitments stemming from his gambling, whether on Baccarat (Punto Banco) or the horses. At one stage he sold one million shares in the Smurfit Group for £4.5 million but still retained a stake in the company which had been established by his late father, Jefferson Snr., whom he idolised. The stake amounted to just over three million shares worth a cool £18 million and in addition he enjoyed an annual income from dividends of £140,000 – before tax.

Betting on horses for him was really a form of relaxation from the pressures of business and it was the same with Baccarat. He accepted that if he was a professional gambler like J.P. McManus or Barney Curley, working to the strict guidelines by which the professionals operate, then he would do things far differently whether he was having a "cut" on a horse on-course or off-course. "Sometimes you win, more often than not you lose. If we did not lose, there would be no bookmakers," he said with a philosophical shrug of his shoulders.

Win or lose, the champagne always flowed when he was in celebratory mood with friends. They knew him simply as "Junior" and he could be the life and soul of any party because his approach was always a big one, in keeping with the bigness of his heart and outlook on life. He liked to think of himself as the human face of the Smurfit Group.

It was inevitable that when the Variety Club Convention brought him to San Francisco that he should journey on to Las Vegas to test his skill not against the slot machines ("only a fool would play the machines," he said) but at the card tables.

You can almost imagine the jet coming in over the Nevada desert, in over the lights of downtown Las Vegas – and Jeff, with his close friends, smoking that inevitable cigar. Now he would be in the mood for play – to have a cut at breaking the Baccarat "bank", for of all the card games, he believed that it came nearest to giving the punter an even-money chance.

Jeff Smurfit, on being formally introduced to Frank Sinatra, found the whole scene that evening in Las Vegas intensely fascinating and at the same time very elaborate. But then it was a scene set for a big game and high stakes.

"Frank Sinatra was very natural in his approach and, as a player, quite experienced," Jeff recalled. "In such a setting as Las Vegas, it wasn't surprising really that you could find yourself playing alongside famous names and also with men who could far outstrip Sinatra in knowledge of the game. It just happened on this particular night that I got an introduction to Frank and found myself playing in his company into the early hours of the morning."

The game of Baccarat (pronounced Baa-Caa-rah) or Punto Banco, as it is known in Europe, is a version of the old game of Chemin-de-Fer. It was introduced to the Sands

202

Hotel in Las Vegas in 1960 by Tony Renzoni. He was a fugitive from the Havana of General Batista and Mayer Lansky, who had the Casino concessions prior to the overthrow of the Batista regime in the Cuban Revolution of 1959.

The object of the game is to wager on the hand (bank or player) which the person playing feels will be closest to 9. The highest hand in Baccarat or Punto-Banco is 9. The lowest is zero (equals 0). The closest to 9 is the winner. Tens and picture cards count for nothing and so also a combination of cards that comes to a total of 10 i.e. 6+4=0 or 10+2=2.

In evaluating a hand, once the total goes over ten, the 10 is deducted.

Thus, for example, if you draw a King and a 3 (that is 10+3 or 13), the total is 3 while a 4 and a 3 becomes a total of 7.

Therefore, you hope to avoid drawing a total of 10 or any two ten-count cards which equals a total of nought. Rather do you want to draw a two-card total of 9, giving you an unbeatable hand. The best the opposite side can do in that situation is to also draw a two-card total of nine. As nobody can draw the third card, it becomes a "stand-off", equalling no bet.

Likewise, a two-card total of 8 prevents the opposite side drawing the third card. The only way you can be beaten with a two-card total of 8 is that the opposite side has a two-card count of 9, then the 9 beats the 8.

The key person or persons acting for the House are the dealer (croupier) or dealers, depending on the type of table, that is mini, midi or kidney-shaped. Table rules are the same no matter which table the game is played on. With the mini or midi tables, only one dealer operates the game on behalf of the clients and the House. The clients have the option of backing the player hand or the bank hand.

The dealer draws the first card from the shoe (containing the cards) and puts it in the player position face down. He then draws the second card and puts in in the bank position face down. The third card is dealt to the player posi-

Player Having	
1 2 3 4 5 10	Draws a card
6 7	Stands
8 9	NATURAL: Banker cannot draw

Banker Having	Draws when giving	Stands when giving
3	1 2 3 4 5 6 7 9 10	8
4	2 3 4 5 6 7	1 8 9 10
5	4 5 6 7	1 2 3 8 9 10
6	6 7	1 2 3 4 5 8 9 10 No.
7	Stands	
8 9	NATURAL: Player cannot draw	

tion and the fourth to the bank position. When each position has got two cards, the cards are turned over and the values are totalled.

A third card may be allowed as per the above chart.

Terry Rogers maintains that the game of Baccarat or Punto-Banco is without doubt the fairest game to either bank or player as the punters can bet with the bank or with the player.

One night at a table in a Las Vegas Casino Terry explained to me how by "tracking" the cards you can get an "edge" on occasions but, of course, you must know what you are doing.

"Over 20,000 hands (or coups), the percentage in favour of the House is 1.32 per cent each time the punters back the player position and 1.28 per cent each time the punters back the bank position," was how Terry outlined it to me.

204

Aficionados of the 'tracking' know that after 50 per cent of the cards have left the shoe, they will have an edge on occasions. They might go as many as three complete shoes before Terry's system can be put into operation. It may only last for one or two hands or it could last right through the remainder of the shoe.

"The best place for a person playing the game is on the mini-table. You can stand and bet when you wish. In recent years a new table called a midi has been introduced. You have to sit at this table which means that you are trapped, in the sense that you have to bet on almost every hand. It rules out the operation of the tracking system in that you cannot bet only when you decide that the edge is in your favour, Terry explained."

I saw Terry Rogers at a mini-table in Las Vegas utilising the tracking technique very effectively and, indeed, there came a stage when he wasn't welcome at mini-tables. They realised that he knew the score too well and was picking and choosing when to bet – and winning.

Terry's favourite place to play Baccarat is in Harrahs in Lake Tahoe.

One night in the Curzon Club in London Terry and his friend Bill Cutler were playing at a kidney-shaped table. When Terry decided that the shoe had come completely in their favour he gave a tic-tac signal to Bill to bet his limit. "We cleared no less than £80,000 on that particular night," Terry recalled.

I have been told by Baccarat experts – though Terry Rogers is not one who subscribes to the theory – that where experience comes into play is that if you get a run, then the approach is to double up. But you have to have a fearless nerve in deciding how far you will let your money ride.

Jeff Smurfit could double the stakes, not out of the calculated approach of the professional, but simply to try and recoup his losses or play up his winnings.

A perfect example of this was seen in the game of Punto Banco in which he was involved on the night of St. Stephen's Day, 1976 after the running of the Sweeps Hurdle at Leopardstown. Jeff got word at the racecourse that

Terry Rogers was having a private game in his residence in Talbot Street.

Terry takes up the story: "Jeff arrived with his aide-de-camp, the late Chris Travers. The game had already commenced and the stakes were between £50 and £200. Jeff asked if he could play. He stipulated at the same time that, if I was agreeable, then he would want to bet up to £1,000 on each coup.

"I agreed to let him play. However, I made it clear that the bank – in which two people present were participating, with me – was being set at £20,000. 'It will not go higher,' I told Jeff, 'so if you succeed in breaking the bank, the game will end. I also made it clear that the game would not go on beyond 2.30 a.m.

"Chris Travers took careful note of every bet which Jeff Smurfit had, confirming each transaction with me. I was happy about this. You see I was very fond of Jeff Smurfit and I always found him to be personally a very nice fellow, polite and sociable.

"Around 12.30 a.m. Jeff asked that the stakes be increased to £2,000. I gave my consent to this, again emphasising that I was not increasing the size of the bank.

"When it came to 2 o'clock in the morning and the last eight-deck shoe was about to commence, Jeff was losing between £108,000 and £113,000. He suggested that for the final shoe the stakes should be doubled to £4,000.

"After reflecting for a moment, I said – 'Okay, £4,000 it is.'

"At that juncture I left the room to go and get more chips. When I returned the game had recommenced. I found that Chris Travers was betting as well as Jeff and two coups were already over.

"Naturally I was upset at this as I knew that Travers hadn't the kind of money that would allow him to bet £4,000 a coup but Jeff quickly interjected to declare: 'I'll guarantee Chris.' What was happening was that Chris was actually betting for Jeff. It meant that Jeff instead of having just £4,000 on with each coup was actually betting £8,000 a go. Therefore, if he got a run, he could wipe out his losses.

"The first coups after that went win-one, lose-one. Then

Jeff hit a really lucky run, switching from bank to player and player to bank. Half-way through I found myself rooting for him because I was still upset at the stupidity of my associate in allowing Chris Travers to bet for Jeff.

"Jeff brought off twelve winning coups in succession at £8,000 a time. In the process he won back £96,000. In the second last bet of the night he actually went ahead by a little over £3,000. He lost the last bet, however, and it was then the end of the shoe. As the hands of the clock had gone past 2.30 a.m. to 2.40 a.m., I announced: 'That's it. The game is over'.

"Jeff in the excitement of his winning run had forgotten completely how he was standing with the bank and when he heard me call a halt, he said: 'But the game is not over yet. I must get a chance of getting my money back', thinking no doubt that he was still well behind.

"I told him – 'Before your last bet, Jeff, you were actually in front. And if you had won that last bet, you would have broken the bank'."

Chris Travers confirmed this.

Jeff was quite satisfied then and settled his account.

"Just after he left, one of my associates, called Joe, went into one of the other rooms to get something and in the process set off the burglar alarm. 'Hell . . . you should have done that half-an-hour ago!' I remarked."

Terry Rogers recalled that over a period of almost fourteen years he played quite a bit with Jeff Smurfit. "We played roulette on several occasions during the fund-raising nights for St. Gerard's School, Bray. I only succeeded in beating him twice. It was the same when he bet on the horses with me. Generally, he came out winning."

When the Eccentric Club's International Hold 'Em Poker Championship was held on the Isle of Man, Jeff Smurfit, then resident there, renewed acquaintanceship with Terry Rogers and actually played in the tournament, which of course was for charitable causes.

At the Leopardstown Christmas meeting in 1976, Jeff Smurfit went for a 'touch' in the Sean Graham Chase (2m 2f) on Bunker Hill, which started at 11/8 with Bannow Rambler an even-money favourite.

Bunker Hill, ridden by Michael 'Mouse' Morris beat Siberian Sun (Frank Berry) by a length in a driving finish and immediately his friends began to celebrate with Jeff Smurfit. I recall being told at the racecourse that day that he stood to win close on £20,000 ("it was more than that," he smiled when I broached it to him later) – and then over the public address system came the announcement of a stewards inquiry, the outcome of which was that Bunker Hill was disqualified and placed second. It was argued that Smurfit could easily have left the champagne party in one of the top bars of the stand and gone down to the ring and laid off enough to have saved his stake, or he could have got someone to do the job for him – as the bookmakers were betting against Bunker Hill losing it in the stewards room.

"All right, I know a professional punter in that same instance would have laid off," he agreed. "but let me repeat that I am not a professional punter. There is a lot of controversy about what happens in the stewards room these days. That could be a good thing or a bad thing. There is no doubt that in certain cases horses deserve to get disqualified."

He admitted to getting a lot of pleasure out of a day at the races – "for me it can be a wonderful day out, a very good social occasion," he said.

He was brought up to know about racing and horses and to experience the scene in Ireland at a young age. His father had a number of horses with Vincent O'Brien early on in the career of the Master of Ballydoyle.

"I can remember going to race meetings with my father," he recalled. "My father never had any real success with the horses he owned. In fact, he gave up racing over losing a race in the stewards room with a horse called Patrickswell."

The race in question was the Blackwater Chase run at Naas on January 8, 1949. Patrickswell, trained by Danny Ruttle and ridden by Mickey Gordon, started 5/2 second favourite. He won by a length from the 9/4 favourite, Blenamirth. But the latter's rider, Jimmy Brogan lodged an objection on the grounds of bumping – and it was sustained.

Jeff Smurfit recalled that his father bought him his first runner, Lady Matador, which was trained by Clem Magnier. She proved herself a very speedy filly and won the Curragh Stakes.

"My father used to tell the trainers he knew that I was a newcomer to the racing scene and he would add that if his sons wanted to make the same mistakes as he had, then that was their funeral. But he did not discourage us."

Jeff Smurfit got his thrills as an owner at racecourses on occasions far from the roar of the crowd and all the atmosphere of Cheltenham in March. He recalled, for example, having a horse with Kevin Bell that gave him some of his most memorable thrills from racing. "It won a few small races for me. I had great fun going to places like Wexford and savouring the special atmosphere of such meetings. I never had a big bet on him but, as I say, I had great pleasure owning him."

The day I called to interview him in late August, 1979 at the Group headquarters at Clonskeagh, County Dublin he was sitting in a black-leathered swivel chair in a fine new office. He never seemed to be without that distinctive big cigar and this particular afternoon he was working in a blue striped shirt, matching the soft pile of the blue carpet.

As he took a call, I realised that at 42 his stake in the Smurfit Group put him comfortably into the millionaire category. Already the tentacles of the Smurfit empire had stretched not alone into Britain and the States but also into Africa, where that same year a new modern corrugated case factory had been established in Nigeria. In the ensuing decade, growth would continue at an even more impressive rate.

Jeff Smurfit was the first to acknowledge that many of the public when they thought of the Smurfit Group, thought only of Michael Smurfit, frequently portrayed as the managerial maestro who had built the Group into a worldwide business, generating staggering profits.

While obviously his own contribution didn't elicit the same level of recognition, it didn't upset Jeff. For he knew the reality.

And the reality, as he explained it to me, was that "our customers do not think in terms of Michael alone. They think in terms of people at the selling end."

Jeff's heart ailment prompted open heart surgery followed by a by-pass operation. It was to get away from the social whirl of Dublin which he knew in his heart was death to him that he retired in 1984 from his posts of Deputy Chairman and Assistant Chief Executive of the Smurfit Group, to the quieter pastures of the Isle of Man (though he continued to serve as a non-Executive Director).

Michael Smurfit himself, however, readily acknowledged what a born salesman Jeff was, acknowledged too the debt the Group owed him and he echoed that regard when he stood at Jeff's 50th birthday party in the Isle of Man and paid him an outstanding personal tribute. Jeff confided later that nothing over the three days and nights of celebrating had touched him as deeply.

When Jeff Smurfit died suddenly in August, 1987 just three weeks after his 50th birthday party and on the eve of the wedding of his daughter Karina, Angela Phelan, the *Irish Independent* diarist wrote of the death of 'The Salesman' under the heading "Just Junior To A World Of Friends."

"Among those he played golf with were Ben Dunne Jnr. and Sean Connery. 'I am doing what I do best . . . after selling,' he would say. When he wasn't playing golf, he was talking about his constant pursuit of excellence in the game that became a major part of his life since he retired.

"A natural host, Smurfit was one of the great party givers in the old, lavish style. The party for his 50th birthday outstripped all others.

"Business associates and rivals were all agreed on one thing. Whether he was selling corrugated paper or new business ideas, no one could refuse his powerful personality.

"He always referred to the pace at which his father lived his life and said: 'Who ever heard of a happy, retired salesman. The selling thing is in your system. Once a salesman, always a salesman'."

As I sat in his office with him back on that August day in 1979, I came to realise why his strength was in selling, saw too the brilliance of his innovative mind and why there would come a day when the price he paid in heart trouble would cause him to say: "I burst a gut for 31 years laying the foundations. I don't need the day to day hassle of endless meetings and meetings . . . about meetings. Let my other brothers, who have their own talents and who have been overshadowed, get in there."

The philosophy he learned when he started out at the age of 16 trying to win outlets for Smurfit products in Britain would stand him in good stead all his business life – right on to the day when he came to have a force of 300 salesmen under him. If people at a race meeting or on a social occasion felt they could readily identify with him, then it was because he was always himself – the natural self. And it was this very quality he looked for in picking a new salesman – naturalness and sincerity.

"I was brought up to think positively," he told me. By that he meant that he took the approach that 99 per cent of people are basically honest.

"I start out from that premise in the negotiation of all sales," he went on. "You will in life always meet at some stage the out-and-out chancer but I believe that it would be wrong to always start from the basis of suspicion in dealing with new clients. If you do not start from the basis of trust, then you are beginning with a definite handicap. The number of times I have been let down has been negligible."

Because he was reared in such a hard school, he could spot the chancers in the business world, but when he was relaxing among the gambling set, he allowed himself to fall victim to unprincipled "sharks" in poker sessions, especially in the era before he gave up alcohol. One insider told me that he made a point of *never* playing cards with Jeff Smurfit when he wasn't in full control of himself or not accompanied by a "minder". But, of course, there were others who played on Jeff's innate faith in human nature.

Young Jeff Smurfit had gone into a market in Britain which was totally new to him and all he had to help him were trade directories and suggestions from helpful people. He told me how he was in Woolworths in Liverpool one day actually jotting down the names of suppliers from a pile of empty boxes when he got a tap on the shoulder from the manager, wondering at the curious activity of a total stranger to him. Jeff told the manager what he was about and the result was that he was shown around the warehouse where, he recalled: "I could take notes of boxes and their makers to my heart's content."

In his first assault on the British market, he won a bridgehead in Lancashire when Jacobs of Aintree asked him to quote for an order of 25,000 boxes (5,000 was big to Smurfits at the time!) and he was still doing business with that firm the day I talked to him.

In between taking notes I got an insight into his high-powered lifestyle, for apart from his involvement at executive level in the Smurfit Group and Harcourt Irish Holdings, he was principal shareholder in a syndicate owning five racehorses, some trained in England and some in Ireland.

That very evening he had a business appointment in Bloom's Hotel at 8 p.m. Now the phone rings and he is asked can he make it across to England to see one of the two year olds run. But he calculates that the Board meeting he will be attending next day will go on to 1.30 p.m. at least – and he could never hope to catch a plane to make it to the races. But he advises his friend to report back to him on the colt's performance.

Then there is a discussion on how effective the Smurfit "hospitality tent" had proved at the Carrolls Irish Open Golf Championship at Portmarnock the previous weekend. Jeff had acted as host to the Group's customers and business friends and there was nowhere in the world he was more at home than in a golf setting.

He was playing at the time off a 16 handicap. The handicap, he confided, was incidental to the intensity of the friendly fourball matches in which he participated at any of the three Dublin clubs – Miltown, Elm Park and Foxrock – of which he was a member or some other course on the metropolitan circuit or out of town in Ireland or maybe on the great championship courses in Britain or in Spain.

"We always have a bet," he told me. "The main bet is never less than £25 a man but there are additional side-stakes for birdies and individual matches inside the four-ball itself. If I lost £100 I would regard it as a bad day – not, I must stress, because of the amount of money involved but because it would indicate that things had gone badly for you in the overall fourball itself and in all the side matches.

"Yes, it's never really the money in golf – it's the talk afterwards and the ribbing you have to endure if you lose. Then you want to settle the score next time out and that's what really makes all the fun – it's no different whether it's 50p or £50 or £100. We try and arrange fourballs so that we will have a very even match and with the side bets going, you might lose the fourball and yet come out on the day winning overall."

Yes, whether it was playing golf, snooker or cards or punting on the racecourse, the crack was always good when Jeff was relaxing . . . a sharp contrast to the business tycoon sitting opposite me in an office in Clonskeagh on an August day in '79, talking about how he had taken up £400,000 of a rights issue that same week and then flicking the ash from his cigar, remarking casually: "That's £1 million in earned income."

At the time of Jeff's untimely death, from a heart attack at the age of 50, the Smurfit Group had become the first publicly-quoted Irish company to exceed the £1 billion valuation mark on the Irish Stock Exchange. A long, long way from an order for 25,000 boxes from Jacobs of Aintree that marked Junior's initial successful assault on the British market.

He was survived by his wife Anne, daughters, Karina (23) and Tina (21) and sons John Jeff (19) and Jason (16).

When wedding bells should have been pealing joyously in Dublin, funeral bells were tolling instead in a Manx churchyard.

Robert Sangster stood beside Ray Burke T.D., then Minister for Energy, representing the Irish Government and former Taoiseach (Prime Minister), Jack Lynch was also

213

there.

As the coffin faced the altar, the congregation sang *Abide With Me*.

In his adopted island he had come to be known affectionately as the "Irish Ambassador" because of his generosity and the positive image he promoted of Ireland there.

Jeff's name became a byword for altruism and he had only recently sponsored a charity for research into paediatric diseases.

Only after the grave had been closed in the Isle of Man did it become known that Jeff Smurfit, gambler and fun-lover, golfer and card player and lavish party-giver, had for ten years secretly followed in the footsteps of his father and funded the Kimmage Ambulance Service.

A small, local service, it provides a 24-hour on-call facility to the local poor who are dying from terminal cancer.

Joe Fennell, who founded and still runs the service, said in tribute to Jeff Smurfit: "There are so many people around here who have benefited from his generosity. The only thing he ever insisted upon was that nobody should know that he helped us. I feel I have lost a great friend. And Dublin has lost one of its greatest charity workers."

No finer epitaph than this to 'The Salesman'.

PART TEN

PATRICK GALLAGHER
*A £750,000 Gamble on
Try My Best*

15

"Come on Vincent,
it's brandy time"

"Come on Vincent, it's brandy time" was the six-word comment that Patrick Gallagher limited himself to in the shattering moment that the seemingly unbeatable Try My Best trailed in last of the nineteen runners in the 1978 English 2000 Guineas.

Vincent O'Brien was as shocked and mystified as the 27-year-old millionaire Dublin property tycoon who had gambled on the Dewhurst winner training on from an unbeaten record as a two-year-old to win at least one, maybe even two Classics.

Patrick Gallagher evaluated Try My Best at £2 million on his achievement in emerging as the undisputed juvenile champion of the 1977 season and decided to lay out at least £500,000 to buy a quarter share in him. He was to purchase that share eventually for £750,000.

In the aftermath of the defeat Gallagher sold back to the syndicate headed by Robert Sangster, deciding to cut his losses rather than endeavour to get back exactly what he had invested in the colt.

At the time he bought into Try My Best he was riding a high tide of success and everything he touched seemed to turn to gold. Later when Merchant Banking collapsed and he ended up in Belfast's Crumlin Road jail, the sum of three-quarters of a million pounds which he had laid out to become a part owner of the son of Northern Dancer looked like the proverbial "peanuts" in comparison with the scale of his financial operations at one stage.

Patrick Gallagher's investment in Try My Best has been viewed by cynics as one of the most spectacular failed individual gambles in the bloodstock field.

It's easy, I know, to be wise after the event but the way he outlined it to me over a drink in a Stephen's Green hostelry at the time showed that there was no sentiment whatsoever in the way the decision was reached. Indeed, it was a pure business transaction by the 6ft. 4ins. head of one of Ireland's biggest house-building property-developing companies, also engaged in merchant banking – and, remember, at that point Gallagher was treating his racing and breeding interests as totally separate from the rest and he was doing "nicely" at the breeding end at least.

Gallagher had plenty of encouragement from expert opinion to pursue the deal without fearing for a moment that he would get his fingers badly burned in the process. First of all, a glance through the form book for 1977 revealed that Try My Best had three outings as a two year old and had been successful in all three. Those who were at Leopardstown on Saturday, September 27 and saw Try My Best win the Larkspur Stakes by six lengths knew that they were looking at an exceptional colt. And that faith was fully justified when he went on to take the Dewhurst Stakes at Newmarket by 1½ lengths from Sexton Blake.

Lester Piggott said as he dismounted: "The colt is without doubt the best two year old we have seen this season. He will have no trouble in getting the Rowley Mile."

Robert Sangster, in whose colours Try My Best raced, had this to say: "We knew Try My Best was something exceptional before he ran. I see him as a Guineas hope at the moment and then a potential Derby winner."

And Vincent O'Brien predicted: "I do not see why he should not develop into another Nijinsky."

Gallagher's approach to the deal was that if Try My Best took the English 2000 Guineas and then went on to win the Derby, he would be valued even higher than The Minstrel (which was to attain a tag of 9 million dollars).

It was an investment, which at the moment it was clinched, looked like paying off very handsomely indeed.

And yet there was an insurance factor in the breeding potential – irrespective of what the future held in the Classics – that you would not always have in a big business deal.

The fall-back position, in effect, was that even if this 'wonder' colt disappointed in the 2000 Guineas and Epsom Derby – and Patrick Gallagher took full cognisance of this in his calculations – the value would still remain at £2 million on Try My Best's two year old performances.

When negotiations began with the syndicate headed by Robert Sangster and comprising Simon Fraser, Danny Schwartz, John Magnier and Vincent O'Brien, it became clear to Patrick Gallagher that the people he was dealing with would see no point in selling "unless they got something for the colt's prospects in the Classics – that is his potential on top of his basic value at the end of the 1977 season."

"As I saw it, he was worth £2 million at that point even if he were to finish nowhere in the 2000 Guineas. But on potential you could put an extra million pounds on his head at least – that is a tag of £3 million. Had he gone on to win the Guineas, I estimated he would be worth £4 million definitely. And if he had taken the Epsom Derby as well, his value would have jumped to £7 million, possibly £8 million.

"After that you had the Irish Derby and if he had maintained an unbeaten record, the sky was the limit. I saw him as the finest colt since Nijinsky. Remember, The Minstrel did not win the English 2000 Guineas prior to taking the Epsom Derby and Irish Derby and then the King George VI and Queen Elizabeth Stakes and we know the price tag he was to achieve."

The very limit Gallagher thought he would go to was £600,000 but as the negotiations progressed, he agreed to £250,000 over and above the £500,000 on the potential of the colt – "that is I paid £750,000 for a quarter share."

The "escape" factor that caused him to pay that extra £250,000 was the pedigree of Try My Best. A bay colt by Northern Dancer out of Sex Appeal by Buckpasser, he represented the best of American blood.

Gallagher reasoned that with American blood so dominant, the stud potential of Try My Best in the States would become all the greater with every race he won as a three year old but even as it was, the world attention gained by his achievements as a two year old had been enough to make him a very valuable stud property.

He flatly and categorically rejected suggestions that he was an innocent abroad when he paid £750,000 for a quarter share in a colt that had to win at least one Classic before he could hope to realise any profit on his investment.

"Let me put it on the record that the way the syndicate treated me in clinching the deal was exceptionally good," he said. "The worst that could happen was balanced against the best that Try My Best could achieve as a three year old. In the world of big business you are gambling all the time. You are gambling in setting up new companies, in going into property deals and you have to learn to steel yourself against disaster.

"Fortunately, I have not known the disasters that have hit others but I have learned that you don't just count your chickens before they are hatched when the risk factor is there in any deal that promises a sizeable profit.

"You have got to be prepared for setbacks, for something going seriously wrong, even the worst happening, and you have got to learn to cut your losses and get out, if the prospect of saving a company or turning some venture into a profit-making one, suddenly evaporates before your eyes."

A decade on from when Patrick Gallagher said this to me his empire had collapsed and he knew what it was like to spend hours alone in a cell . . . contemplating the might-have-beens.

However, in the spring of 1978 – in the era when he knew only a champagne lifestyle – he would have scoffed at the thought, if you had the temerity to suggest it to him, that there would come a day when he would have to listen to a judge impose a jail sentence on him because he could not meet the £500,000 balance of a £1 million sterling fine imposed on him by a Belfast court.

In that golden spring of '78, in the countdown to the

English 2000 Guineas he was already planning the victory party to celebrate what he was convinced by then would be a sweeping initial Classic success for Try My Best. And what a champagne party it was going to be.

Later when the crash came, men remembered how the flamboyant financier and racehorse owner had hired a private jet to bring a party of family members and friends over for the race and a London night-spot had been booked in advance to continue the festivities after the champagne corks had first been set popping at Newmarket itself.

He still managed to put a brave face on things in the aftermath of the total eclipse of Try My Best, coming up with the classic comment: "Risks are taken every day. Some come off, some don't. You can't sit around crying when they fail to come off."

So the party went ahead anyway, even if lacking in the heady effervescence that would have marked it if the colt had triumphed in the manner expected of him.

There would come a day when Patrick Gallagher, winging it home in the private jet, would be happy to be able to purchase the cheapest Apex ticket between Dublin and London, wanting the lowest possible profile in economy class where once it was unthinkable that he would not automatically travel first class or club class.

And the chauffeur-driven car whisking him around town as he pulled off his mega-deals would soon be added to the pile of abandoned perks.

That was after the racehorses and the studs had been disposed of, also the Rolls Royces and the magnificent six-bedroom Georgian house in County Meath overlooking Bective Abbey and the River Boyne. And after the fair-weather acquaintances and hangers-on who had quaffed champagne with him in his peak days in the Seventies had vanished into thin air (but there were loyal friends who helped him and his wife Susan pay the school fees for their sons, Matthew and Patrick in St. Gerard's School in Bray and later at a top public school in Britain).

Try My Best was quoted at 3/1 for the Epsom Derby when Alan Smith visited Ballydoyle in March '78 and *The*

Sporting Life under the banner headline "Try My Best Leads Another Cashel Fleet of Destroyers" quoted Vincent O'Brien as saying: "I'm very pleased with my colt's development. He must be a live contender for the Guineas. I hope he'll progress to stay the Derby distance."

Those who had plunged on him at all available odds during the winter could take heart also from Lester Piggott's verdict: "I see no reason why he shouldn't stay a mile and a half."

The 2000 Guineas then seemed but a mere formality, and more so after Vincent O'Brien gave him a warm-up outing in the Vauxhall Trial Stakes over seven furlongs at the Phoenix Park on Saturday, April 8 with the going officially described as "yielding".

Raceform Notebook said the colt had gained in strength during the winter, looked very fit and ran a supremely satisfactory Guineas trial. He won going away by two lengths from Columbanus, which would go on to win the Tetrarch Stakes and then finish third behind Jaazeiro and Strong Gale in the Irish 2000 Guineas.

On the big day itself at Newmarket on May 6, the going was described as "soft".

The build-up was immense and there was that air of expectation in racing circles both in Ireland and Britain that had not been experienced since Nijinsky opened his bid for the Triple Crown here in 1970.

Disquieting rumours had emanated that all was not well with the colt and instead of starting at odds-on, in keeping with his tremendous reputation, Try My Best was easy enough to back at even-money on the day. Did the bookies know something that the ordinary punter was not aware of?

Try My Best broke well enough from the stalls in the swampy conditions but at no stage held out any hope of reaching a challenging position. When asked to quicken by Lester Piggott shortly after half-way, he drifted left-handed, found nothing under pressure and dropped steadily back through the field – to finish a dismal last of nineteen.

Thus the colt that had cost 185,000 guineas as a yearling and which on his potential before the Guineas was valued at £3 million, was unplaced behind the 28/1 outsider Roland Garden, which cost only 3,200 guineas as a yearling.

The form was too bad to be true. Was it the heavy going? Was it a virus? Or could Try My Best have been got at?

The famous English professional punter, the late Alex Bird argued in his autobiography that Try My Best was 'got at' the same as Gorytus before the 1983 Dewhurst Stakes.

Vincent O'Brien, when I questioned him in the summer of 1992, on that point, rejected the 'got at' theory but he had no doubt on one point: "The colt was sickening when he ran in the Guineas – he must have been; otherwise he could not have run as badly as that. He was listless and had lost weight after the race."

Patrick Gallagher did not believe that Try My Best was 'got at'. But he shared Vincent O'Brien's conviction that there was something radically wrong.

"The horse was not right on the day. Of that there is no doubt. He purged himself on the way to the ring and in the ring itself. He was also sweating up and was very much on his toes – quite different from his behaviour in any previous race.

"I believe now he was the victim of a virus and, my God, I know from experience with my own horses how much can go wrong when a virus gets into a yard.

"Try My Best's running was completely contrary to the impression he had created in all his previous races and certainly could not be explained away by the going alone," he added.

When I asked him about reports that he had advised against running Try My Best on the prevailing going, he replied: "I did not say that the horse should not run. It was for the trainer, Vincent O'Brien to take that decision."

But he revealed to me that about a fortnight after the Guineas, he suggested to Vincent O'Brien that in his opinion the horse should not run again. "But at the same time, I realised that the trainer was the only man in a position to judge what was the right thing to do."

Try My Best did not run again. He was retired to stud –

and thus it became one of the great unanswered questions whether he would have won the Epsom Derby if he had gone to post running in the form he had displayed as a two year old.

Vincent O'Brien himself explained to me the reason for the decision: "After the Guineas I had to give him a rest and when I started to do a bit with him, I found he didn't stand up to anything. I decided then we should retire him."

Regarding the stories that circulated before the Guineas concerning Try My Best, particularly the persistent rumours that the colt was "wrong of his wind" and "making a noise", Vincent was most emphatic: "That rumour was everywhere but there was never any truth in it."

Patrick Gallagher told me that the deal he concluded when selling back his share to the syndicate was "a very amicable one."

"I did not get back what I invested, but I was happy. My gamble on the potential of the colt was not realised – so I could not expect to get back all I had risked."

Gallagher was deep into racing and breeding at the time of Try My Best's Guineas failure and so spectacular were his "killings" in the property-development sphere that he could easily shrug off any loss he had incurred in the deal.

He had seventeen horses in training, two of them in the National Hunt game. Looking relaxed in his dark pin-striped suit, he was talking to me at that time as one of a family that had been in racing for years and had known quite a deal of success.

For example, he had Godswalk in training with Christy Grassick in 1976, winning four races, including the Norfolk Stakes at Royal Ascot by four lengths. Later he sold out to the Robert Sangster syndicate. Godswalk went on in 1977 to become one of the leading sprinters of the season, taking the King's Stand Stakes at Royal Ascot in the course of three successes. He would stand at stud at Coolmore.

Other horses of note that passed through the hands of the Gallagher family were Yellow God, Candy Cane and Balliol.

They described him as the man with the Midas touch

such was the success that attended the mega property deals he executed in Dublin in the Seventies. And when other entrepreneurs were adopting a more cautious route to profits in the recession that followed the oil crisis, young Gallagher remained convinced that he could still gamble on property – and make millions.

And he did.

In the late Seventies he clinched a deal for the purchase of one of the capital's most prestigious properties, the 78,000 square feet neo-Georgian office block on St. Stephen's Green, which had been named Sean Lemass House (now Edmund Farrell House). He bought it for £5.4 million and five days later sold it to the Irish Permanent Building Society for £7.5 million.

He disposed of a batch of properties including the Old Jury's Hotel (now a Bord Telecom office), a series of buildings in Clare Street (now the Department of Energy) and various old houses on St. Stephen's Green en bloc to AIIB for £11 million.

The policy of buying buildings on strategic sites and then demolishing them to make way for new offices that he knew would be wanted by Government Departments and semi-State bodies was bringing rich dividends. He brought this policy into play successfully also by providing the offices within a stone's throw of Leinster House (seat of the Dáil and Seanad) that he guessed would be wanted by the European institutions. Despite howls from those with an eye to Ireland's historic past, Molesworth Hall was demolished – but Patrick Gallagher was again smiling all the way to the bank as the European Parliament and European Commission ended up with offices side by side to each other.

It was estimated that prior to the '82 crash that Patrick Gallagher was worth at least £20 million net on paper. In fact, he was reputed to have stocked up his wine cellar with claret and champagne to the value of £100,000 on one occasion – in order to beat a budget being brought in by the Fianna Fail Government of the day.

He enjoyed living life as befitting a multi-millionaire building tycoon and financier. He was fortunate that the attractive girl he married shared with him a love of horses and the racing scene. Susan Craigie's father, Eric, a member of the Premier Dairies family, was a former Master of the Ward Union Hunt.

Together they dined out at the "in" restaurants, the most fashionable ones you could name, and with the children enjoyed the most exotic holidays in the sun.

Susan showed total loyalty after the '82 crash and never wavered in her support for her husband, exclaiming: "Patrick will be back again." She displayed immense courage as she watched with inner pain everything the family owned being sold off under the supervision of the High Court. She took an injunction restraining the court-appointed liquidator from seizing furniture and paintings which she had owned before her marriage.

She had to say goodbye forever to the luxury of Straffan House and its lovely setting by the Boyne.

She followed Patrick to London, staying in a small apartment in Kensington with him as he tried to re-establish himself in the property field. She used her hunting connections to set up a travel company selling hunting holidays in Ireland.

In 1987 as the couple's business interests in London improved, they bought Balsoon House in Bective, County Meath for £250,000. Susan returned to Ireland, while Patrick commuted home for weekends, returning to London for work on Mondays.

But a year later she experienced the worst hammer-blow imaginable. Her husband was arrested in London following a two-year investigation into the collapse of Merchant Banking (Northern Ireland) Ltd.

The charges brought against Patrick Gallagher in the Belfast High Court were of false accounting, theft and conspiracy to defraud.

Again she rallied wonderfully as she endeavoured to have him released initially from custody in Belfast. She spent an entire day and night on the phone ringing friends in an attempt to organise the substantial six-figure sureties required by the court. Her dilemma was that she could not ring any of their many wealthy friends in the Republic as offers of bail from the Republic are not acceptable in Northern courts. She could only contact people in Britain and in Northern Ireland.

She succeeded, however, in her effort.

The 1982 debacle left Patrick Gallagher's companies with liabilities of £34 million as against net assets of more than £26 million.

His fall was a classic example of liquid funds drying up at the moment when the banks, who had been so willing for so long to fund his speculation on the property market, began to apply the kind of pressure that just had to be met.

He could have staved off the banks and survived if his gamble on the Slazenger size on St. Stephen's Green had come off. His plan was to buy it and sell it quickly and it would be 'a turn' that would net him a profit running into millions. He knew that Irish Life were interested.

He would have to go to over £10 million to purchase it but when negotiations got going with Irish Life, it was obvious that by the time a deal was clinched, the sum he would get would certainly not be less than £15 million and he was hoping for higher than that.

In fact, reports circulated in some quarters at the time that Gallagher got greedy and looked for £16.5 million, that Irish Life dug their heels in at £15.75 million and that was his undoing, as the banks had closed on him before signatures could be put to a final agreement.

Whatever about those 'inspired' reports, in the final analysis a crux arose that Patrick Gallagher could never have foreseen – just as he could not have foreseen when he gambled on buying a quarter share in Try My Best that the colt would fail so dismally in the English 2000 Guineas.

Irish Life wanted to buy the Slazenger site subject to vacant possession. Gallagher could not comply with this request – the Green Cinema, subsequently purchased by hotelier P.V. Doyle just months before his sudden death, was under lease following a deal done some years earlier.

Gallagher had meanwhile bought another site in Earlsfort Terrace for an estimated £9 million to £10 million on the assumption that everything would go smoothly in the end with his deal with Irish Life – in effect, that the £5 million profit from that would put him right with the banks on the Earlsfort Terrace gamble.

But the Green Cinema, standing out like a sore thumb in a site that harboured all his dreams of survival, became like Leningrad in Hitler's progress towards Moscow. It wouldn't go away.

So the Gallagher Group found themselves in the quicksands of a cash crisis – even with assets of £26 million. The banks wanted their money, but with the Slazenger site unsold, the £15 million that would have provided the necessary funds to satisfy them simply didn't exist.

Every throw of the dice by Patrick Gallagher in that last desperate period before his empire collapsed had gone wrong.

He had sought to purchase the cash flow of the H. Williams supermarket chain for £4.25 million from the Quinn family but this fell through.

At the time when on the surface all was going well with the 45 companies he headed with his brother Paul as joint managing director, he had even paid £3 million for the now-defunct Phoenix Park racecourse, thinking no doubt that if it pulled in the crowds on a regular basis – outside of the big days – it could be developed into a real money-spinner. However, that was another misguided throw of the dice. And even if he hoped for the fall-back position that the land might in time be utilised for building, resistance to that option was so strong that it was not a credible 'insurance policy' at the time of the investment.

On April 30, 1982 the Gallagher Group, one of the country's largest privately owned companies, was placed in receivership at the behest of Allied Irish Investment Bank, the Bank of Ireland and Northern Bank Finance Corporation.

The bubble had finally burst.

With the Slazenger site gamble, Patrick Gallagher had gone a bridge too far.

At the time of the collapse the Group was described in the High Court as a "large conglomerate with its headquarters in the Cayman Islands."

In analysing the reasons for the Fall, there were those

227

who argued that Patrick Gallagher had come to the big-time too young and to heady success far too soon.

At the 'tender' age of 17 he was already well into active speculation in property in the business created by his father, Matt. And when Matt died, he found himself at the age of 22 running the entire empire.

The approach at the outset was to buy up large tracts of land, then secure planning permission and sell on to developers at a sizeable profit, sometimes splitting the site to achieve ever greater gain.

The boom years when there was a dramatic spread in Dublin's suburban areas, as more and more people came to the metropolis from rural parts, were good years for Patrick Gallagher.

He had his first Rolls Royce when he was 22.

In the Budget introduced the day after Patrick Gallagher had concluded the deal with his uncle James for the purchase of the Earlsfort Terrace site, the then Minister for Finance, John Bruton said that the Government shared the public concern about large windfall gains on the sale of development lands. A special capital gains tax for disposals of development land was introduced at a rate of 45 per cent.

In the early Sixties Matt Gallagher had set up Merchant Banking Ltd. Over the years there was a very close relationship between the Gallagher Group and Merchant Banking. Too close for the comfort of the Central Bank.

In May, 1982 a liquidator was appointed to Merchant Banking. Deposits with the bank were estimated to be in the region of £1.3 million. The Central Bank had been watching closely for some time the activities of the bank.

During the liquidation proceedings it was stated in the High Court that the affairs of the bank had been "grossly mismanaged" and that the matter was under investigation by the Fraud Squad.

When he moved to London, Patrick Gallagher worked out of an office in Knightsbridge – doing what he had known best from the age of 17 but on a much smaller scale now than in the golden Seventies. He would find sites and buy and sell them and sometimes he would work with others in the property field, taking a 'piece of the action'. Naturally the banks were wary but they were willing to back his small operations once he showed them letters of guarantee from monied friends and business associates.

But while all this was going on a time-bomb was ticking away.

Merchant Banking Ltd. at the time of the Gallagher Group's collapse owed £5 million to depositors. In the North other savers had placed £3.5 million sterling with an offshoot of Merchant Banking. A sum of £1.4 million sterling was recovered from the Bank of England's deposit protection fund. The rest appeared to be lost.

The RUC claimed that money belonging to Merchant Banking was used to buy two paintings (by Jan Vogel and another artist called Keino), which were not subsequently listed as assets of the bank and which were used as collateral for further loans raised from the Bank of Ireland in Dublin.

I was in London for an international rugby match between Ireland and England, writing on the game for the *Sunday Independent*. I planned to stay over until the Monday as I had arranged to interview Patrick Gallagher about his effort to fight his way back into the big-time property development league and in the piece I would incorporate a throw-back to the time I talked to him in Dublin after he had bought that quarter share in Try My Best.

When I rang his secretary on the Monday morning to confirm the time and place of our meeting, she apologised for the fact that it would not be taking place that day after all. Other appointments had also been cancelled. She wasn't certain when he would be back

I decided to return home and to leave the interview for my next visit to London.

If I had waited over, I might have got the last interview with Patrick Gallagher before he was arrested by RUC officers in the English capital and taken to Belfast to answer a series of fraud charges which resulted in a two-year jail sentence being imposed on him on Monday, October 1, 1990.

Behind the permanently manned watchtowers, the glare

of powerful spotlights and the barbed wire-topped high granite perimeter wall of Crumlin Road prison, the man who flew by private jet from Dublin for the 1978 2000 Guineas and booked a London night-spot for the victory celebrations, now found himself suddenly in a regime where he could expect no special facilities or preferential treatment. The wheel had turned full circle and terribly cruelly at that. The only consolation he had as he stood in the dock, flanked by two white-shirted prison officers, was that he would only be required to serve half of the sentence handed down by the judge.

When I got the news that he was lodged in a grim Victorian jail in Belfast, I felt sad, remembering how he had met me as a journalist back in the late Seventies. I had no fault to find with him then, or any other time I ran into him at the races. It only struck me how young he was to be 'King' of the property scene.

Footnote: Walking into The Horseshoe Bar in Dublin's Shelbourne Hotel on Wednesday evening, September 23, 1992, I had a totally unexpected meeting with Patrick Gallagher. Over a casual drink, he first of all apologised for failing to keep our London appointment after the rugby international. I told him not to worry. I understood.

Our conversation ranged over the Try My Best days and the shattering Guineas failure. He recalled the nice little 'touch' he had on Godswalk at the Royal Ascot meeting in 1976 that covered all the expenses of bringing over the family. The conversation switched, amazingly enough, from horses to Yeats and Kavanagh – "I have no difficulty with them but I must admit I have with Joyce." Then he recalled his schooldays when he sat beside Bob Geldof in Blackrock College and it was then that he learned to play poker.

He told me about the trauma of the breakdown of his marriage when the Crash was behind him and how he was starting a new life in Africa.

I wished him well as we shook hands and I walked out into the Dublin night.

PART ELEVEN

ROBERT SANGSTER & JOHN MAGNIER

Spearheading 'The Syndicate' in The Golden Seventies

16

A Lunch Hour Break At The Hyatt Regency

Almost invariably at lunch hour in the Hyatt Regency Hotel in Lexington, Kentucky during the Keeneland July Sales, you will find Robert and Susan Sangster in the company of John Magnier. And Vincent O'Brien's brother, "Phonsie" of the genial and affable manner will be there also.

A break from the front lines as it were for Robert, John and "Phonsie" but even then they will be assessing what they have seen in their rounds of the barns from early morning and what they must see in the afternoon when not actually in the auditorium itself during the sales sessions.

Relaxing over a drink at the luncheon break, whether it is a Papa Doble (Hemingway's Key West elixir), a Coco Loco or a Marguerita or simply a gin and tonic, is part of the ritual of the day during the frenetic period of the Select Yearling Sales.

They come in from Ireland and Britain and all parts of the globe the men (and women) who in the space of a few short days turn the Keeneland Sales into a centre of high hopes and dreams, of prices attained that may go far beyond the anticipated reserve or fall sharply below it, into a centre where all the knowledge of some of the greatest world experts on breeding is concentrated.

The world of the high rollers of the bloodstock arena, those who gamble on their eye for a potential champion and their knowledge of breeding lines and crosses, who know that if you get it right in one final bid there can be a lot to gain but equally if you get it wrong there can be a hell of a lot to lose. No world can be as cruel as this one. And none can teach such sobering lessons.

The ultimate dream is, of course, to buy one that will turn out to be on a par with Sir Ivor (amazingly enough purchased for a mere $42,000 – $18,000 below Raymond Guest's top limit of $60,000) or The Minstrel (bought at Keeneland for just over $200,000 and later valued at $9 million) or Secreto (purchased for $340,000 and destined to find his way to David O'Brien's stable and beat Vincent's 'wonder colt' El Gran Senor in the 1984 Epsom Derby) or Golden Fleece (bought at the Select Sales for $775,000 and which after winning the 1982 Epsom Derby in a new record time of 2 minutes 34.27 seconds for that classic, since electric timing was introduced, was valued at about $25 million).

Dubai's Sheikh, Bin Rashid Al Maktoum (better known now to racing followers everywhere as Sheikh Mohammed) and his brothers, Maktoum Al Maktoum, Hamdan Al Maktoum and Ahmed Al Maktoum arrange for their trainers in Britain, Ireland and France to be either Concorded to the States or to arrive in Kentucky on first-class air tickets, as often as not left for them for their convenience at the chosen airport from which they will fly to America.

Sheikh Mohammed and his entourage will arrive in his private jet and automatically take some of the best suites in the Hyatt Regency and it is in this hotel that you will meet his trainers. The *Racing Post*, owned by the Sheikh, is available at breakfast, specially flown in.

The Japanese stud owners pay their bills in the Hyatt Regency with Gold American Express cards (you feel rather small presenting an ordinary American Express card!).

You don't hear anyone – among the high rollers at any rate – enquiring about the "going rate" at Mrs. Williams' select guesthouse down the highway or asking the overnight rate at the cheapest of the Motel chains.

You leave yourself outside the action and the conversations over breakfast if you decide to save by opting out of the hotels where the top racing personalities gather.

"Life is about timing," Robert Sangster said to me one morning in the Berkeley Court Hotel when I talk to him over coffee.

And he emphasised that the timing was "just right" when he became involved with Vincent O'Brien and John Magnier as the main partners in 'The Syndicate' – established to buy yearlings, mainly American-breds, at sales such as Keeneland – and in the creation of the world-renowned Coolmore Stud complex, of which John Magnier is boss.

At that point in the Seventies Sangster, whose father, Vernon had founded Vernon's Pools in 1926 (Sangster himself would sell it eventually for "an offer I could not refuse" in order to clear off £40 million in loans raised from the banking institutions) had already been in horses for about five years and had acquired a property near Macclesfield in Cheshire that would eventually become the Swettenham Stud.

The challenge was now there: could he go into racing and breeding on a big scale and make it pay? The fateful year was 1974 – the first year of stallion involvement.

Fate decreed that his path and that of John Magnier, boss today of Coolmore Stud, should cross at the very moment in time that was most opportune for both of them.

John Magnier comes from farming background. And while he will never miss a rugby international weekend in Dublin and, depending on Ireland's fortunes, further afield, he takes a keep interest in the national game of hurling also. Whenever I meet him before the start of a championship season, he will ask my opinion on prospects, in particular the prospects of Cork and Tipperary.

He is son of the late Thomas Magnier, who farmed extensively in the Fermoy, County Cork area. John's father actually stood the great National Hunt sire, Cottage (died 1942) at the 300-acre Grange Stud.

After school in Glenstal, John Magnier went back to work on the family farm and it was he who was responsi-

234

ble for switching the emphasis from dairying to horses. Later he would joke with friends that he got tired of milking cows at all hours and that horses were an easier option.

He had taken over the running of Grange Stud after his father's passing and had founded Castle Hyde Stud in 1971 when he teamed up with Robert Sangster. Together they got involved in Sandville Stud.

But the whole scenario changed dramatically once they hit on the idea that it was foolhardy to be in direct competition with other Irish breeders with whom they had a lot in common and finding themselves constantly in the position that they were bidding against one another. Why not a pooling of resources?

Coolmore Stud, a few miles north of Fethard and owned by the internationally-renowned Tim Vigors became a member of Coolmore, Castle Hyde and Associated Stud Farms, a title which confirmed the link of the Magnier family in the new venture. Grange and Sandville and Beeches Stud (owned by Robert McCarthy, Tallow, County Waterford) were also in the new title. Soon two more studs, Longfield and Thomastown Castle were incorporated in the complex.

The base of the Coolmore empire as we know it today had been established.

"We decided that we would make our own stallions," recalled Robert Sangster. Still vivid in his mind is the day John Magnier and himself went to see Vincent O'Brien at Ballydoyle House. "It was the day we virtually put The Syndicate together," added Sangster.

Share ownerships were merged with Tim Rogers of the Airlie Stud to avoid clashing head-on for the same animals. "But we never did manage to get our two syndicates together," Sangster noted.

Initially Stavros Niarchos, the Greek shipping tycoon was involved with Coolmore and The Syndicate but later he would pull out.

The dynamic three were Sangster, Magnier and Vincent O'Brien.

A three-year plan was devised. The inspired move was

235

the decision to make the best of American blood available to European breeders through Coolmore.

The year 1975 saw the first major assault by The Syndicate on the Keeneland Sales.

A package of horses was brought back to Ballydoyle that included The Minstrel, Alleged, Artaius and Be My Guest. There were a few outstanding purchases at sales in Europe also. But really the epoch-making event was the successful invasion of Keeneland.

The Vincent O'Brien/Robert Sangster/John Magnier team planned their approach to the Keeneland Sales with military-like precision. The attention to detail that Vincent O'Brien had always displayed as a trainer was brought now to the task of ensuring that nothing was left to chance in pinpointing the colts and fillies that he decided The Syndicate should go after – and seek to acquire. They had not to contend with the oil-rich Sheikhs at that time in the mid-Seventies.

In May the advance guard moved in, going round all the farms not alone in Kentucky but in Maryland and Pennyslvannia, an area close on 100,000 square miles, searching out and looking over the yearlings of quality.

Meanwhile, back in Ballydoyle, Vincent O'Brien would study his advance copy of the catalogue, putting a mark opposite the ones with the right blood and which he would look over himself when he arrived in Lexington.

John Magnier could be described as the Field Marshal of the Syndicate in its heyday. He could be seen going round the barns with other expert members of the team and the yearlings he wanted to look over were pulled out for him. Notes were taken.

Then would come the moment when Vincent, the Commander-in-Chief, cast a Master's eye over the short list and, as Robert Sangster put it to me – "in the final analysis, it was Vincent who invariably took the big decisions; it all came down to him really."

It's Sunday, July 17 – eve of the 1988 Keeneland Select Yearling Sales – and I have chosen to follow Vincent O'Brien and his team around the barn area. Despite the intense heat, I found it a most fascinating experience. he is personally greeted at the Claiborne barn by Arthur Hancock, son of 'Bull' Hancock, who bought Sir Ivor at the Keeneland Sales. And, of course, Nijinsky was to stand at Claiborne.

Vincent is asked to stand to be photographed with Mrs. Will Farrish with whom Queen Elizabeth stayed while visiting Kentucky.

Vincent's progress around the barns is like the progress of royalty – but he is not thinking of it that way, as his concentration is totally on the yearlings, on their conformation – the head, the ears, the neck, everything, in fact, right down to the front feet which he once said to me should be "sprung like good dancers feet." He cannot look into the heart of a yearling, cannot state conclusively whether it will have the courage that may be demanded in a finish of heads in a classic but from years of experience, he can look into the eye of the animal in front of him and there are telltale signs that will help him in forming his judgement.

When first he saw Nijinsky at E.P. Taylor's Windfields Farm in Canada the colt "filled his eye" and struck him as a real champion in the making. In fact, Vincent has told me himself that Nijinsky had the "look of eagles." To discover that was for the Master of Ballydoyle a moment he can never forget – like a prospector in the mountains in the Old West hitting a golden vein.

Vincent O'Brien and Sheikh Mohammed and their advisers naturally would never hit the same barn area at exactly the same time. It was as if an unwritten schedule had been formulated to guard against this.

"My advisers give their view, but eventually I decide yes or no," said the Sheikh – and in this he was at one with the Master of Ballydoyle.

There was a unique picture by Jacqueline O'Brien carried in the *Irish Racing Annual* a few years back of Sheikh Mohammed in full Arab dress with red spotted head-dress standing with falcon in hand, a noble figure silhouetted against a desert background.

The falcon is at the heart of his philosophy as he sums up his approach to racing. "I have a falcon at home. Some days when I take him out to fly, he does not feel himself and may fly sideways. Horses, and people too, can also have their off days. All you can do is attempt to buy the best horses and give them to the best trainers. If everyone tries their hardest and you still do not win, there's nothing you can do about it."

A day was to come when Sheikh Mohammed and his brothers would become the dominant figures in the bidding at Keeneland, assuming the mantle that had been the preserve of The Syndicate in the Seventies. If they spared nothing in having the finest advice possible available to them as they went after the best yearlings, in a way, they were following the trail that had been blazed by Vincent O'Brien and his trusted lieutenants.

The Sheikh Mohammed "machine", as it operates during the Keeneland Sales, is the most streamlined imaginable and one that left a deep and lasting impression on me.

John Leat has been the Sheikh's personal assistant for almost twenty years. Anthony Stroud, the racing manager, might well be described as the Commander-in-Chief in the battle-field. Without doubt he has a major role to play in the circle of experts and everyone has a specialist job to do. Charles Spiller has the task of studying and analysing the pedigrees. Nothing is left to chance. There is even a man with the sole responsibility of arranging the transport while the Sheikh's "army" is in Lexington. it's impressive, highly-impressive.

The Sheikh's trainers will look over the yearlings that have been picked out and each makes his own personal notes and gives his opinion to Anthony Stroud. The list may be cut down according to the advice advanced by the experts. New ones may well be added, not earmarked in advance.

Michael Osborne, former Manager of the Irish National Stud and then for a time attached to the North Ridge Stud in Kentucky, returned to Ireland in April, 1986 to assume responsibility over Sheikh Mohammed's bloodstock interests in Ireland, overseeing at the same time the tremendous operation that is the refurbished Kildangan Stud. Michael is a central figure during the Keeneland Sales, almost invariably at the Sheikh's elbow as he looks over the yearlings.

Contrary to what many people outside of the racing and breeding industry might be inclined to imagine, it's not a question of "money's no object" with Sheikh Mohammed when it comes to purchasing yearlings at Keeneland or any of the other yearling sales. He and his team of experts are quite selective. If they don't like something or turn it down on conformation or for some other reason, they won't make a bid at all – even if American trainer D. Wayne Lukas and the other big players are right in the thick of the action.

But when they really go after a colt or filly, they will normally get it – once it's around the ceiling they have pencilled in opposite it on the catalogue.

In July 1988 – the year I was at the Keeneland Sales – Sheikh Mohammed did not go after the Nijinsky colt out of Crimson Saint that had caught the eye of Vincent O'Brien and which he was determined to acquire on behalf of Classic Thoroughbreds and Robert Sangster. Eventually, having gone into the front trenches himself at the height of the bidding, he had to face a bid of 3.4 million dollars from D. Wayne Lukas.

Vincent, in yellow shirt and white boater, quietly responded with a final bid of 3.5 million dollars – and Lukas indicated that he was finished.

Described by Hubie De Burgh of the Derrinstown Stud to me as "the best looking colt in the sale" and lauded by Vincent O'Brien himself for being so correct in conformation, this yearling which was to be named Royal Academy was just touched off by Tirol in the 1990 Airlie/Coolmore Irish 2,000 Guineas and, then having won the July Cup, climaxed his career by winning the Breeders' Cup Mile (Turf) at Belmont Park, New York in the hands of Lester Piggott. Today he stands at Coolmore.

It proved beyond any shadow of doubt that Vincent O'Brien had not lost his eye for a champion in the making.

But by the dawn of the Nineties the heady days for The Syndicate were past and they had given away to the financial muscle of the Sheikhs.

Everything, however, that the Sangster-Magnier-O'Brien

team had touched over a decade from 1975 to 1984 had turned to gold. Godswalk, Golden Fleece, El Gran Senor, Sadler's Wells.

And while Assert was not bought by Vincent, he carried the Sangster colours to victory in both the French Derby and the Irish Derby (trained by Vincent's son, David and ridden by Christy Roche).

A flood of victories in Europe's top races ensured that each champion was stamping himself in the process as a valuable stud property to realise profits from syndication that became the envy of the world in the boom days.

"The Seventies and early Eighties were highly-profitable years for us," said Robert Sangster. "The market crashed in 1985 and 1986."

"Highly-profitable" might even seem an understatement when you look at some of the figures from those glorious years.

After winning the Prix de l'Arc de Triomphe for the second year running in 1978, Alleged was syndicated for 13 million dollars (Sangster originally paid only 120,000 dollars for him after Billy McDonald had picked him out).

The Minstrel bought at Keeneland for 200,000 dollars was syndicated for 9 million dollars. Assert, purchased in France by David O'Brien, cost only £16,000 and Sangster sold 50 per cent of the colt for 14 million dollars.

Even when colts did not train on to realise as three year olds the potential they had shown as juveniles, a "killing" could still be made.

There was no finer example of this than Storm Bird. The Northern Dancer colt (out of South Ocean), closely related to Nijinsky and The Minstrel, was picked out by Vincent O'Brien at the Keeneland Sales and bought by the BBA on behalf of The Syndicate for 1 million dollars.

Rated the top juvenile in Europe after five successive wins as a two year old, Storm Bird was installed winter favourite for the English 2,000 Guineas and at the same time was viewed as a potential Epsom Derby winner. At that point, according to Robert Sangster, he was valued at 20 million dollars.

It's history now how Storm Bird missed the English

2,000 Guineas and the Derby – after disappointing in his final gallop for the Epsom Classic.

Few stories in the racing and bloodstock sphere compare with the way Storm Bird was sold for twenty-four times his original purchase price – even though he failed to win a Classic and, indeed, was beaten in his only outing as a three year old in the Prix du Prince d'Orange at Longchamp on Sunday, September 20, 1981 – a race that was supposed to be a refresher for the Prix de l'Arc de Triomphe. But he never did contest the Arc.

After he had finished breakfast with Vincent O'Brien and John Magnier in the Hyatt Regency Hotel in Lexington that summer, Robert Sangster was contacted by bloodstock agent George Harris about the possible sale of Storm Bird, and when he asked Sangster what value he would put on the colt, the response came: "15 million dollars."

For Sangster it was just an opening shot and he thought nothing about it until Harris met him that same evening and said he had a client who was willing to start negotiations at 15 million dollars.

After private discussions involving Vincent O'Brien, John Magnier and Robert Sangster, it was decided not to sell for less than 25 million dollars. Eventually in George Harris's suite the deal was clinched at 24 million dollars.

"Every time I reflect on that amazing day, I just cannot believe how smoothly the whole business went," Robert Sangster told me. "At the time 24 million dollars became like so many chips in a big poker game in Las Vegas in the cut and thrust of negotiation. You know what I mean, you forget momentarily the astronomical sums you are dealing with, as you battle to clinch the deal."

George Harris was acting for Robert Heffner, an oil and gas magnate from Oklahoma (and no relation of Hugh Hefner).

Storm Bird was later syndicated for 30 million dollars to stand at the Ashford Stud in Kentucky – a part of the Coolmore empire – and it was here also that El Gran Senor was to stand.

As a sire carrying on the valued Northern Dancer line, Storm Bird did not lack patronage and soon the winners began to flow. El Gran Senor, for his part, may have lost the 'wonder colt' tag of the 1984 season when short-headed by Secreto in the Epsom Derby photo finish but, despite fertility problems, he was to become an outstanding success at stud and sired Rodrigo de Triano, who won the 1992 English 2,000 Guineas and the Irish 2,000 Guineas in Robert Sangster's colours but was unplaced in the Epsom Derby and beaten into fourth place behind the Dermot Weld-trained 25/1 winner, Brief Truce in the St. James's Palace Stakes at the Royal Ascot meeting with Kentucky Derby failure, Arazi again a deep disappointment, as he could only finish fifth.

The good times were rolling again for Robert Sangster. His partnership with his 29-year-old son-in-law, Peter Chapple-Hyam brought him right into the Classic limelight in 1992 – fifteen years on from The Minstrel's win in the Epsom Derby. And, of course, it fulfilled at the same time his "Manton Dream". He had always wanted it to be a training centre for the production of champions but initially everything went wrong in the high-profile days of Michael Dickinson. Indeed, Manton, with all its lavish amenities, had the "For Sale" sign on it until taken off the market by Sangster in 1991. Again the timing was just right, as on Derby night '92 Peter Chapple-Hyam's staff were celebrating a third Classic triumph in the space of a month in the Trelawney social club on the estate.

Rodrigo de Triano may have failed to complete a Classic treble for his trainer and disappointed the legion of Lester Piggott fans in the process but Chapple-Hyam, in only his second season as a trainer, still had the joy of turning out the impressive winner in Dr. Devious, ridden to victory by County Down-born John Reid. Dr. Devious had earlier finished seventh in the Kentucky Derby and obviously didn't like the dirt.

Robert Sangster could so easily have been leading in the winner if he had not decided to sell the colt before he won the 1991 Dewhurst Stakes to the Italian, Gaucci Del Bono for 400,000 dollars on condition that he stayed at Manton. Then Dr. Devious passed on to the American, Sidney Craig, given to him as a 2.5 million dollar present for his

60the birthday by his wife, Jenny. Mrs. Craig wanted, in fact, to see her husband leading Dr. Devious in a winner of the Kentucky Derby. He thought she was "out of her mind" in spending so much on one horse – but Epsom vindicated her "big splash" and Sidney Craig was overjoyed.

And how did Robert Sangster feel about letting Dr. Devious pass out of his ownership? The emphasis in the case of Sangster's operation these days is very much on selling. As he put it himself: "I did not mind how well Dr. Devious did after I let him go because the more winners you sell, the more buyers will return."

He had the additional satisfaction of having a 40 per cent stake in Dr. Devious's dam Rose of Jericho.

Robert Sangster has always liked a bet. I know that one of the bets he had on El Gran Senor to win the 1984 Epsom Derby was £30,000 to £20,000 at 6/4 with Hills.

John Magnier didn't see any need to bet on El Gran Senor – "as I owned a bit of him." So he put a saver on Secreto – £10,000 each-way at ante-post odds of 16/1 with Ladbrokes.

John still has the cheque for £170,800 framed in his office at Coolmore. "Ladbrokes closed my account after paying me that cheque," he told me with a smile.

Of course, if El Gran Senor had gone to stud with no blemish whatsoever on his record, his value would have been enhanced all the more and the £170,800 that Magnier received from his Secreto wager would have appeared a mere drop in the sea.

John Magnier presides over an empire at Coolmore which with its American off-shoot, the Ashford Stud, commands today some of the most sought-after sires in the bloodstock world. Sadler's Wells and Caerleon are already firmly established and the victory of Dr. Devious in the 1992 Epsom Derby provided a major boost for his sire, Don't Forget Me, a son of former Coolmore sire, the ill-fated Ahonoora, which was killed in a freak accident in Australia while on dual-hemisphere duties Down Under.

It's hard to believe at times that John Magnier is still in his early forties, such is the pressurised world he lives in as one of the most influential figures in the bloodstock arena on a global scale. Coolmore itself has become a byword for excellence and innovation.

John Magnier and his wife, Sue, who is Vincent O'Brien's daughter, live with their five children in a Georgian house in the Coolmore complex itself.

The only time of the year that the boss of Coolmore can take an extended break is in January and then Sue and himself will head for Barbados, where the big annual Pro-Am golf tournament, sponsored by Robert Sangster, is staged over the Sandy Lane course.

The action takes place along a strip of the island's west coast known as 'The Golden Coast' or 'Platinum Coast' and it was here in March, 1989 that I interviewed 'Scobie' Breasley, sitting on the patio of his bungalow-style home, for my biography of Vincent O'Brien.

The Sangsters stay at their beachfront holiday home, 'Jane Harbour' right next to the Palladian-style Sandy Lane Hotel, where you rub shoulders with Britain and Ireland's racing elite and, indeed, racing personalities from many parts of the globe, also celebrities, who constantly make the social columns and who annually are on the invitation list for the golf tournament.

Of course, some celebrities like Chris de Burgh, now a racehorse owner, and R.D. Hubbard, the Texan tycoon – "call me 'Dee'" – are happy staying in old colonial-style houses which can be rented on the edge of the golf course.

The professional golfers are generally to be found in The Buccaneer Hotel, just down the road from the Sandy Lane.

This is a time for the wearing of T-shirts and shorts in the Caribbean sunshine where at Royal Ascot the high rollers would sport topper and tails.

You would have found it hard to play in anything but shorts in the January '91 Pro-Am tournament as it was 86-degrees heat out on the course.

But it's amazing how men like John Magnier and J.P. McManus and intrepid bloodstock agent, Billy McDonald and John Leat and Robert Sangster himself can forget the heat as they battle for their pride – and also to win all kinds of side bets.

"Nobody really talks horses during the competition. But the golf is really competitive," Robert Sangster told Deirdre Frenand of the *Sunday Times*.

Reporting on the January '91 "bash", she described that "damnable midday sun" as being far too hot, adding that the most soothing sound to the spirit was "the rattle of ice cubes."

Going on to stress how much stamina went into partying over the week, she graphically described the "punishing schedule" which started on the Sunday night: "It began with a dinner at the pink stucco Royal Pavilion Hotel (hot smoked salmon mousse and lamb noisettes) where even the hoteliers, used to the bacchanalian whims of the rich, were amazed at how much fine wine was drunk. One table of eight ordering a grand cru at £100 a bottle, soon notched up a wine bill of nearly £2,000.

"Monday was relatively quiet with a cocktail party around the pool at the Sandy Lane . . . the next night Dee Hubbard threw a small impromptu party for a few friends at his house. The table groaned under the weight of a suckling pig and 60 people dined under the stars to the strains of a steel band.

"On Wednesday, the Sangsters, the most generous hosts on the island, threw a birthday party for their friend, Anthony Speelman, the art dealer . . . by popular request Chris de Burgh sat down at the piano to sing *Lady in Red* and then everyone danced the night away, the disco music wafting along the beach.

"It was left to the Irish contingent, including John Horgan, to entertain the Sangster set when they were 'at home' on Thursday night in Horgan's rented house. A grand time and a good binge was had by all.

"And Friday? Well, by the end of the week few could remember where they had been or who their host was anyway.

"Win or lose (at the golf), the sporting spirit never once disappeared during the week. The alcohol flowed, the Bermuda shorts grew brighter and the conversations never seemed to vary."

She added that with so many of the world's high rollers

getting together in Barbados at that time in January, it was little wonder that "thousands of pounds" were wagered on golf.

Come to think of it – we somehow didn't get to know exactly who emerged as the winners and the losers in the big side bets.

But then the winners one day may be the losers the next as the 'circus' rolls on to the next watering hole.

PART TWELVE

ALEX BIRD & PHIL BULL

17

Yes, You Can Beat The Bookies!

Alex Bird was unquestionably the most successful professional punter in Britain after the Second World War – and, in fact, he must rate as one of the most successful of all time.

Yet right up to the time of his death at his £400,000 Cheshire manor at the age of 75 on December 12, 1991, he continued to assert that he was not a gambler but an investor. "If I had been a gambler in my early days, I would have become a millionaire when things were going well. I am too cautious for a gambler," he said.

Nevertheless, he made a fortune backing horses, principally by fearlessly supporting his own judgement and not being swayed by racecourse tips and rumour.

Like a true professional, he never regarded betting as a chancy business. You were rewarded at the level of the hours you spent studying the form book and eliminating all the factors that might militate against your final choice justifying a substantial wager.

It was nothing to Alex Bird to spend two to three hours studying a single race. It entailed also making sure that the horse could act on the prevailing going ("I think it won at Ayr last year on heavy ground. I must check up. I'll go through every race he's run in the last three years.").

And, of course, the odds had to be right to his money before he would make an investment ("If I think a horse should be 3/1 and the bookmaker is offering only 2/1, I won't back it, no matter how much I fancy it. However, if I think a horse should be 3/1 and I'm offered 4/1 or 5/1, I'll have twice as much on because I'm getting terrific value").

He saw gambling on horses as much the same as playing the stock market, a business in which emotion and hunches had to be ruthlessly suppressed. "It requires a similar type of brain. Again you have to be prepared to study for hours if you are to be a success at stocks and shares. I couldn't do both. I just wouldn't have the time," he admitted.

He never deviated from the principles formed early on in his betting career. "I never back in doubles, trebles or accumulators," he once said. "That's for the mugs."

Also for the mugs was betting on every race on the card. And when asked by a newspaper interviewer on one occasion for one golden piece of advice, he responded with a cryptic four-word gem: "Never chase your losses. It has been the ruination of many a punter."

He worked to the time-honoured dictum of the born professionals in that he knew when to fold.

Once he found himself down £250,000 after a bad losing run (even professionals don't win all the time but they know how to cope with a run like that in order to survive).

"I pulled myself up short," he recalled. He vowed that he would get the money back in three months. Overnight he reduced his stakes by 90 per cent. "I didn't have to wait three months to get it back. I was again smiling on my way to the bank inside three weeks."

In his prime he was betting very big – aiming for a return of 4 per cent on an annual outlay of £2 million. He admitted that he never in those days bet less than £500 on a horse and generally the sums ranged from £5,000 to £50,000.

Once he put £50,000 on a horse in a photo finish – just to win £1,000.

But in case you think that was crazy, you have to remember that he discovered the formula to making a succession of killings when the photo-finish was first installed in Britain. As his close friend Richard Baerlein of *The Observer* recalled: "He quickly realised that people were making mistakes about which horse had won in the photo through an optical illusion. In those days almost five minutes elapsed between the time the horses passed the post and the time the photo was developed and the winner announced. This gave plenty of time for backers and bookmakers to do a lot of betting and hedging.

"Alex took up a position in line with the winning post and completely ignored the horses. He just looked straight across the course to see which horse's nose passed between the line first. If the one on the far side had won there was no bet, for the public always thought the one on the far side had won. This was the optical illusion.

"If, however, the one on the near side had won, there was no limit to the amount Alex was prepared to put on. He would put on £50,000 to win £5,000 or £50,000 to win £1,000. So confident was he of his judgement that he would put on any sum of money he could get on.

"In those years when he was betting really big on photo finishes he made only one mistake. It happened at Epsom.He had been going sometime by then but he told me that if it had happened in the early days it would have shaken him so much that he might not have continued with his scheme."

By 1952, Bird claimed to have won 500 consecutive photo-finish bets, each worth an average of £500.

His profit from this source reached £750,000. That is a lot of money to-day and it was a fortune then.

The betting on the photo finish died a natural death when the photo was developed in much quicker time and when the bookmakers put their own men on the line and realised what Alex Bird had been doing all this time.

Outside of photo-finish bets, some of Alex Bird's biggest wins were achieved on a race popularly regarded as a lottery – the Aintree Grand National.

It was not surprising in a way that he had a soft spot for this race as it was the medium of one of his initial successful coups. He had £10 to win and £1 a place on Battleship for the 1938 National and the reason he didn't have any more on the 40/1 winner was that he couldn't afford it.

His reasoning about the great Aintree race – before they

modified the fences and it became an "easier" jumping event, with many more finishers – was that the odds were good, the market was strong and one could narrow the field down to a handful of runners who could be depended upon to get round.

He won £70,000 when Freebooter took the 1950 National at 10/1 and another £50,000 through the success of Teal in 1952, coupling this one also with Dramatic for the Lincoln Handicap.

That same afternoon – in '52 – he hit the bookies for an additional £50,000 when his own horse, Signification scored for him in a minor race at Liverpool and, incidentally, this one was to go on and win the Ebor in the same year.

Geoff Hamlyn, who was for over 45 years Starting Price reporter for the *Sporting Life*, recalled in a fascinating contribution to the *Irish Racing Annual* the details of the Signification coup, as related to him by Bird himself over dinner in December, 1975. "Alex knew that, although the horse had little previous form, he had something to go to market with. Accordingly, he arranged for three or four professionals to approach the then immensely strong members' rails at a given signal.

"Betting at Aintree in those days were William Hill, Max Parker, Willie Preston, Jack Burns and Laurie Wallis amongst others. Alex chose to approach the last-named himself, and was laid a bet of £50,000 to £3,000.

"After that, the ring quickly came alight. After several thousands had been invested on Signification the last price taken was 7/2. It was difficult to get 7/2 at the off, as backers were tumbling over themselves with shouts of '£1,000 to £400' or 'three-and-a-half monkeys' and these requests were all refused as the horses went on their way. Signification was a very easy winner, and to the astonishment of everyone, paid 33/1 on the Tote!"

The year 1954 saw Alex Bird coming within a neck of landing his most fearless gamble of all on the Grand National – one that would have netted him a cool £500,000.

In its preparation for the National, Tudor Line won three times in a row and on each occasion Bird had a big bet.

Now Richard Baerlein takes up the story: "Alex used the money won on these three races to back Tudor Line ante-post for the National from 40/1 down to 100/3. Even on the day, in spite of the big sums already invested, he put a few more thousand on, so confident was he of success.

"It so happened that Tudor Line was one of the unluckiest losers in the history of the race, going down to the Vincent O'Brien-trained Royal Tan by a neck. At one stage he was practically tailed off but came with such a storming run in the last half-mile that it was only the brilliance of Bryan Marshall that kept Royal Tan going long enough to gain a narrow win.

"Tudor Line had a habit of going out to the right and to prevent this a pricker was put on in his three winning races prior to the Grand National. This was left off in the National itself because it was thought he had been cured of the habit. Unfortunately, this proved not to be the case and he covered far more ground than any other horse.

"Alex Bird did not add up the exact final sum he stood to win. He preferred to put his vouchers in the waste paper basket. The sum was obviously fantastic. He had been reading the race to Mrs. Trulove, owner of Tudor Line and, as the horses passed the finishing line, he calmly turned to her and said: 'Bad luck, you'll probably win it next year.'."

As it happened, Tudor Line was second again the following year.

Needless to say, the 1954 reverse was not the only one suffered by Alex Bird during his racing career. In 1951 heavy rain brought the going right for his horse, Newton Heath in the Lincolnshire Handicap. He backed it to win £60,000 and it was coming home a comfortable winner when the saddle slipped and Barnes Park came and beat it half a length.

Alex Bird was born, you might say, into the racing and punting life. His father ran a coal merchant's business from the ground floor of their premises in Newton Heath, near Manchester and a bookmaker's business from an office at the top of the stairs in an era when it was illegal to be in the kind of business he ran. "But the police turned a blind eye," Alex would explain in later years. "They knew that the ordinary working chap couldn't bet on credit, which was the only betting legal then off-course. My father left bags in factories where the workers would place their wagers. Ninety-five per cent of betting was conducted in that way in those days."

Alex knew how to make a book almost from the time he could walk.

When he was 10 he was already a keen student of the form book. "My dad would see my bedroom light on under the door at three in the morning. And I wasn't reading novels either."

On leaving school at the age of 14, he worked for his father full-time. It was a serious business. And, as David Ashforth noted in a tribute to him in the *Sporting Life* on his death: "When he married Evelyn in 1937, his father was too busy to attend the wedding and the bridegroom was under strict instructions to be back in the office at 5 p.m."

Alex struck up a close friendship with Jimmy Park, the man who persuaded Richard Baerlein to join him on the *Evening Standard* ("he was known in the press room as the greatest of all", is the tribute paid him by Richard Baerlein).

One golden rule which Alex learned from Jimmy Park was: "Never rate a two year old in the highest category, no matter how easily it has won, until it has done a time."

That piece of advice was to stand Bird in good stead and win a lot of money for him. Like Park, he was to become a keen student of the stopwatch.

Eating caviar and popping oysters and, of course, quaffing champagne became part and parcel of the lifestyle that he came to know and relish as a successful professional punter.

If it is true as the saying goes that you never see a bookie on a bike, then you don't expect your average punter to graduate to a Rolls-Royce Silver Cloud from backing horses. Not alone was he able to afford from the winnings he accumulated one sleek limousine but a number of them, also his own plane, butlers and maids, a string of racehorses, his own box at Manchester United's Old Trafford ground, a private dining room at Aintree and holidays

254

with his wife and family in the most exotic places you can care to name.

He was able to put his three sons through public school and afford to buy a sixteenth-century moated manor, described thus by Steve Turner when he went to interview him for the *Sunday Telegraph Magazine* in March, 1987: "In a large rosewood-panelled living-room with an open log fire, he sits down by a window which looks directly over the moat. Ducks and swans slide across the surface; pike, bream, tench, roach and carp swim beneath. On the walls of the room are oil paintings of children and landscapes but, surprisingly, none of horses."

Another writer who visited him described how he could spin for pike from his bedroom window and once or twice a week motored sedately to the races in his blue Rolls-Royce. Or he would park it in front of Macclesfield station and take a train.

He stood 6ft. 1in. tall, cutting a striking figure in his sheepskin coat, racing glasses at the ready and the inevitable large cigar (in fact when driving he was wont to hold the cigar aloft over the steering-wheel as he made a point). A burly man, rosy-faced, balding in front but with wisps of hair blowing in the breeze on a blustery day, and outside of that rich Manchester accent, the eyebrows perhaps were his most distinctive badge of all (shooting up "like startled caterpillars", as Nick Guitard put it in a feature on him).

He reckoned that he must have invested £70 million in a lifetime as a professional punter but the difference between him, of course, and Terry Ramsden was that where Ramsden recklessly gambled that amount and more away in the space of five years, Bird was happy to make £750,000 a year, saying of that profit margin: "It pays for the oysters."

Once the Taxman assessed him for £50,000 a year tax on his winnings. "The argument went on for five years, by which time I was supposed to owe them £250,000. Then I pointed out that if a professional punter was liable to pay tax on his winnings, he would have to be allowed to claim against his losses during a bad run. A fortnight before I was due in court, the Inland Revenue people dropped the case."

The betting tax and levy of over eight per cent caused him to go into what he described as "semi-retirement" as a professional gambler. "Some say I'm a legend and I don't know if that is true," he said in 1983 to Terry Manners of the *Daily Express,* who was to "ghost" his best-selling auto-biography, *Alex Bird – The Life And Secrets Of A Professional Punter.*

"But it is a fact that men like me will never come again. Not because I am anything other than flesh and blood but because the opportunity to build a life backing horses is not there anymore. Betting tax has seen to that. I'm retired now but I bet about £250,000 a year – just for fun."

His successes as a punter have been well tabulated. Suffice it to recall that even when he was beginning to slow down, he was still fearless when it came to backing one he "expected" or judged a certainty on the form book. "At the time of the 1990 Goodwood meeting Peter Walwyn came into our garden – where Alex was sunbathing and study-ing his formbook – and said he thought Mukaddamah would win that afternoon," recalled Richard Baerlein. "Quickly going through his ratings, Alex came up with a positive response and put £10,000 on that colt who duly obliged."

In 1986 he backed Dancing Brave to win £100,000 in the Epsom Derby, only to see it beaten into second place by Shahrastani. Believing the colt to be one of the best horses he had ever seen, he continued to put money on it and got back his Derby losses with wins in the Eclipse Stakes, the King George and Queen Elizabeth Stakes and the Prix de l'Arc de Triomphe.

In November he flew to California with the aim of hav-ing £20,000 on Dancing Brave in the Breeders Cup at Santa Anita. In a preliminary race he had £1,000 on the French horse, Last Tycoon. He reckoned it would pay around 6/1 on the Tote but the actual return was 35/1. Alex cleared £31,000 and put the lot on Dancing Brave in the fifth race and it got beaten. He had the consolation of knowing that he was out of pocket only on his expenses for the trip to the States.

Five years before his death Alex had a fall on the steps in his son's house at Kingston after a dinner. From that moment he gave up his beloved champagne, which he had once described as "bottled sunshine." Richard Baerlein asked him if he had consulted a doctor before taking such a drastic decision (Bird thought nothing of drinking four bottles a day). When he said "no" to his friend's query, Baerlein remarked: "You will be lucky to last two years after such a sudden-cut-off."

The man who became the bane of the bookmakers and was known to the small every–day punters as 'Lucky' Alex Bird was paid the tribute, under the heading "Last Of The Turf's Great Gamblers", by Richard Baerlein in *The Observer* in 1963: "He has beaten the bookmakers but there can never be another Alex Bird, for the number one unwritten rule of all bookmakers today is – 'Thou Shalt Not Win'. And that is rigidly enforced."

At his passing, Baerlein recalled in the *Sporting Life* what he had written almost twenty years beforehand, finishing his final salute thus: "He was as straight as a die and it will not only be on the racecourse where he will be missed. As I wrote in an article in 1963: 'There can never be another Alex Bird'."

Alex Bird, with all the success he enjoyed as a professional punter, may have been egotistical at times but he had the redeeming quality that while he was not a very religious man himself, he respected his wife's beliefs ("she says her prayers every night") and bowed to her when she admonished him for his superstitions, like periodically touching wood during a conversation ("I gave up being superstitious when my wife told me that it showed a loss of faith in God").

Phil Bull, however, had an outsize ego that led him to publicly rubbish those who believed in God and practised their religion. It was ill-befitting the *Timeform* organisation, of which he was the founder, to give permanence to his outlandish attacks on religion by including them in their "final selections from his writings and utterances" as if they were gospel.

If Bull couldn't rationalise something with his philosopher's approach, then it had to be rejected out of hand. Therefore he saw belief as "prejudice" and religion (whether Christian or otherwise) as "not a matter of rational conscious thought on one's part and largely a geographical matter of where one was born." Thus he concluded that *"all* religions are to be rejected because they are all founded on superstitious beliefs with no basis in reality."

Phil Bull was a man to be listened to on horses but certainly not when addressing the Gloucester Philosophical Society or giving an interview to the *Halifax Courier* on matters pertaining to religion. The cobbler should stick to his last.

If he had become a legend before his death as "The Man Who Started Timeform", it has to be remembered that he was also a very successful punter. It was through the medium of some spectacular winning bets on Dante that he really established himself on the Turf in 1944 and 1945. Bull was the first to grasp Dante's enormous potential when the colt won at Stockton on his debut in the spring of 1944. What really made him sit up and take special note was that the time of the race was so exceptional. And, being a time expert from the very outset, he realised that here was a horse right out of the ordinary.

Bull backed Dante substantially every time he ran subsequently. the colt was beaten only once in his career – by Court Martial in the 2,000 Guineas and then rather unluckily. When he took the Derby, Phil Bull had the win of his life on him. Indeed, over two years he won a fortune on this horse.

His next major coup was on Nimbus in 1949. He was entirely responsible for the breeding of the colt and when Nimbus won the 2,000 Guineas and Derby, he had his maximum on both times. That would have been £5,000 at least and he could have gone to £10,000, which at today's figures would be ten times that.

His next jackpots came three years running in the Gimcrack, with Eudaemon, Pheidippides and Be Careful.

The last time he really went to town was with William Hill's filly Cantelo as a three-year-old. He won a great deal on her in the Cheshire Oaks, lost when she was beaten by Petite Etoile in the Oaks, but got it back with interest when she won the St. Leger.

Yes, he was certainly one of the most influential players in the ring in his prime.

The son of a Yorkshire coalminer, Phil Bull grew up in the small town of Hemsworth – a world where the working men talked of bringing off their doubles and trebles and naturally he caught the racing bug. He remembered his father as a powerful speaker on political platforms and his uncle became the local M.P. with the biggest Labour majority in the country.

Bull won a scholarship to Leeds University where he obtained a B.Sc. degree. He came to London in the Thirties. "I earned £173 a year as a schoolmaster and divided my spare time between attending sociology lectures at the City Literary Institute and going to the races."

After a time he tired of teaching. Already he was making money from betting on horses. He would not have gone into the racing game as a punter if he had accepted the common assumption that because bookmakers win, punters must lose. "This is not logical because 'punters' does not mean necessarily *all* punters."

Just before the outbreak of the Second World War, he was running what he called Temple Racetime Analysis. Advertised in the *Sporting Life* as William K. Temple, B.Sc., this consisted of issuing a list of horses to clients each week. "My recommendations were based on the time figures recorded on my own stopwatch and the conclusions I drew from them."

They proved quite successful and, backing them on a level stake, punters made a substantial profit each year. Indeed, so successful did they become that William Hill saw fit to close the accounts of a number of Bull's clients.

Bull remonstrated about this. Hill met him over the issue and the outcome was that the two joined forces for a number of years. Bull acted as a kind of personal assistant to Hill and used to go racing with him during the War. He also ran Hill's advertising for him, the lay-outs and ante-post prices for the firm.

He was quite successful as an owner-breeder, winning a Lincolnshire Handicap during the War with the filly, Lady Electra, which he bought at the Newmarket Sales for £3,500, having been impressed by her at the Newmarket July meeting (he actually outbid the late Aly Khan, recalling that he only had £2,500 at the time and had to borrow the rest). Lady Electra won ten races in all and was a successful brood mare, a founder member of Bull's stud.

Pheidippides won the Gimcrack Stakes for him in 1957 while his fillies Ariett and Aureoletta were placed in the 1,000 Guineas and Oaks respectively. His only Derby runner, Guersillus, was fifth in 1957.

It was the knowledge that he brought to his gambling that made Phil Bull a rich man and, as in the case of Alex Bird, brought him all the trappings of wealth, including a Rolls-Royce and a historic mansion a few miles outside Halifax, The Hollins, standing on 66 acres in secluded woodland overlooking the Calder Valley. With its tower, turrets and battlements, Bull had every reason to describe it as "a miniature imitation castle." Inside, the visitor's eye was immediately caught by the magnificently-elegant Adam fireplace in the drawing-room and on the mantelpiece were displayed the trophies that Bull's triumphs as an owner had brought him.

He drank the best wines and numbered retired snooker champion Joe Davis among his guests when he threw parties during the race weeks at York and Doncaster (incidentally, he was no mean snooker player himself, he would play Joe Davis, and reckoned that there were not many men in Yorkshire who could beat him). He was married three times.

In line with the approach of J.P. McManus, Barney Curley and Alex Bird, he advanced the rule that you should never bet – unless you reckoned that the odds were in your favour. "If I am offered only evens about a horse I judge to be a 6/4 chance, I will not bet. If, however, I get 2/1 then I *will* bet. And if 3/1 is offered about the same horse, then it is a Bet with a capital B."

Compared with J.P. McManus, Barney Curley, Alex Bird and Noel Furlong he would certainly not have been rated in the premier league as a punter. His normal bet on a horse he reckoned to be a "good thing" on the book was £1,000. It was only rarely that he had £5,000 on.

He didn't claim to win all the time but over a year his winnings worked out roughly eight per cent on turnover. To the professional that is a good return.

His seven golden principles for the ordinary punter to observe were: (1) Don't bet unless the odds are good value; (2) Don't bet beyond your means or try to make your fortune in a day; (3) Don't concern yourself with staking systems – increasing stakes after a winner or so many losers and so forth (stakes should be varied only according to the chance of the horse and the odds); (4) Don't buy tips or systems, geese that lay golden eggs are never for sale; (5) Don't fail to read your bookmaker's rules, especially the small print; (6) Don't bet ante-post (before the day of the race) unless you know that the horse is an intended runner; (7) Don't bet each-way in handicaps or other races with big fields; a place bet at one-fifth the odds is rarely good value.

He had a reputation for being gruff and blunt – his critics would say that he could be downright rude at times – and he could never suffer fools gladly. But at the same time he was an immensely knowledgeable man and no one understood better the business of betting and its place in racing.

With his razor-sharp brain it was inevitable that he should turn increasingly to racing politics and he became notorious as an anti-establishment figure. Nothing was more forthright than his speech as the winning owner at the Gimcrack dinner in 1957 and most of the radical proposals he made (overnight declaration of runners, camera patrols, starting stall and so on) were subsequently implemented. In 1977 he made a 40,000-word personal submission to Lord Rothschild's Royal Commission on Gambling and his logical and lucid attack on the humbug of betting office regulations led indirectly to the many improvements in facilities for betting-office punters.

When he passed away at the age of 79 in June, 1989, Geoff Greetham, twenty-one years with Timeform at that

point and one of its longest-serving Directors, acknowledged in the course of a personal tribute to him that none
of his considerable achievements could match that of setting up Timeform, leading on to the creation of the Timeform Black Book, The Timeform Racecards, the Timeform
Phone Service and the prestigious 1,000-page *Racehorses*
annual (Flat) and its counterpart *Chasers & Hurdlers*
(National Hunt).

Punters owe him a lasting debt for taking the mystery
out of the approach the professionals adopt. With Timeform at hand, you could assess with greater certainty a
horse's correct distance, also the kind of going it wanted
and if it lacked courage in a finish – or worse.

PART THIRTEEN

JIMMY FITZGERALD
The Man from the Horse and Jockey

18

Gambles that Rocked the Ring at Cheltenham

After the 1984 Cheltenham Festival meeting, Jimmy Fitzgerald went home to his training establishment in Malton bitterly disappointed that Forgive 'N' Forget had not won the Sun Alliance Chase.

In 1983 the gelding had landed a tremendous gamble that rocked the ring at Cheltenham and saw him start a raging hot favourite at 5/2 when capturing the Joe Coral Golden Hurdle Final in the hands of Mark Dwyer from Ashbourne, County Meath. Fitzgerald himself had gone for a real "touch" at 8/1 ante-post.

Mark Dwyer, because he suffered a dislocated shoulder in a fall from Canny Danny at Haydock, missed out on partnering Forgive 'N' Forget at the 1984 Festival meeting. Jimmy Fitzgerald engaged John Francome, then performing on such high plains of excellence that there were men who had seen them all back to Martin Molony who put him on a pedestal apart among English horsemen of his era.

Fitzgerald was fully confident that Forgive 'N' Forget had simply to get around safely to win over the course for the second year running — and backed his judgement accordingly. But Forgive 'N' Forget had to be content with second place behind A Kinsman.

The Man from the Horse and Jockey — the little village not far from the Cathedral town of Thurles in County Tipperary — there and then backed Forgive 'N' Forget at odds of 33/1 to capture the 1985 Gold Cup.

That was confidence, indeed...

But there was a long way to go to the race and Burrough Hill Lad, who gave Jenny Pitman her first Gold Cup triumph in 1984 as an eight year old, dominated the ante-post betting all through the winter months into the spring of 1985 and, really for many, it seemed to be only a one-horse race.

Then at breakfast on the Monday prior to the race Jimmy Fitzgerald was reading *The Sporting Life* and saw that Burrough Hill Lad was a doubtful runner. His confidence soared.

In walked his son Tim and it was the same as if he had dropped a grenade when he said: "Never mind Burrough Hill Lad, Guv'nor, we've got troubles of our own. You had better come quickly and take a look at Forgive 'N' Forget."

"The horse had some heat in his off-fore foot," Jimmy Fitzgerald recalled. "We were very worried at that point that we might not be able to get him to Cheltenham. When, however, the vet came to see him, he could find nothing wrong in the foot and eventually it cooled down."

The public, engrossed with the headlines being made through the exit of the favourite from the race, never realised the drama that was being played out at Malton. And it was only on the eve of the Gold Cup that the vet gave the all-clear that Forgive 'N' Forget could run.

"He had steel shoes fitted and, suspecting it might have been a thorn that he had picked up, I didn't dare take off the shoe, so he ran in three plates and one ordinary shoe," said Jimmy Fitzgerald.

"On the morning of the race I worked him on the course and he came up the hill like a greyhound. That made me a lot more optimistic."

Those ante-post bets executed twelve months beforehand at 33/1 were looking good, especially when one recalls that in the ring itself that day Forgive 'N' Forget was to finish up at 7/1.

Mark Dwyer had been out of action for a long time at the start of the 1984-'85 season — again with a recurrence of that dislocation in his right shoulder. In fact, it was popping out so frequently that he decided to have an operation on it — and, fortunately, all the pieces of the jig-saw came together perfectly on the day as the Jimmy Fitzgerald-Mark Dwyer combination enjoyed the greatest triumph of their careers.

Dwyer rode a beautifully-judged race, making ground steadily and then taking up the running over the last. Righthand Man (G. Bradley) and Earls Brig (P. Tuck) both threw down challenges but they were safely and authoritatively contained as Forgive 'N' Forget had one-and-a-half lengths to spare at the finish from Righthand Man.

Fate had decreed that Jimmy Fitzgerald would not win the Gold Cup as a jockey. He had only two rides in the race before a horrific fall at Doncaster put an end to his career "over the sticks" in 1967.

He was left lying in hospital with a fractured skull, complete deafness in his left ear and dizziness for a year. It was twelve months before he regained his balance again but he was never to recover the hearing in his damaged ear (any journalist interviewing him will be asked to sit on his right side).

Jimmy reckons that it was a blessing in disguise that his career as a jockey ended when it did — "because it launched me into training at just the right time".

"I purchased my 120-acre farm in Malton before prices started to rocket. Today I consider myself very lucky to have such a place of my own."

In over thirty-five years he has not once missed the Festival meeting. Naturally as one from the South of Ireland — and County Tipperary especially — the love of steeplechasing is in his blood. He will admit to you that Cheltenham has always held a special fascination for him. And nowadays the thousands who travel over from Ireland and the many in Britain who follow his stable, take it almost for granted that there will be a spectacular "Fitzgerald gamble" any National Hunt season he has one or two capable of delivering for him.

Nothing, he admits, gives him a greater thrill than to have a winner at Cheltenham. "To have a winner there makes the whole season seem worthwhile."

Even if Burrough Hill Lad had not been withdrawn from the 1984 Gold Cup, the connections of Forgive 'N' Forget would still have "put the money down" on the course — that is those who may have missed out on backing him at fancy ante-post odds.

"I had to be frightened of Burrough Hill Lad before he dropped out, but I always thought we had a great chance," was how Jimmy Fitzgerald himself put it.

What gave him a special thrill about this victory was that he was winning for one of his greatest patrons, Tim Kilroe, who had emigrated from the West of Ireland to England as a young man and like so many others made his fortune in the building and construction business and then contributed handsomely to racing. It was fitting that Forgive 'N' Forget, a gelding by Precipice Wood, should have been bred in Ireland.

When Tim Kilroe lost Fairy King and Brave Fellow he wanted Jimmy Fitzgerald to find him another horse. "I didn't think I'd ever get anything to match Fairy King, unquestionably the best horse I've trained."

"For me Fairy King was Cheltenham Gold Cup class, but I wasn't sure if he would stay three miles. If he did I knew I'd got a Gold Cup horse. I was trying him over three miles at Kempton when he broke his back at the second last. A tragedy.

"Then along came Forgive 'N' Forget. When he won the Coral Golden Handicap Hurdle Final, I knew I had a bright chasing prospect, indeed a possible Sun Alliance Chase winner and maybe after that, even a Gold Cup winner."

If the bowl of Prestbury Park has provided Jimmy Fitzgerald with some of his greatest thrills, it has also given moments of searing heart-break. He is still convinced that Forgive 'N' Forget would have captured a second Gold Cup but for breaking a hind leg at the top of the hill in 1988. "I'd never had him better in my life. He was only cantering."

Forgive 'N' Forget had been third in the 1986 Gold Cup behind Dawn Run and Wayward lad, beaten 3½ lengths. In

1987 he won the inaugural running of the Vincent O'Brien Gold Cup (later to become the Hennessy Cognac Gold Cup Chase) at Leopardstown. "That was a tremendous thrill," said Jimmy Fitzgerald. "Vincent O'Brien is a man I have always admired, ever since I was a kid. He has done everything that no one had done before and is unlikely to do again."

When Forgive 'N' Forget stormed up the hill to win the Coral Golden Hurdle Final, the bookmakers could see the irony in the name of this Festival winner. They could not forgive or forget as they looked into their empty satchels!

But then Fitzgerald of the ruddy complexion, bright eyes and greying hair is a man who readily admits to a liking for bookmakers' money and the list of gambles he has landed has made him a folk hero among racing followers in Ireland and Britain. Yes, he is a man who sends shivers down the bookmakers' spines when he goes for a real assault on them for they know that there is no one better at planning and executing long-term betting coups.

Fortunately for the bookmakers at the 1983 Cheltenham Festival meeting, Fitzgerald didn't go for a "touch" on Canny Danny in the Sun Alliance Chase as the stable gambled on Forgive 'N' Forget in the Coral Golden Handicap Hurdle Final. In fact, Fitzgerald admitted that he "didn't have a penny on Canny Danny" who, starting at 33/1, rallied in thrilling style on the run-in in the hands of Niall Madden to snatch a dramatic short-head victory from Jonjo O'Neill and Torreon.

Later as the champagne flowed and the Fitzgerald party went on into the night, the trainer smiled: "We were unlucky it wasn't a treble because Direct Line would have won the Mildmay of Flete Cup if he hadn't blundered at the second last. He finished fourth."

Jimmy Fitzgerald was born to want only one life — and that was in racing. He started riding when not long out of nappies and was out in the hunting field as an eight-year-old, he revealed to Tim Richards when interviewed for the 1983-'84 edition of the *Irish Racing Annual*.

After starting as an apprentice with John Oxx Senr. at the Curragh, increasing weight meant a return to Dad's farm before joining Dan Moore's stable, where he spent two years, and then he gained further valuable experience with Willie Rooney.

Venturing across the Irish Sea, he was associated first with Bobby Renton, who trained Freebooter to win the 1950 Aintree Grand National. Next he joined Ted Gifford and his first winner was Roberts Choice for that stable at Southwell in 1956. He then moved on to Pat Taylor at Beverley before linking up with Arthur Stephenson for the first two seasons of his successful career.

Jimmy rode 225 winners, seven of those wins being on Magic Court, the best horse he was associated with, though he didn't partner him to his 1964 Champion Hurdle triumph.

Fitzgerald has always believed in managing a balanced, mixed stable. "I like to have a dual-purpose yard because if you find yourself with a bad bunch of one category, you can have a second chance under the other code," was how he put it to Tim Richards. "It makes it hard work, of course, as we never really get a long break but I must admit that it has gone well for us."

Again the bookmakers would have preferred if Jimmy Fitzgerald had never ventured into Flat racing. For in this sphere too he has hit them with some sickening coups, the three most notable of recent times being Kayudee's triumph in the English Cesarewitch of 1985, Sapience in the Ebor at York in 1989 and one of the most spectacular of all, the ante-post gamble landed when Trainglot (returned at 13/2) won the 1990 Cesarewitch by six lengths easing up.

He had come a long way from the 1983 'Coral' success of Forgive 'N' Forget when Michael Seely went to the Norton Grange stables to talk to him for the 1990-'91 *Irish Racing Annual*.

Standing in the kitchen he delivered his verdict that placing an owner's horses to the best advantage was the key to lasting success as a trainer. Allied to that when you went for a coup, you had to engage a top jockey in whom you had complete trust.

He sees the gambling, though it captures the headlines,

as only the froth on the serious side of the business of training.

"If you've got a potentially good horse, you've got to make a long-term goal and go for it. If you miss your chance, you sometimes miss the whole season. It's not the same with ordinary horses because you have another chance next time out."

Nothing illustrates Fitzgerald's philosophy and approach in this respect than his handling of Sapience to win the 1989 Ebor Handicap.

In opting to get Pat Eddery to ride, Fitzgerald was leaving nothing to chance and Eddery delivered — as expected. "Engaging a top jockey is the most important thing when you've done all you can with the horse," he stressed. "If you put a fellow on a horse and he gets into trouble or is not as good as the man alongside, you've lost. And you can only blame yourself."

Sapience, which got into the Ebor with only 8-4, subsequently proved what a "good thing" he was in the Ebor when finishing second to Michelozzo in the St. Leger.

Over the jumps, Fitzgerald's partnership with Mark Dwyer has been a most rewarding one and, apart from those notable successes on Forgive 'N' Forget, Mark also won the Hennessy Gold Cup in 1985.

"He's as good as any of them," is Fitzgerald's tribute. "Not one of them could give him a pound. He's got a great way of settling a horse and never gives one a hard ride if he's beaten. A jockey should be like a musician; he must have good hands and a good head."

The trainer has a very high opinion also of Derek Byrne, whose enterprise and dash were shown to the full when he won the valuable Victor Chandler Handicap Chase at Ascot on Meikleour in January '90 and then took the Swinton Insurance trophy at Haydock in May of the same year.

Turning to one of his pet subjects, bookmakers and the ante-post market, he had this to say: "I do like to have an ante-post bet if I fancy a horse. The only time to bet is when the odds are in your favour and you have a little in hand of the handicapper. I never take a short price. And the bigger the price, the more you should have on. At long odds you can afford to get beat. If you get one up, you can stand an awful lot of hammer before the next winner."

Things have changed, he argues, from the bad old days when trainers had to bet to survive. "Prize money was so poor that you could not get enough money that way to buy the really good horses. So you had to try to collect a bit to have a bet."

Like all his colleagues, Jimmy Fitzgerald has had to compete with Martin Pipe, the Wizard of Wellington. Strands of Gold was removed from Norton Grange to Nicholashayne and won the Hennessy Gold Cup Chase the following season (1988).

Michael Seely asked Fitzgerald about his rival and the already high colour deepened and the blue eyes flashed.

"You're on dangerous ground there," warned the trainer's wife, Jane.

Fitzgerald's sense of humour swiftly got the better of him. "I never thought there was any secret to training," he said, "but Martin Pipe seems to have found one."

He went on then to describe to Michael Seely a day spent pheasant shooting on the Yorkshire Wolds. "This bird came rocketing over and I pulled right through it," he recalled. "The beater said it was the highest pheasant they'd ever seen shot at Garrowby."

He almost fell over as he swung an imaginary gun vigorously over his right shoulder.

He might have been up there on the hills overlooking the Cheltenham course aiming towards the bookies in the ring — and pulling right through them as he landed another spectacular gamble.

Because in the final analysis shooting high pheasants on the Yorkshire Wolds and emptying the bookies' satchels both come alike to the Man from the Horse and Jockey and he is every bit as deadly no matter which is occupying his attention at a given time.

The name of Ryan Price will always be linked with the Schweppes Gold Trophy Handicap Hurdle (now the Tote Gold Trophy Handicap Hurdle) and run at Newbury in February.

271

From the moment of its inauguration in the early Sixties, Price decided that this was a race for which you could "lay one out" and take the bookies to the cleaners in the process at good odds to your money.

He took the first two runnings in 1963 and '64 with Rosyth but the Stewards of the National Hunt Committee were clearly dissatisfied with the horse's form in the run-up to this second success. Shortly after the race Price was warned off and his stable jockey, Josh Gifford suspended.

When the disqualification was lifted four months later, Price immediately set his sights on the Schweppes once more, winning it in 1966 with Le Vermontois, a 15/2 shot and with the seven-year-old Hill House in 1967. Hill House, which carried 10-10 and was ridden like Le Vermontois by Josh Gifford, started at 9/1 in a field of 28.

Fierce controversy stemmed from the victory of Hill House. As he passed the winning post twelve lengths clear of his nearest rival, Celtic Gold, there was a storm of booing. Once more Price and Gifford were sent before the Stewards of the National Hunt Committee.

Following a series of inquiries that dragged on for months, the Stewards accepted veterinary evidence that Hill House could have produced his own cortisol and that this could have affected his performance in the race. They were satisfied that nothing other than a normal nutrient had been administered to the horse before the race.

But a shadow remained over some at least of Ryan Price's triumphs in the Schweppes and coloured what was in many other ways an outstanding training career that saw him turn out a total of nearly 2,000 winners from the time he started at Hambleton in Yorkshire in 1937 until he retired at the end of the 1982 season. At that point he had been concentrating on the Flat from his Soldiers Field (Findon) base. He had won the Cesarewitch in the Sixties with Utrillo, Persian Lancer and Major Rose. His first Classic triumph came in 1972 when Ginevra won the Oaks, to be followed three years later by Bruni's runaway win in the St. Leger.

The nearest he came to winning the Epsom Derby was when Giacometti finished third in 1974 behind 50/1 winner Snow Knight and the colt was second in the 2,000 Guineas to Nonoalco and runner-up also in the St. Leger to 11/10 favourite Bustino.

When he passed away in August, 1986 George Ennor concluded his tribute in the *Racing Post* thus: "Ryan Price was a man for whom drama might have been invented. His successes alone were enough to make him a man to remember, even if there had been no episodes of a less happy nature."

Newmarket trainer, Neville Callaghan is a man who is no stranger to controversy – a man also who has always enjoyed a good old-fashioned tilt at the ring and who has enjoyed more than one nice "killing" during his career.

During the Newmarket '91 July meeting when I met him in his home in Hamilton Road, adorned with two paintings of Lester Piggott, who lives just across the road, he certainly didn't hide the fact that he likes to have a cut when he believes that one of his charges is in with a good winning chance.

"I am very much a punter," he said frankly. Indeed, he confided that the gambling bug had already caught him when he was a schoolboy in his native County Cork and one of his first winning bets was on the Vincent O'Brien-trained Quare Times to win the 1955 Aintree Grand National. The reason nowadays that he preferred to go for a "touch" on one of his own horses was – "because you are more in control of the situation."

"Like all people, I like to win when I put the money down and if the one I have backed fails to repay the investment, it hurts – but not for long. I can take defeat."

He doesn't favour betting ante-post. "Generally, too many imponderables can arise. In a nutshell I like to bet on something that I know will run."

Corrupt did him a few good turns during the '91 season. He got 20/1 when the colt won on his first outing as a three-year-old in the Bonusprint Easter Stakes at Kempton in March.

That run convinced Callaghan that Corrupt was a far better horse than those assessing the potential Derby candidates had concluded. In fact, he believed he was one to "go to war" on. The stable connections got in at 8/1 on Corrupt for the Maxims Club Derby Trial Stakes at Lingfield in May. The Lear Fan colt, in the hands of Cash Asmussen, showed a fine turn of foot inside the final furlong in winning comfortably by four lengths from previous winner, Young Buster, the 9/4 favourite. Corrupt started at 9/2.

Cash Asmussen retained the ride for the Epsom Derby but the 4/1 joint-favourite (with Toulon) was left with a lot to do in the straight and Neville Callaghan, whose motto is that if someone does not perform to his satisfaction, he is not afraid to say so, commented frankly: "Cash did not excel on him."

However, the trainer added at the same time that Corrupt "did not fire" on the day as he had at Lingfield. Corrupt had to be content with sixth place behind the highly-impressive winner, Generous who went on to frank the form in no uncertain terms subsequently. Corrupt compensated to an extent for his Epsom Derby defeat by taking the Great Voltigeur at York at 5/1 in the hands of Pat Eddery from the 11/8 favourite, Saddler's Hall, ridden by Lester Piggott.

We basked in the July sunshine as Neville Callaghan's wife Jenny served a poached salmon lunch in the garden. Later in the company of a few friends, I would have a game of snooker with him in the Newmarket club frequented by the racing fraternity.

His staunch patrons, like bookmaker-cum-professional punter, Michael Tabor of the Arthur Prince chain of S.P. offices (who, incidentally, according to Callaghan is "one of the shrewdest and most-feared punters in Britain") have never wavered in their loyalty to him. And, of course, he has a few Irish owners, self-made millionaires, who identify with his volatility. – a volatility, I might add, that has caused him to make more than one headline.

Over a gin and tonic before lunch, I had cast his mind back to the time in 1975 when he found himself in deep hot water for allegedly insulting the Queen during the Loyal Toast at a dinner in the Subscription Rooms Club in Newmarket. Callaghan had always firmly denied that he had made the remark attributed to him and equally firmly rejected the accusation that he had remained seated during the toast.

Five years after the event the *Daily Express,* for some reason that Callaghan will never understand, resurrected in two gossip column items, the allegation against the Newmarket trainer, who immediately sued for libel. He was awarded £15,000 damages with costs by Mr. Justice Russell in a reserved judgement delivered in Manchester.

Describing it as a "very serious libel," Justice Russell said that Mr. Callaghan had always emphatically denied any disloyalty to the Queen. He went on: "In my judgement the defendants have come nowhere near justifying what was written in either of the articles five years after the event and I suspect that had they taken the trouble to investigate the matters with more depth, the features would not have appeared."

The Judge stressed also that there had not been even a hint during the case that by word or deed, before or since the dinner, Mr. Callaghan had displayed animosity towards the Crown or any interest, let alone support, for the IRA.

Neville Callaghan himself recalled: "I regularly attended those dinners in the Subscription Rooms Club. In season you could find yourself sitting down to pheasant or grouse supper. The attendance normally totalled about 50 or 60.

"I never had the slightest trouble in standing with the rest for the Loyal Toast. I have never been a supporter of any causes and I would be the last person to give any support to the IRA.

"As the Judge said in his summing up during the libel case, the Queen is a great patron of the sport of racing and for years now I have been making my livelihood out of it. so the last thought that would cross my mind would be to do anything disrespectful to Her Majesty. I respect the Queen as much as anybody else.

"You stand automatically for the Loyal Toast and I invariably did so at the dinners in the Subscription Rooms Club and toasted the Queen with everyone else at table. If I had remained seated, as I was accused of doing, there would have been an outcry there and then from the others beside me at table. There was none."

The pain of being a week in court in London and "being put through the hoops" and, what was worse, having to endure the agony of waiting a further three weeks until the reserved judgement was given in Manchester still rankles deeply when Neville Callaghan reflects on it.

But he was prepared to go through with the case, no matter what it cost him, for as he told me: "I never felt so strongly about anything in my life. I didn't mind if I lost everything but I had to clear my name."

A stay of execution for 28 days was allowed the defendants in the libel case while an appeal was considered. Neville Callaghan went to the William Hill awards lunch and was introduced by Charles Benson to Lord Matthews, then in a top executive position in Express Newspapers.

"We have just had a case with you. I don't want to discuss it in the event that we appeal," said Lord Matthews.

Callaghan flushed with anger. "If you want to lose any more f——— money, I would appeal if I were you and it will suit me fine."

"And that ended that conversation very quickly," recalled Neville Callaghan.

There was, in fact, no appeal.

PART FOURTEEN

P.J. PRENDERGAST
The Man They Knew As
"Darkie"

19

"The only problem is that two of us know now."

It was the era when Christy Roche was riding as first jockey to the late Paddy Prendergast and from that partnership flowed five Irish Classic triumphs – the 2,000 Guineas on Ballymore (1972) and Nikoli (1980), the 1,000 Guineas on Sarah Siddons (1976) and More So (1978) and the St. Leger on Mistigri (1974).

Over a decade later after the Rossmore Lodge maestro had passed on, Christy revealed to me how the man they knew affectionately as "Darkie" brought off some of his cleverest coups. Contrary to what many people thought, it was not always on the "flying machines" – that is the brilliantly speedy two year olds in the category of Windy City and Floribunda. No, it was on maiden three year olds that he had assessed to a tee.

Sometime before they had even made their first appearance of the new season, he would have judged the ones that were just short of Classic standard. These were real betting propositions, literally "thrown in" against rival maidens he knew were totally outclassed on a line through other animals in his stable, formed the previous season.

"I was very, very close to P.J." said Christy Roche. "He was like a father to me. I remember this day he was very ill and he called me to his room. He said: 'Christy, I have this horse lined up and I want you to ring up this friend of mine and tell him to do the needful for me.' I knew then that it wasn't medicine he was looking for but that he was going for a real old-style touch. I told him his instructions were already as good as carried out.

"As I walked towards the door, he called me and, as I turned back, he remarked: 'The only problem is that *two* of us know now.'

"In a situation like that P.J. seldom if ever failed – and the one he had lined up on that particular occasion romped home."

It could be argued that Christy Roche was a biased observer when putting Paddy Prendergast right up there on a pedestal as one of the greatest of all Flat trainers that Ireland has produced.

But while accepting the deep affection he displays when speaking of the man who was his first Guv'nor, it has to be remembered that Christy's own record as a top jockey qualifies him eminently to look right across the spectrum of years and assess, for example, the difference of approach between 'Darkie' and Vincent O'Brien. He rode for both of them and also for David O'Brien and when David decided to give up training, when still in his early thirties, the Man from Bansha became first jockey to Jim Bolger – the finest tribute to his talent.

And if one were not prepared to accept the verdict of Christy Roche, then there is that of Lester Piggott, who rode Meadow Court to victory for Paddy Prendergast in the 1965 Irish Sweeps Derby. "There's no doubt he was a great trainer," said Lester. "He was a self-made man, who grafted for success and went right to the top of his profession from a difficult start. But he was a fantastic judge of horseflesh."

Christy Roche, when I breakfasted with him during the course of the research for this book, had come a long way both in terms of success as a jockey at the highest level and in the confidence gained from riding colts of the calibre of Assert (French Derby winner and Irish Derby winner for David O'Brien in 1982) and Secreto (Epsom Derby winner in 1984, again for David O'Brien) and the filly Jet Ski Lady (English Oaks winner for Jim Bolger in 1991) since he started out as an apprentice with 'Darkie' Prendergast. St. Jovite (Budweiser Irish Derby) followed in '92.

Peter O'Sullevan in his autobiography, *Calling The Horses*, described Paddy Prendergast as "an Irish volcano" and Christy Roche said frankly that "he was a hard man to ride for." Indeed, not many finished their contracts with him and when one of the Australians left, for example, before the end of a given season, Christy would invariably be called upon to fill in for the rest of the season. 'Darkie' had a set way of doing things and no one – literally no one – was allowed to break the mould. You could take your papers and leave if you wanted it otherwise.

In an age when there were no big syndicates, no Arab oil money about, 'Darkie' Prendergast could go to the yearling sales and buy small by the inflated standards of later years and pick out potential world beaters or he could purchase them away from the sales ring.

One of his most inspired purchases was that of Pelorus, which was to prove such an anchor to the stable over an eight-year period. Peter O'Sullevan relates in his book how the chestnut gelding by Sea Serpent out of Dinah's Daughter was knocked down to Kerr & Co. for 30 guineas in the sales ring at Ballsbridge on September 30, 1941 and 'Darkie' Prendergast bought him from Bertie Kerr for £200 on behalf of one of his patrons.

When it came to turning out fast two year olds, Paddy Prendergast was "the artist supreme" in his day, according to Jack Doyle.

Tony Sweeney noted in an authoritative historical review of Irish racing in Noel Phillips Browne's *The Horse in Ireland* (1967) that between 1950 and 1965 Prendergast was responsible for no less than twelve of the sixteen Irish two year old champions (colts and fillies who were allotted top weight in the Madrid Free Handicap) including youngsters of the calibre of Windy City, The Pie King, Paddy's Sister, La Tendresse and Young Emperor.

"He was an outstanding judge of a juvenile," said Jack Doyle. "I never saw 'Darkie' pick a bad-looking horse. You could go to the parade ring at any racecourse and pick out the Prendergast horses without a programme, as you could also do with the Ryan Price runners.

"There is an old saying among the real judges and that is

Kate Horgan, wife of John Horgan of Cork, holds the Airlie/Coolmore Irish 2000 Guineas trophy high in triumph after Tirol's victory in the 1990 Curragh Classic.

The brothers Jim and John Horgan of Cork and (below) Tirol (Pat Eddery), on inside, gets the better of Royal Academy (John Reid) in the last furlong to win the 1990 Airlie/Coolmore Irish 2000 Guineas by a neck.

Tirol (Michael Kinane) takes the 1990 English 2000 Guineas by two lengths from Machiavellian (Freddie Head) and (below) the enthusiastic scenes in the winner's enclosure at Newmarket.

Seamus Purcell and his wife Phil proudly lead in Buck House (Tommy Carmody) after his magnificent triumph in the Queen Mother Champion Chase at the 1986 Cheltenham Festival meeting and (right) successful trainer Michael 'Mouse' Morris. And (below) Mrs. Purcell holds the trophy aloft after My View had won the 1992 Coral Golden Handicap Hurdle (Final) at 33/1.

Dunmore, County Galway-born Dr. Michael Mangan with Monksfield after he had won the Champion Hurdle for the second successive year in 1979 and (below) Dessie Hughes (left) and Jonjo O'Neill on Sea Pigeon taking the last to produce a battle of unforgettable quality to the line.

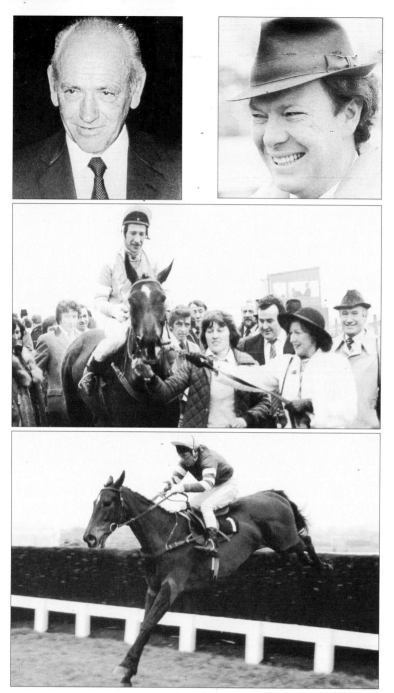

The late Tony Murphy of Cork, the man at the centre of the "Gay Future Coup" and, right, Edward O'Grady, trainer of Gay Future. Tommy Carberry shares the glory of another win on Anaglog's Daughter with Bill Durkan, (behind) and Tony (on right) while, below, Carberry is seen winning the Arkle Challenge Trophy Chase at the 1980 Cheltenham Festival.

Michael Heaslip (left) of Galway gives a victory wave to the crowd after For Auction's 40/1 victory in the 1982 Champion Hurdle and (below) successful trainer, Michael Cunningham, Danno Heaslip and jockey Colin Magnier show their joy as they display the imposing trophy.

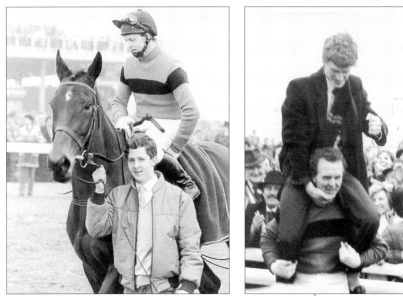

Dawn Run and Jonjo O'Neill being led in the parade by John Clarke before the 1986 Gold Cup and, right, Jonjo chairs Tony Mullins in a memorable moment in the winner's enclosure while, below, Paddy Mullins is pictured with the gallant mare who died that same summer in action in France.

that you cannot buy solely on looking up a horse's pedigree – in a word you cannot train paper. You must see for yourself and let your eye be the judge if the right conformation is there, and real quality."

I reminded him that Vincent O'Brien had said to me once that you could, with an experienced eye, select an animal with the right conformation and with class in every line of its frame but you could not look into its heart or know if it had that over-drive that the true champions of the turf can produce in the finish of a Classic.

Jack Doyle accepted that there were imponderables that went beyond the human eye and yet he recalled 'Darkie' Prendergast picking Windy City – a veritable flying machine – which others had let go by that day in the sales ring and brilliant ones like The Pie King, Royal Duchy and Gold Cup that this wonderful judge of potential two year old champions could select, they were not all fashionably bred.

There are those who maintain that in this age the cheque book can dictate who gets the potential champions. "There have been those backed by millions who have failed to purchase Classic winners," Jack Doyle noted. "Vincent O'Brien hadn't millions behind him when he was starting off. He had to depend on his eye. Likewise 'Darkie' Prendergast did not have rich patrons at the outset of his training career though he did acquire them later. He too had to depend on his eye."

'Darkie', he went on, was one of the few successful trainers who was also extremely successful as a punter. Vincent O'Brien too was invariably outstandingly successful in his tilts at the ring before the era arrived when, with millionaire patrons in his stable, he no longer needed to bet. And like 'Darkie' he seldom if ever left it behind with the bookmakers.

Prendergast was at his deadliest, according to Jack Doyle, when backing the ones he trained himself because then he knew what he had to "go to war" with and similarly when Vincent O'Brien laid one out for a target he had set his mind on winning, the bookies took a real caning.

"You could say that I was on the outside looking in at

some of those great gambles – though it wasn't terribly difficult to know at times when one of those good things was well nigh past the post.

"You had only to look at the board of the great Dick Power (David's grandfather) and he would simply put up a one (evens). And then perhaps take an even £5,000 or £10,000 when bets of that size were awesome when set beside the money terms of today. Dick Power would not flinch and what I admired about him was that he was prepared to take his hiding like a man as one trotted up. A marvellous individual, old Dick Power – a man who set standards as a bookmaker and created a tradition, which I am happy to say David has maintained in admirable fashion."

'Darkie' Prendergast controlled things with an iron hand in his stable. "He had some wonderful work riders like 'Chalk' Doyle, Billy Tutle, Johnny Winters, 'Spur' Nolan, etc. and two great jump jockeys in Connie Eddery (Pat's uncle) and Toddy White," recalled Jack Doyle.

"He was wont to deceive the 'gallop watchers' when he knew he had a real two year old flier. Not everyone in the stable would know either.

"He used Gordon Richards a lot when he first went raiding in England and Gordon was able to give him an accurate estimate of a particular colt or filly.

"Later, of course, he had such jockeys as Jack Thompson, Ron Hutchinson, Des Lake and Garnie Bougoure, who had an extraordinary record of coming out on top in photo finishes, and he also used the services of another great Australian, Bill Williamson."

Jimmy ('Corky') Mullane, whose style and particularly his "sit" on a two year old made him a joy to watch in his prime, will be remembered especially for his contribution to Paddy Prendergast's fabulous record in the Phoenix Park '1,500'.

Prendergast was only able to entice the great Sydney champion, Jack Thompson, to stay in Ireland for one season, but he won the 1950 Irish Derby for him on Frank More O'Ferrall's Dark Warrior. It was on the specific recommendation of Thompson that Ron Hutchinson came to ride for Prendergast and immediately made his mark by winning both the 1960 Irish and English 2000 Guineas with Kythnos and Martial while the same season he won on Typhoon and Floribunda at Royal Ascot.

The 1962 season would see Garnie Bougoure riding for the Prendergast stable. He was successful on Display and Tender Annie at Royal Ascot. The 1963 season, however, would be his most memorable. He was victorious on Ragusa in the English St. Leger and Irish Sweeps Derby, rode Noblesse to Victory in the English Oaks and won the Irish St. Leger on Christmas Island – all for 'Darkie' Prendergast. And then in 1964 he took the English 1000 Guineas on Pourparler for his retaining stable.

Jack Doyle admitted to me that his own relationship with Paddy Prendergast was "an up-and-down affair", sometimes even a stormy one but then this was understandable when reflecting on how his closest friends and admirers all accepted that P.J. was nothing if not volatile.

"We even fell out for periods but there was that link between us that never died. I remember his last visit to York and some time before he had said to me at the Curragh: 'Be sure to be at York.' I duly arrived and I am almost certain that it was the week that marked the beginning of his last illness. I had gone into the weighroom to try to get Lester to go to Woodbine in Toronto for the Rothmans. When I had finished talking to Lester, I turned round and saw 'Darkie' sitting on a bench in the room. We started to chat. He proceeded to tell me his two-year-old runner that day would win. I remember saying to him " 'is this one of the old-fashioned ones, Darkie?', meaning, of course, could one bet on it as we had gone in on such as The Pie King and Royal Duchy. He winked and said: 'Yes'.

"I knew that his great friend and my own good friend also, the late Joe McLoughlin would be backing the horse for 'Darkie'. I asked him to put me on a monkey on him. The horse in question was Pollerton and he won at 8/1."

Paddy Prendergast had training greatness thrust upon him through the refusal of an Army recruiting board to induct him into Britain's fighting service at the start of the Second World War. Of all things they suspected that he might be a terrorist bomber!

P.J. brought his family back from England and then returned to Britain with the intention of joining the Royal Air Force. Before he could do so he was arrested by the Liverpool police on suspicion of being a member of the I.R.A. and deported back to Ireland. "That was the turning point in my life," he would tell friends later.

A few months afterwards a chance meeting in a bar got him his first patron and his first horses, Spratstown and Rare Rajah. He took out a licence and set up in a couple of boxes lent him by Mick Connolly.

It would be nice to write that Paddy Prendergast like Fred Winter, Jonjo O'Neill and Dessie Hughes had been an outstanding jockey before turning his hand to training. But in actual fact he was not a particularly distinguished jump jockey and there is no body of writing extant about his singular achievements in this arena. But he did have the distinction of belonging to that select group of riders who broke their necks and lived to tell the tale!

Louis Gunning, who chronicled his exploits over a thirty-five year span, made the point that Prendergast's rejection as a potential pilot in the Royal Air Force must have been the cause of bitter regret by many an English trainer in the post-War years. "Because, having decided to fight on another front, when normality returned to the English racing scene, he had mustered a panzer corps of speed merchants which were to prove the scourge of English trainers on all their best-loved courses," said Louis.

"They consisted mainly of two year olds, not as has sometimes been said, because the dynamic young trainer's special expertise was in the selection of potentially quickly maturing racehorses, but as Paddy himself would point out; because owners at that period were mainly interested in a quick and profitable return on their outlay. And that outlay was microscopic compared with the prices paid for yearlings in later decades."

Success came slowly for Paddy Prendergast at the outset of his career. The apocryphal story is told of him cycling through Newbridge with a bale of hay on his bicycle, of Cecil Boyd Rochfort writing to him and telling him that if he didn't make a go of it, there would always be a job for him in his stable and 'Darkie', with complete faith in his own ability, writing back to inform Boyd Rochfort that if he ever fell on bad times, he would be looked after with a position in the Prendergast stable!

Paddy Prendergast had reason to be thankful that the exploits of Pelorus, a rattling good handicapper on the Flat and a first-class steeplechaser into the bargain, kept his name before his peers and the racing public – and the wolf from the door.

By 1946 he had got his first two year old flier, Port Blanc, whom he produced to win at Goodwood. She cost her owner, Sam Henry, who played a notable role in building up the Rossmore Lodge stables, a mere 350 guineas. She was to bring him further glory at Royal Ascot.

The flamboyant American, Ray Bell acquired Windy City for 700 guineas when his original owner, The Hon. Richard Stanley, according to Louis Gunning, had to opt out of the transaction for political reasons which would seem ridiculous nowadays. Windy City, having won in sensational style at Chester, cantered away with the Phoenix Park '1,500', won York's Gimcrack Stakes and then got beaten a short head for the Prix D'Arenberg at Longchamp after Charlie Smirke and his flying machine had the misfortune to be facing in the wrong direction when the tapes went up.

Windy City, like so many other precocious Rossmore Lodge youngsters, was sold to America after his first season. His subsequent career included a head defeat by Hill Gail in the Santa Anita Derby.

Sixpence, Gold Cup and The Pie King were other legendary two year olds from that period in Paddy's career that brought fame and many a small fortune to their owners.

"But," as Louis Gunning recounts, "a new breed of owner was being attracted to the Curragh powerhouse of predominantly first season talent. These were people who, while delighted to bask in the glory of such brilliantly-speedy Ascot, Goodwood and York winners as Floribunda, Paddy's Sister, La Tendresse and Pourparler, had the cash

285

to pay, and all the time in the world to wait, for the greater glories of Classic victories."

The late Frank More O'Ferrall, a great admirer of Paddy's training skills, introduced many wealthy patrons from the other side of the Atlantic, to 'Darkie', including Frank McMahon and Max Bell and Mrs. Pansy Parker Poe.

Now the skill of Paddy Prendergast with three year olds and older horses was to blossom to the full and by the close of the 1966 season he had won eleven Irish and four English Classics. By 1980 – the year he passed away – the record read – 17 Irish Classics and four English Classics.

He never realised his ambition of winning the Epsom Derby. But I have no doubt that he would have gone into the racing history books with that achievement to his credit had not Meadow Court had the misfortune in 1965 to come up against Sea Bird II, rated by Jack Doyle as the No. 1 middle-distance colt and Derby winner he has seen and he would even put him ahead of Nijinsky and Sir Ivor. Incidentally, when I asked Vincent O'Brien to name the greatest colt he had seen in his time (outside, of course, of those handled by himself), he also plumped for Sea Bird II.

Meadow Court, running in the colours of the Canadian Max Bell, and ridden by Lester Piggott was beaten just two lengths by Sea Bird II (T.P. Glennon) at Epsom – there was a field of 22 – but made ample amends when landing the Irish Sweeps Derby for Prendergast some weeks later.

On the eve of the Curragh race Max Bell sold shares in Meadow Court to his very good friends, Frank McMahon and Bing Crosby.

Bing, like Max Bell and Frank McMahon, was appropriately refreshed at Rossmore Lodge on his way to the Derby meeting and, after Meadow Court's triumph, he was in the mood to add shownmanship and gaiety to the occasion by singing "When Irish Eyes Are Smiling" in front of the crowded Grand Stand. All who had the privilege of being there that day will never forget that moment.

The victory of Meadow Court meant that 'Darkie' Prendergast had become the first trainer to win the Irish Sweeps Derby twice though, of course, Vincent O'Brien would later emulate and surpass that feat through the suc-

286

cesses of Nijinsky (1970), The Minstrel (1977), El Gran Senor (1984) and Law Society (1985).

The first of Prendergast's two triumphs, that of Ragusa in 1963 may, in the viewpoint of Tony Sweeney, have been a "fortunate" one.

The French colt, Relko who had romped to a six-lengths win in the Epsom Derby in the hands of Yves Saint-Martin, with Ragusa third, went lame on his way to the start for reasons that have never been satisfactorily explained and had to be withdrawn before coming under starter's orders. Taking advantage of the mishap, Jim Mullion's colt overcame considerable difficulties in running to win comfortably.

The admirers of Ragusa would contend that the Epsom Derby came a bit too soon for him and that he would have turned the tables anyway against Relko had the two renewed rivalry at the Curragh. The arguments about their relative merits were never settled as the two horses did not meet again.

However, Ragusa's subsequent career, which included victories in the King George VI and Queen Elizabeth Stakes, the Great Voltigeur Stakes, allied to an effortless English St. Leger triumph and, at four, victory in the Ardenode Stakes, would tend to lend credence to the argument that he was something special. Supporters of Relko, on the other hand, rest their case on the one cold statistic that Ragusa was nine lengths behind Relko in the Epsom Derby.

The genius displayed by Paddy Prendergast in spotting potential champions was never better illustrated than in the way he purchased the Ribot colt for his patrons, the Mullions, after the American-bred had been cast aside from another quarter as being a "ragged or weedy" yearling.

The friendship between Paddy Prendergast and the Mullions was to be of tremendous benefit to Irish racing and the Irish breeding industry. And it would last right up to the time of Paddy's death in June, 1980.

The Mullions ploughed much of Ragusa's winnings and more besides into forming a new stallion stud as an extension to Ardenode and named the Ragusa Stud.

They had the satisfaction of seeing Paddy's Sister produce Ballymore, who made history by winning the 1972 Irish 2000 Guineas on his first appearance on a racecourse and at the same time gave Christy Roche his first Classic triumph.

Tom McCormack tells the story of how Paddy Prendergast came to pick out one of the fastest two year olds he trained on one of his annual autumn inspections of the Ardenode yearlings.

Having viewed them all, he spotted this yearling colt in an adjacent paddock and put the query to Jim Mullion: "What's that over there?"

"THAT", as it so happened, was "Floribunda", as then unnamed, of course, and segregated from the rest because of the habit he had of biting at the tails of the other yearlings.

"I'll win for you at Royal Ascot with that fellow," predicted 'Darkie' Prendergast with the confidence and assurance of a man whose eye had already told him that in Floribunda's frame were the qualities of another flying machine.

Floribunda won the Norfolk Stakes (then the New Stakes) in 1960 in the hands of Ron Hutchinson and the following year the Princely Gift colt proved himself the champion sprinter by his stunning defeat of Cynara and Bleep-Bleep in the Nunthorpe Stakes at York.

At the outset of the 1965 Flat season Paddy Prendergast had every reason to feel that it was going to be the greatest he had enjoyed. Four three year olds in the stable, Hardicanute, Prominer, Carlemont and Meadow Court, had been placed at or near the top of the 1964 English and Irish Free Handicaps.

"Indeed, they looked to have a great chance of winning all the colts' Classics between them in both countries – a feat never yet approached," recalled Tony Sweeney. "Then in the early spring of '65, the coughing epidemic hit Rossmore Lodge and every plan had to be torn up. Hardicanute never ran again. Prominer – in my opinion, anyhow – was never as good afterwards. Carlemont, possibly the best of them all, won the 'prestige' Sussex Stakes at Goodwood as a four year old but his three year old career was wrecked. The only one of the four to survive was Meadow Court."

Yet, despite the shattering effect of the cough on some of his finest talent, Paddy Prendergast established a record in that same year in that he topped the list of champion trainers in England for the third successive season. Few English trainers could claim that hat-trick and it was quite unprecedented for a trainer based outside the country.

Tom MacGinty, who came to know 'Darkie' Prendergast very well during a spell of close on thirty years as Racing Correspondent of Irish Independent Newspapers, contends that it was indeed tragic in the sporting sense that P.J. did not realise his ambition of winning an Epsom Derby before his death, especially when one considers that he won all the other classics in Britain and Ireland.

"I remember one September, 'Darkie' kindly offered me a lift from the Doncaster St. Leger meeting to Manchester Airport. Before the motorway system was fully developed that was an arduous journey but on the occasion in question, the time and the miles passed unnoticed.

"Paddy was great company and a marvellous raconteur. His tales of battles lost and won and characters he met were fascinating, often hilarious. But in a serious and ruminative moment he suddenly said: 'You know, Tom, I have had a great life. I have won and made a lot of money and have invested in farms and cattle and no matter what I do now, I couldn't go broke. But before I finish I want to train the winner of the Derby. It is the greatest race'."

Louis Gunning maintains that of all the courses in England on which 'Darkie' Prendergast left his mark as a master of his art, York was the one for which he had a real yen. "And I think it stems from an historic confrontation there in August, 1953.

"In the previous September, the English Jockey Club Stewards had banned him from running horses in England following an inquiry into the running of a horse called Blue Sail, which believe it or not had been beaten in a race at Ascot! The Irish Stewards refused to follow suit but the English ban lasted for nearly a year.

"It was lifted in time for Paddy to stage a blitz on the York meeting which yielded four winners – Panalley, Sky Gipsy, My Beau and Blue Sail – from five runners.

"As Paddy stood in the winner's enclosure awaiting the first of them, Sir Humphrey de Trafford, the senior member of the body that imposed the ban, shook him warmly by the hand, saying: 'Welcome back, well done, Paddy.' It was the sort of gesture to strike a responsive chord in his own impulsive good nature."

His sons Kevin and Paddy Jnr. followed him into the training profession, with their establishments on the Curragh.

Had 'Darkie' Prendergast arrived in the era of the prize-money that can be commanded today by a colt or filly that sweeps the board in a given season and if too he had enjoyed the patronage of the oil-rich Arab Sheikhs – which no doubt he certainly would with his talent – I am convinced that he would have left an even more indelible imprint on racing records.

Suffice it to say, over a decade after the "Year of Ragusa", he remarked rather ruefully to Louis Gunning that this outstanding colt's successes netted about £146,00. Update that haul to the financial terms of the Eighties and Nineties and you can see why 'Darkie' had reason to think he had been rather short-changed! But, of course, it was the same for Vincent O'Brien when he started out.

Paddy and Vincent made up for what they lost in their cut of less-substantial prize-money by taking it from the bookmakers.

Peter O'Sullevan came to know both of them extremely well and even did commissions for them. I quote no finer tribute than that of 'The Voice of the BBC': "It should always be remembered that Vincent and his long-time contemporary Paddy ('Darkie') Prendergast did more than any two personalities to put Ireland on the international racing map."

PART FIFTEEN

VINCENT O'BRIEN
*An Incomparable Record
on Two Fronts*

20

A Council of War at
The Jockey Hall

Vincent O'Brien had called a "Council of War" for lunch-time at the Jockey Hall restaurant on the Curragh on the Saturday of the 1949 Irish Cesarewitch. He had invited Nat McNabb from Dublin and Bob Mulrooney from Limerick to be present. These were his two trusted lieutenants – the men who did the commissions in the ring when the stable went for a "killing". Also there were Vincent's two brothers, Dermot and "Phonsie", owner Harry Keogh and Dermot McDowell, a Dublin solicitor and a great friend of the Keoghs.

The lead-up to that luncheon gathering was a piece of work on the gallops in Churchtown, County Cork between Hatton's Grace and Knock hard.

Now Vincent spelt it out for those present. "We worked the two at home together and Knock Hard pulverised Hatton's Grace for speed. We have something to go to war with and the reason I have brought you here is that I want to make sure we get the best price to our money."

Looking straight at Nat McNabb, as silence fell over the table, he said: "Knock Hard meets Hatton's Grace on 10 lbs. better terms today than in the gallop. What do you think?"

Nat's reply was: "Well, Vincent, in that case he must be a racing certainty."

He qualified that statement, however, by adding: "but there is one thing we must not forget, Hatton's Grace is the

292

type of horse that never gives in. He will be staying on when most of the others have cried enough over the two miles of the Cesarewitch."

There was another important consideration also. "Hatton's Grace had this knack of fooling you at home and he didn't really give of his best on the gallops. He was a different horse on a racecourse. The excitement seemed to electrify him in some strange way and stir him into giving some wonderful displays," recalled Moya Keogh in whose colours he won three successive Champion Hurdles (1949-'51).

But on the basis of what the gallop had revealed, the O'Brien stable had concluded, in the words of "Phonsie", that "Knock Hard was a cold-stone certainty if held up to make the best use of his acceleration in the final furlong."

The plan decided over lunch was that the man entrusted with the task of ensuring that the major gamble to be landed on Knock Hard would be at the highest possible odds, would go in first on Hatton's Grace. And to put the bookies off the scent, those who invariably kept tabs on the movements of Nat McNabb and Bob Mulrooney in the ring would be left in no doubt that Hatton's Grace was the one the stable was on.

Nat McNabb arranged with his wife Eileen that she would position herself in a certain spot on the stand wearing a hat. "When we had finished the job backing Hatton's Grace and I knew that the price was right on Knock Hard, I would give her a pre-arranged signal from down below in the ring and then she would touch her hat. That would be the sign for the others in the front-line trenches to go over the top."

Nat knew there had to be perfect timing. "We had to act in complete concert, hitting the books together, snapping up the best odds to our money before any of the bookies realised what was happening."

The overall strategy for the day worked like a dream. Hatton's Grace came down to 3/1 as Knock Hard's price was pushed out to 6/1, then to 7/1 and even to 10/1 on some boards.

As Nat McNabb and Bob Mulrooney and the "troops"

under them went to war, the ring was rocked with the money poured on Knock Hard. He came down to evens favourite as Hatton's Grace drifted to 8/1.

Once again the bookies had been completely out-foxed by Vincent O'Brien.

The trainer's implicit instructions to Bert Holmes, the rider of Knock Hard, was that under no circumstance must he hit the front until inside the final furlong. "The horse, however, was going so easily as they turned into the straight that Bert Holmes let him go on," said Nat McNabb. "Hatton's Grace was a terrific stayer and under the power finish engineered by Martin Molony, he caught Knock Hard within sight of the post and beat him."

Naturally, I posed the direct question to Nat McNabb: Why did Hatton's Grace have to come like that and spoil the party?

"No one would ever dream of telling Martin Molony not to try. Anyway, after the gallop and, remembering that on the strength of it Knock Hard had a good 10 lbs. in hand, it was possible to allow both horses run on their merits and, as Vincent visualised it, Hatton's Grace should succumb to Knock Hard's finishing speed."

Vincent O'Brien had read it perfectly – only that Knock Hard was not held up to the very death.

Because of the money put on Hatton's Grace early on, the stable did not lose as much as would have been the case had the commission been solely on Knock Hard.

Nevertheless, Vincent O'Brien was not a man who liked leaving any of his money with the bookmakers. He was hardly back in Churchtown that evening from the Curragh when he began devising his plan to execute a coup where there would be absolutely no danger of anything going wrong.

He looked ahead five months to the 1950 Irish Lincoln. And again he very cleverly outwitted the bookmakers.

He showed real shrewdness in running Knock Hard in a novice chase at Naas, which he won, incidentally. This was a fortnight before the Lincoln and the bookies, like some of the big professional punters, concluded that this success over the jumps would have blunted his speed for the big

294

Curragh handicap event. And into the bargain Knock Hard had been set to carry 8 st. 12 lbs.

In what seemed an open race on the face of it, betting took a wide range initially. Then, as Louis Gunning reported in the *Irish Press*, "an avalanche of money hit the bookmakers to make Knock Hard a tight 2/1 favourite."

The immense stable confidence was completely justified as Knock Hard, with T.P. Burns in the saddle, beat the opposition to a frazzle.

Knock Hard, whose middle name was "versatility" as he could win on the Flat, over hurdles and over the major obstacles, was sent over to contest the Coventry Plate (1 mile 2 furlongs) at Worcester with "Phonsie" O'Brien having the ride. This race for amateurs was worth a mere £138 but that didn't worry Vincent O'Brien.

The stable in another awesome gamble took something like £14,000 out of the ring that day. Nat McNabb put the scale of that win in perspective for me when he told me that it was in the era when "you could buy a new suit for £4 and a pint was only 10d."

Christy Kinane, who was one of those who graduated from the Vincent O'Brien "college" and whose training establishment is in Cashel, County Tipperary, maintains that Vincent was "the Daddy of them all" when it came to getting a horse ready for a stable coup and he had no equal in the art of bringing them off.

"I know from working under him that he was a genius," said Christy. "He might be galloping two horses and then he would put a third in to test further the one that was being prepared for the job.

"As far as he was concerned there would be no question of one that was expected getting beaten because it was even one per cent short of the required peak of fitness. Horses won for Vincent that would have won under no other trainer. He got the very best out of them.

"Furthermore, you often hear it said of certain stables that their success is not due entirely to the trainer himself but maybe to some man under him. Vincent was *totally* in control in the days I worked for him. A few new hands might arrive and on the gallops the very next morning he would know them by their first names. He knew everything about every horse in the stable with a knowledge that amazed you again and again.

"He left no stone unturned when going after particular targets. From the very moment he started to climb up the ladder he was aiming for the chief prizes at Cheltenham and Aintree and later at Epsom and Royal Ascot and Longchamp and further afield. He set a record over the jumps that can never be beaten and it was the same on the Flat. He was uncanny.

"The pressure at times was immense, especially in the countdown to Cheltenham. But no man could take it like Vincent O'Brien. They didn't all win, of course. There were setbacks and even in one case at Cheltenham, you had a runner from the stable – Alberoni – 'got at' when the nobblers put acid under his shoes. Overall, year after year, until he reached the point in his career when the stable didn't have to bet anymore, Vincent, as the ledger he kept showed, came out well on top in his tussles with the bookmakers."

Like an army commander keeping mementos of battles long ago, the O'Brien ledger revealed to me that the amount invested on Ahaburn in the County Handicap Hurdle in 1952 was £1,452. That might appear to younger readers to be but "peanuts" compared to J.P. McManus or Barney Curley having £10,000 and more "on the nose" on a prime fancy. But when translated into the money values of today the £1,452 becomes over £20,000.

Aubrey Brabazon was riding Ahaburn. In the parade ring beforehand, Vincent said quietly to 'The Brab': "I think this one should win."

When Vincent ventured something like that, Aubrey knew that the horse was fancied no end.

"We were only cantering at the second last and I said to myself – 'This is going to be easier than Vincent himself imagined.' Then Ahaburn stopped as if he had been shot and finished in the ruck in ninth place," recalled Aubrey.

Vincent was mystified and very dejected at what had happened but he didn't say a word to his jockey.

It wasn't until two days later that it was discovered that

the horse had burst a blood vessel internally. "In such situations instead of bleeding from the nose, the blood will be retained in the system and it's the droppings that reveal to you what has happened," said Aubrey Brabazon.

Ahaburn was injected for the problem. Vincent O'Brien laid him out to win the Irish Cesarewitch later that same year, which he duly did – and recouped with interest the money loaned, you might say, to the bookies at the Festival meeting.

And Vincent's conviction in 1952 that Ahaburn was a made-to-measure potential winner over hurdles at Cheltenham was confirmed three years later when with T.P. Burns in the saddle, he landed a major gamble in the Birdlip Hurdle – the selling hurdle later withdrawn from the Festival programme.

Dermot O'Brien told me that one of the biggest coups of all was brought off on Gladness in the Broughton Plate at Manchester on November 16, 1956.

Dermot went in to have £1,000 with William Hill for "openers" and that representing some salvo thirty-six years ago. The money poured on Gladness as if there was to be no day of reckoning. She went off at 8/11. Considering that in subsequent seasons, she would win the Ascot Gold Cup, the Goodwood Cup and the Ebor Handicap by seven lengths with top weight (9st. 7lbs.) and finish second in the King George VI and Queen Elizabeth Stakes, you can imagine what a cold-stone certainty she was in a big field of maidens over twelve furlongs at Manchester.

Her only previous run had seen her finish unplaced exactly twelve months earlier in the Swilly Maiden at the Curragh.

After a trial against first-class material at Gowran Park, Vincent O'Brien knew that there was no way she could get beaten – bar a fall. And he bet accordingly.

While acknowledging three decades on, that he enjoyed planning coups and bringing them off, he added: "But it was a great strain. My career depended on it absolutely."

"Before the English bookmakers woke up to how good Vincent really was at preparing a horse to win the race he had it earmarked to win, we took them to the cleaners more than once," Nat McNabb told me.

"Yes, we stung them very badly with Hatton's Grace the first year he won the Champion Hurdle in 1949. I know the starting price was 100/7 but we backed him ante-post at 33/1, 25/1 and 20/1 and continued to back him right down the line."

Reflecting on the day – November 19, 1952 – that Knock Hard, with Tim Molony up, ran in the Nuneaton Hurdle at Birmingham, Nat said: "He must have been the greatest certainty of all time when you consider that he had won the Irish Lincolnshire with 8st 12lbs."

Nat's commission on that particular day was to get £10,000 on if possible – a truly massive amount by today's values.

"Knock Hard won even more easily than Gay Future did on an unforgettable occasion at Cartmel. He was actually passing the post when the others were only jumping the last," he noted.

Dermot O'Brien thinks that Vincent's outstanding achievement was the unparalleled record he set in the Gloucestershire Hurdle. Now the Supreme Novices Hurdle, it used to be run in two Divisions as the curtain raiser to the Festival meeting. The record reads: ten winners out of twelve runners in the period 1952-'59. the other two, Knockabout and Courts Appeal, finished second, beaten by two outstanding horses in Tasmin and Albergo respectively.

There came a day, after the successes of Cottage Rake and Hatton's Grace and those successful Gloucestershire Hurdle gambles, when the English bookmakers were no longer taking any chances with runners from the O'Brien stable.

Often when asked to try and pinpoint the basis of his success, Vincent O'Brien has summed it up by saying that it came down to hard work and attention to detail. Total concentration also in trying to avoid mistakes in any direction.

These of themselves would not have sufficed if he didn't have flair in the way he picked potential champions and brought them to the requisite peak of fitness on the day that really mattered. Once he took a liking to a horse he would not be put off, and this was never better illustrated than in the case of The Minstrel, bought for 200,000 dollars and later valued at 9 million dollars.

No one went to the lengths that Vincent went to when it came down to "attention to detail". Noel O'Brien who lives today with his wife, Margaret and family in Glashganniff House – the old O'Brien homestead in Churchtown – pointed out to me the rolling acres of "The Galloping Field" (where cows graze now) over which Vincent exercised his charges when he was establishing himself as a trainer and, significantly, it had the Cheltenham-style uphill climb that tested a stream of winners at the Festival meeting.

Later at Ballydoyle when developing the gallops, Vincent ensured that he had a downhill sweep on one gallop that made it an exact replica of the sweep into Tattenham Corner and again this gallop had an uphill climb at the finish – like the finish at Epsom.

He went for jockeys whose ability he could trust – Martin Molony of the superb horsemanship, electrifying in the way he drove a horse into the last and powered his way to victory; Aubrey Brabazon, who rode to the dictum "hands, very sensitive and delicate, are essential for a successful career with horses"; T.P. Burns, who rode brilliantly over hurdles and on the Flat; the late Tim Molony, Martin's brother, who according to Nat McNabb "conjured victory from the impossible" when winning the 1953 Gold Cup on Knock Hard.

For his Aintree Grand National triumphs, he went for two born horsemen in Bryan Marshall and Pat Taaffe. And Marshall was to oblige by winning in successive years on Early Mist (1953 and Royal Tan (1954) while Pat Taaffe scored on Quare Times (1955) to complete the historic three-timer and, of course, Pat would win the race again in 1970 on Gay Trip for Fred Rimell.

Vincent O'Brien ran four in the 1955 Grand National – Royal Tan (Dave Dick), Early Mist (Bryan Marshall), Oriental Way (Fred Winter) and, of course, Quare Times (Pat Taaffe). Long before the actual day of the race and once he knew what horses he would be entering, he lined up the jockeys he believed would be best for the job on hand.

Again his one hundred per cent attention to detail was shown in the way he gathered the four jockeys in his suite in the Adelphi Hotel on the eve of the race and ran films of the two previous Nationals. As Bryan Marshall had won on Early Mist and Royal Tan, Vincent asked Dave Dick, Fred Winter and Pat Taaffe to study closely the tactics employed by Bryan in victory and advised them to use these tactics as their guidelines. He played the films not just once but a number of times. And, as Pat Taaffe recalled for me: "He pointed out what he felt we should avoid and indicated too the best route to take, especially in the case of the very tricky run to Becher's Brook."

When Vincent held that meeting on tactics, it looked as if the going would be goodish. But it rained all night and he had Pat Taaffe back up in his suite next morning to discuss new tactics.

Apart from Quare Times winning the race, two of Vincent's three other contenders finished the course, Early Mist taking ninth place and Royal Tan Twelfth. Oriental Way was brought down at the eleventh fence.

When the Keoghs decided to switch Hatton's Grace, Royal Tan and Castledermot to Churchtown in the summer of 1948 from the Barney Nugent stable, Vincent O'Brien would only take them on condition that they would not see a racecourse for quite sometime and he let it be known that he was prepared to wait a year with the trio, if necessary.

"Vincent was determined that he would be given time to build up the horses we sent him. He wanted to do his own thing. He didn't want to be hurried or rushed into anything. He did not let us see them until October. Vincent's patience was tremendous and, of course, it paid off handsomely," recalled Moya Keogh, whose husband died in 1964.

Vincent was true to his word, as Hatton's Grace didn't see a racecourse for five months and had just two outings in 1949 before he won the Champion Hurdle for the first time.

Moya Keogh, who looks the very picture of elegance in the old prints of her leading in Hatton's Grace, brought me back to the Cheltenham that Vincent O'Brien knew as he was beginning to make his way up the ladder to international stature as a trainer. A Cheltenham that was more intimate than it is today. Wooden stands where now there is concrete. No executive boxes in which business concerns dispense lunch and largesse and interminable drinks to patrons whose interest in racing may be nil or at best very casual.

Charter flights were as yet unknown. The invasion of the Cotswolds that the Eighties would bring was still a long way off. There was no question of putting a limit on the crowd for Gold Cup Day (now set at 50,000) and certainly no question of selling Club badges in advance for all three days. It would have been unthinkable for the then manager of Cheltenham racecourse to come across to Ireland – as Edward Gillespie did before the 1988 Festival meeting – to explain why they were compelled to go all-ticket.

"We didn't fly initially," Moya Keogh recalled. "We went over by boat and took the train on to Cheltenham. Later we would take over the car in the ferry to Liverpool and drive the rest of the journey. The Queen's Hotel and The Plough (now no more) were the centres of much of the action for the Irish. We always stayed outside the town, the first year in an old Manor House that had a big blazing fire. Dan and Joan Moore stayed there that year also. Someone said it was haunted. I got a funny feeling myself. We didn't stay there again.

"I remember the gatherings – the O'Briens and their friends and we and our friends. Nat McNabb, of course. Aubrey would be there at dinner. It was like a family gathering. No hectic late nights. Nothing but race talk. They would talk racing until the cows came home. Vincent and Aubrey and Nat McNabb talking about the opposition, talking tactics and you had to be impressed with the knowledge they showed. You got the feeling of people being keyed up, an air of expectancy about the morrow."

Hand-in-hand with Vincent's successes at Cheltenham and Aintree went a growing total of victories on the home front and naturally it led to jealousy. It seemed unthinkable to those "up country" that a Churchtown-based stable should make such a mark both in Ireland and in Britain. It intensified after the move to Ballydoyle in 1951 and there was no diminution in his record of success. "The stewards, 95 per cent of them, came from up country," Vincent himself noted.

Reflecting on the occasion when Vincent first lost his licence in 1954 for three calendar months over alleged discrepancy between the English and Irish form of four horses trained by him (namely, Royal Tan, Lucky Dome, Early Mist and Knock Hard), Dermot expressed the view that on the broader plane it was only natural and human that there should have been jealousy of his brother's success, extending right across the board, even to owners who did not have horses in the stable and to trainers who could not match his strike rate. And as Vincent at that point was still winning his biggest prizes in the National Hunt arena, especially in Britain, one could expect that in a country where racing over the jumps meant so much, trainers of National Hunt horses had to be envious.

Later would follow the terrible pain and hurt for Jacqueline and himself, as they had to leave Ballydoyle for a year and Phonsie took over the training of Vincent's string, when Chamour was found to have one ten thousandth of a grain of something resembling methylamphetamine in his system after winning a race for maidens worth just £202 at the Curragh in April, 1960 when starting at odds of 4/6. And the stable didn't have a penny on him. I have recounted the full details of that extraordinary episode in Vincent O'Brien's career in my biography of The Master of Ballydoyle. Suffice it to say here that Vincent fought tooth and nail to clear his name, even to the extent of bringing the Stewards of the Turf Club to the High Court and forced from them a humiliating admission over a wrong entry in the *Races Past Plus Calendar* (Bound) for 1960, and an apology "for any suffering and injury caused to him and his family.

At the end of the 1958 Flat season – a season marked by the astonishing triumphs of Ballymoss and Gladness – the

Sunday Times hailed Vincent O'Brien as "the greatest train-er since Fred Darling."

If Cheltenham first revealed O'Brien's great talents as a jumping trainer, Aintree set the seal on them.

He acquired the patronage of American John McShain and bought five yearlings for him, all of which won, and the batch included Ballymoss. Vincent never looked back from that moment.

When his concentration was principally on the jumps, he took what horses were offered to him. And, as he put it to me, "the people I was training for liked to gamble and they had the money to gamble."

"We did all right," he added. A classic of understatement.

Now he had the financial backing to pick and choose. The new breed of owners patronising Ballydoyle wanted to experience the thrill of owning Classic winners – horses with the potential to win the Epsom Derby, which for the Americans was the parallel on this side of the Atlantic of their own glamour race for three year old colts, the Kentucky Derby. They dreamed too of leading one in at Longchamp on Prix de l'Arc de Triomphe day and even taking the Washington DC International Stakes, as Sir Ivor did in the hands of Lester Piggott in 1968.

Anyway, Vincent did not disappoint these wealthy Americans. He won the Epsom Derby for John Galbraith with Roberto and before he died at 54 in 1971, Charles Engelhard had the thrill of seeing Nijinsky win the Triple Crown.

Enter now yet another millionaire into the world of Vincent O'Brien, who unlike Charles Engelhard and John Galbraith – both American to the core – was Irish natural born, a self-made man who represented the classic example of one who made it right to the top of the ladder from the humblest beginnings.

John A. (Jack) Mulcahy, who was born in Dungarvan, County Waterford took the emigrant ship to the United States when the foundling Irish Free State (later to become a Twenty-six County Republic) was still only finding its way after a disastrous and bitter Civil War, returning a millionaire, he bought Ashford Castle and turned it into one of the best hotels in Ireland; he also built the Waterville Lake Hotel in County Kerry in the mid-Sixties and beside it a golf course which was to prove as tough a test as one could find anywhere in the world. He brought top golfers, including big-name Americans, to play there, testing their skill against its long fairways and large greens and when he was 65 he was still playing to a four handicap.

Vincent O'Brien was introduced to John Mulcahy by the latter's brother Dan, an old friend of the O'Brien family and attached to the Munster and Leinster Bank (now A.I.B.) in Cork, where Vincent had maintained an account since he started training after his father died in 1943.

So a new partnership was born and with it a complete change in Vincent's modus operandi.

Already Vincent and 'Bull' Hancock of the Claiborne Stud Farm in Kentucky had become close friends. John Mulcahy, with his shrewd business brain, saw immediately how this could be utilised.

The idea simply was that instead of all the Claiborne yearlings being sent to the sales, some of them would be trained by Vincent O'Brien and another percentage in the States (a number running in 'Bull' Hancock's own colours and others in his friend's Bill Perry's colours).

Vincent and his patrons not alone got Apalachee and Lisadell in the first lot but also a slice of the action.

And one of the most successful horses of all that arrived at Ballydoyle through this concept was Thatch, rated the outstanding miler in Europe in 1973 after winning the St. James's Palace Stakes at Royal Ascot and the Sussex Stakes at Goodwood, partnered by Lester Piggott as he carried the Mulcahy colours to victory in both these races. Later he would stand at Coolmore.

Like all owners John Mulcahy had his ups and downs and he regarded it as a "hell of a loss" that Cloonlara, carrying a foal by Northern Dancer, should have been killed by lightning at Claiborne.

He never realised his great ambition to be part owner of an Epsom Derby winner.

But the influence he had on Vincent O'Brien was in a

way more invaluable than if he had seen his colours carried to victory at Epsom by a horse trained at Ballydoyle.

Having won three successive Champion Hurdles, four Gold Cups, including a three-timer with Cottage Rake and three successive Grand Nationals, Vincent O'Brien took the Epsom Derby six times through Larkspur (1962), Sir Ivor (1968), Nijinsky (1970), Roberto (1972), The Minstrel (1977) and Golden Fleece (1982) and the Prix de l'Arc de Triomphe three times through Ballymoss (1958) and Alleged (1977 and '78) among innumerable big race triumphs.

As I write in 1992 the overall record reads sixteen English classics, twenty-seven Irish Classics and one French Classic, making a total of 44. If you add to this figure the three Prix de l'Arc de Triomphe victories, the three successes in the King George VI and Queen Elizabeth Stakes and the two big races on the other side of the Atlantic namely the Washing DC International Stakes and the Breeders' Cup Mile (Turf), you get a grand total of 52.

It was the challenge, according to Tom MacGinty, that really inspired Vincent O'Brien and brought out the genius in him – the challenge of selecting, or breeding, a young horse and bringing it to a racing peak.

"He was, and still is, essentially a very private person but I recall how he once quietly reflected and then expressed 'surprise' that Paddy Prendergast was campaigning with others for a Tote monopoly on the basis that it would put Irish racing on a firm footing. 'Paddy and I owed more to our successful dealings with bookmakers than most people,' said Vincent almost nonchalantly – but it was an acknowledgement from the Master of Ballydoyle of how important the gambles had been in the early days as he climbed up the ladder. With a Tote monopoly, the price wouldn't have been right when carefully-planned coups were landed.

While acknowledging that 'Darkie' Prendergast was unlucky to run up against Seabird II with Meadow Court in 1965, Christy Kinane felt that Vincent's strike rate in the Epsom Derby put him ahead of the Master of Rossmore Lodge. "No, as far as I am concerned, Vincent stands head and shoulders above them all. We will not see his like again."

Vincent O'Brien celebrated his 75th birthday on April 9, 1992. While his youngest son, Charles, the Heir Apparent, was by now dealing with much of the nitty-gritty of day-to-day responsibilities and taking much of the work-load from his father's shoulders (including handling calls from the media), the Master of Ballydoyle was still maintaining his regular routine of being out on the gallops with first lot each morning. "He's amazing for a man of his age," said Charles.

When I asked Vincent if he had any idea of stepping down, he replied simply: "It's hard to break the habits of years."

PART SIXTEEN

'MINCEMEAT JOE' GRIFFIN
His Life And Times A Film Script In Itself

21

Going for a £100,000 touch on the National

When Vincent O'Brien told "Mincemeat Joe" Griffin that Early Mist would win the 1953 Aintree Grand National, the intrepid Dubliner backed the horse to win £100,000 – an absolute fortune in those days – in just two bets with English bookmakers, Wilf Sherman and Jack Swift. The latter had the cheque framed in his office.

In the period 1950 to 1953 the man to whom they gave the tag of "Lucky" achieved what members of the aristocracy and money barons had spent their lives trying to achieve and yet failed to realise. He won the Grand National not just once but twice in succession and could have made it three-in-a-row had he taken the advice of Vincent O'Brien and purchased Quare Times when it was offered to him for £2,500 – and if his fortunes had not taken a plunge in the meantime.

In three short years he won £65,000 in stake money and winning bets brought that figure well beyond the £100,000 mark. Multiply it by ten and you can quickly calculate that he was in the millionaire class as a successful owner.

But like Terry Ramsden, who came after him and who spurned all the dictums on betting that the professionals would regard as sacrosanct if you are to survive, he was picked clean by the bookmakers as the vultures pick clean the bones of a dead body under a hot desert sun. One year after Jack Swift had framed the cheque he sent to "Mincemeat Joe", the same bookmaker was in the position that Griffin had liabilities extending to £65,000 to him. That in itself gives an idea of the extraordinary level of "Mincemeat Joe's" gambling.

In the books of racing records, like *Ruff's Guide to the Turf*, you read simply "Mr. J.H. Griffin" in the space where the name of the winning owner is carried after the Grand National triumphs of Early Mist and Royal Tan. For most racing folk, however, the entry, "Trained M.V. O'Brien in Ireland" has far greater significance. In fact, the name J.H. Griffin would mean nothing to many of the younger generation today.

To bring back the veil on the era of "Mincemeat Joe" is to relive a flamboyant career that would outscore the most vivid portrait painted by any fiction writer. Dick Francis, I am sure, could write a thriller around the life and times of Joe Griffin and readers would not believe that it was based on fact. "You know, they could make a film of my life and they would be queuing at the box office to see it," said Joe himself twenty-two years after the collapse of his business empire and racing interests. A further fourteen years on and the film Joe dreamed of had still not been made.

The script would have shown how he graduated from a humble home in Dublin's heartland to a millionaire's mansion in Templeogue, from an ordinary spectator at the Sport of Kings to the Prince of the Turf, from a few shillings-a-day punter to a £5,000-a-race gambler.

It would have shown how he was born in Dublin's Montague Street – the kind of area immortalised in Sean O'Casey's *Juno and the Paycock* and *The Plough and the Stars*. He was christened Joseph Harold Griffin but from the time he was nine years old, he was known as nothing else but "Lucky" Joe. The "Mincemeat" tag would come later. On the strength of a borrowed £16 he built an export empire that would make him the envy of men who knew more about business and figures than Joe had even begun to learn.

He remembered always what his mother had said to him when he bought two tickets for a Christmas raffle at the age of 9 and won the hamper: "Joe, it's better to be born lucky than rich."

Subsequently, he never forgot belief in his own star and the feeling that his luck would always hold became almost pathological with him.

At one stage he had 500 workers employed in the Tallaght factory of his Redbreast Preserving Company.

Now the film director would have had the cameras zoom in on the tragic climax, culminating in the Black Friday in July, 1954 when he was adjudged a bankrupt and he closed the door for the last time on his magnificent Georgian residence, Knocklyon House, standing on 24 acres with orchards, paddocks and gardens, which he had bought for £8,000 and on which he had spent £30,000 in decorating and renovating to palatial standards (its accommodation included four reception rooms, eight family bedrooms, a ballroom and a billiards room).

The cameras would have caught the moment when Joe's wife asked their little daughter how – in Joe's own words – "she felt about leaving such a grand place."

"Mammy," she replied, "sure I would never get a boyfriend if we stayed out there!"

And a tragedy that would have done justice to the last climactic scene of *Juno and the Paycock* did not end there.

Two bailiffs, on the Sheriff's instructions, had gone to Vincent O'Brien's Ballydoyle stables and impounded all Joe's horses, including Grand National winner, Royal Tan. Joe looked on helplessly as all his other possessions – even down to his racing binoculars – passed into the hands of the bankruptcy court's official assignee. Subsequently, even his two Grand National Gold Cup trophies – gold cups each weighing 50 ozs. – were auctioned in Dublin.

In what one newspaper described as "The Best Show In Town", hundreds thronged to the R.D.S. in Ballsbridge for the sale of the Griffin horses. The newsreel cameras whirred as, in the presence of many leading racing personalities, on that grey November day in 1954, Royal Tan was knocked down to the representative of Prince Aly Khan for 3,900 guineas and Early Mist was sold to Vincent O'Brien for 2,000 guineas.

Galatian, winner of eleven races, including the Old

Newton Cup at Haydock Park and runner-up twice to Sir Ken in the Champion Hurdle, was also knocked down to Vincent O'Brien for 1,900 guineas. "I like to keep old friends," said the trainer.

Teapot II, for which Joe Griffin had paid £10,000, fetched a mere 40 guineas.

The eight sold realised 8,178 guineas. "Mincemeat" Joe had paid £20,000 for three of them.

It was undoubtedly his blackest hour. "All the world's in a state of chassis," he could have cried with Captain Boyle at that moment.

But there had been a time when it seemed that the days of wine and roses would last forever.

Joe was small and stocky with twinkling eyes – the direct opposite of the archetype business tycoon that you would expect to leap out of the screen at you from a film like *Wall Street*. But he had a sharp brain and that native Dublin cunning that made him see a good business opportunity.

In the food shortages that still persisted after the Second World War, the English hankered for 'goodies' that were taken for granted in Ireland. "Joe, we haven't seen mince pies for years," an English friend remarked to him. His mind immediately began to tick over.

He bought on 'tick' from the Greek Government a £100,000 shipload of dried fruit, a cancelled order from a British grocery chain. He used the fruit in mince pies and sold the product in jars to the same British grocers for £20,000. It was easy to pay the Greek Government on the resultant profit. Joe was on his way with the tag of "Mincemeat" that he never subsequently lost.

The Redbreast Preserving Company was on the crest of a wave for a time, turning over, according to Joe Griffin; "£½ million to £2 million a year in exports for three years and that at the time was a lot of money coming into the country for a single exporter."

After the fall, however, Joe would admit: "I had no background training for big business. I had nobody to help me – it was a one-man show. I brought in an accountant whom I hoped would have been able to keep everything

311

on a proper legal and financial footing. I had the brains to do things and to sell but I lacked the experience to control the finance."

Without the necessary control, the "unorthodox" accounting practices that came to light at the bankruptcy trial, were certain to happen. One of the most bizarre was the disclosure that a cheque drawn on the company for £5,565 and entered in the ledger under the heading "raw materials" was for the purchase of Early Mist.

The bankruptcy hearing was the final humiliation for Joe Griffin, leading to the point where he was forced to promise that he would not go to the Grand National of 1956. His passport had been taken away and it was only given back to him when he gave a categorical assurance that he would not travel to Liverpool.

The nightmare of his two-year legal grilling in the bankruptcy courts would haunt him for years.

It took a court stenographer three and a half days to read the record of the bankruptcy proceedings at a subsequent trial in the District Court.

"Nobody was persecuted the way I was persecuted," Joe said bitterly when ten years after he had left Ireland and was living in Orpington in Kent, making a living out of a small family business, *Sunday Independent* feature writer, Frank Byrne tracked him down for an absorbing and brutally-frank series of articles.

"My trial became a public showpiece," he went on. "I remember once arriving at the Four Courts and there was a queue extending right on to the quayside. The usher had to push his way through the crowd to let me into the court."

Joe could not hide his conviction that a certain group was involved in hounding him into bankruptcy.

"There was somebody behind the whole thing because it was all too nasty to be even half genuine. A fortune was spent on the barristers and solicitors in both the liquidation of my company and in my own bankruptcy. And it was only when there was no more money left to pay the lawyers that my examination in the courts stopped," he claimed.

During the bankruptcy hearing "Mincemeat" Joe had to

spend a month in jail for contempt, having, in the opinion of Mr. Justice Budd, failed to answer the court's questions satisfactorily. "I think you have wasted a lot of time. I think you have prevaricated and you have failed to produce a lot of information that you could have produced," Justice Budd told him. "You have lied quite shamelessly and have been deliberately evasive."

Men and women who had cheered him the night he came home to a hero's welcome to his native city, heading Early Mist in the great victory parade through Dublin's O'Connell Street, now watched in silence as "Mincemeat" Joe was led away to prison between two Gardai after saying goodbye to his weeping wife. All he carried with him were his pyjamas and shaving kit in a small bag.

Many friends deserted the ship. The hangers-on had long since gone. But not everyone forgot Joe in his hour of torment.

Two of his English business associates, Bill Smith and Fred Pontin of Pontin Holiday Camps arrived at his home with a case of champagne. "They knew all about me and they came to bring me a little solace in my darkest hour," said Joe who a decade on had still not forgotten that hands-across-the-Irish Sea gesture of true friendship.

And he never forgot either the magnanimous gesture of Paddy 'Darkie' Prendergast, who sent a messenger to the house with an envelope addressed to his wife containing five £100 notes and a little note to say, 'just in case you're short of money.'

"So I still had some friends left – they weren't all just hangers-on."

Even jail for contempt did not end the torture and torment. He was to find himself behind bars again after purging his contempt.

Later he would say: "What I do regret is that I did not liquidate my company in 1954. Had I done so then, I would still have had all my horses and all my profits; if I had ignored the business and my 500 workers then, I would still be a very wealthy man today."

He blamed his collapse on the fact that he had guaranteed all his creditors personally – "a very stupid thing to do."

"But I was only in my thirties and had no training in these matters. The London finance company, which had a mortgage of £20,000 on my factory, sued me personally under my guarantee and naturally they got judgement. The news appeared on the front page of a Fleet Street daily and, needless to say, everybody jumped in to claim even the £5 notes that were due to them."

His second term in prison he blamed on the fact that he "was not able to get off the ground. One had to get money by fair means or foul."

"I got some goods on credit for a friend who paid me a percentage and I didn't pay for the goods. That was the sum total of my sin."

At one point he received a six months' suspended sentence for a forged £20 cheque and then went to prison for fraud.

During his twelve months in Mountjoy Prison, his spirit never broke. He managed to survive.

"I have never been totally shattered psychologically, because I just would not allow that to happen to me. Even the doctor in Mountjoy said to me – 'I don't understand it, Joe, men of far lesser achievements would be in a mental home if they had to go through what you have gone through'."

Again far from the adulation and back-slapping he had enjoyed at Aintree on the days that Early Mist and Royal Tan triumphed, he had to listen to one Grand National on a transistor radio in the recreation yard in Mountjoy.

"I know I gave everyone the winner of that race. All the prison warders had backed it and there was great cheering when it came in. Naturally, I was treated with the height of respect in Mountjoy. I was the Lord of the Manor."

He even claimed that he had been put in charge of the kitchen and the cooking in Mountjoy. When he was leaving the officer in charge said to him: 'Joe, I hope you won't come back but if you do, you'll come straight down here to the kitchen because you're the best cook we ever had'!"

In Mountjoy jail he had ample time to remember the Camelot days . . . the fabulous victory parties in the Adelphi Hotel in Liverpool (the bash after Early Mist had triumphed in 1953 costing £1,500 and I had started myself as a cub reporter on *The Tipperary Star* in Thurles in 1950 at a salary of £2 a week!) . . . the success his Redbreast Preserving Company was enjoying with profits running in the region of £1,000 a day with the result that money had lost its value for him and, as he put it, "you just spend and spend." There was never a cloud in the sky.

"Money for me is for spending and for making people happy. I have made a lot of people happy – even though I realise now that a lot of them were just hangers-on. I should have chosen my friends more carefully but I have no regrets about spending the money," he would say later, putting a brave face on things – but you wondered.

His wife blended in perfectly into the new world that Joe had discovered and every minute of which he was living to the full and relishing as if the tap from which the finance was coming would never run dry.

On the morning of the 1953 Grand National, Peggy Griffin handed Bryan Marshall a St. Christopher medal and said to him – "Well, if you don't win, at least don't break your neck."

Bryan won by 20 lengths and received a present of £5,000 as Joe Griffin netted a six-figure sum in winning bets.

Joe and Peggy gave a diamond bracelet in platinum, worth £1,000 then, to Joe's secretary, Rose O'Duffy and later it would emerge in the bankruptcy court that Rose pledged the bracelet for £600 and gave a loan from this money to Mrs. Griffin.

Joe had perhaps his proudest moment when a civic reception was accorded Early Mist on his return to Dublin. Thousands turned out to watch as the horse was paraded through O'Connell Street to the Mansion House where the Lord Mayor, Andy Clerkin officiated. It culminated in the gelding receiving a pat on the neck from the Lord Mayor as Joe posed for photographers.

The now-retired Harry McDonald, later to become Head Porter at the Adelphi Hotel – a position he still held when I met him on Grand National eve, 1988 – was a junior porter in the heady days. He recalled for me as if it was only yesterday the sign writers coming in once the result of the National was known and putting up the name "Early Mist" and then "Royal Tan" a year later on a banner flung across the spacious lounge area where the guests at Joe Griffin's fabulous parties would dance after dinner into the early hours to a full orchestra.

The restaurant they now call the Sefton was known then as simply "The French Restaurant" and it was appropriately enough fitted up in green foliage in honour of victory for the Emerald Isle. The tables set in alcoves overlooked the dance area. There was Guinness aplenty for those who tired of champagne. And Irish whiskey also. Whatever you wanted, in fact.

Harry McDonald would never forget the atmosphere generated by those nights with "Mincemeat" Joe at the Adelphi.

Later he would see Roy Rogers bringing Trigger into this same lounge – the famous horse mounting the stairs as thousands of kids screamed in welcome. He remembers Gregory Peck and the adulation he engendered. And "our Harold" (Wilson) smoking a cool pipe as he arrived to talk to his constituents – and of how he loved dear old Liverpool town. And lester Piggott arriving in the days when there was Flat racing at Aintree. The old steam train coming into Central Station before the underground overtook it and the porters going down to meet the train and bringing up the bags.

Harry McDonald remembered great occasions also when Liverpool Football Club used the Adelphi for celebratory dinners, and they added to the store of trophies brought back to Merseyside. But somehow in the whirling nostalgia as we chatted in this same lounge area beside the Sefton Restaurant where they shot scenes for the film on the sinking of the Titanic, it was unmistakably clear to me that the nights created by Joe Griffin had left an imprint on a young porter that could never be erased, especially the memories of the champagne dinner after Early Mist had won "Mincemeat" Joe his first National in 1953.

The Keoghs, Harry and Moya owners of triple Champi-

316

on Hurdle winner, Hatton's Grace, would sell Royal Tan to Joe Griffin to win for him his second National.

Moya Keogh recalled for me the unusual circumstances in which she found herself at the lavish Early Mist victory party in the Adelphi.

"Jacqueline O'Brien was expecting and so did not travel over with Vincent when he left for Liverpool. But as she listened to the commentary on the race, she caught the excitement of Early Mist's 20-lengths win. She rang me immediately and said simply: 'We'll go over, Moya.' Of course, it was all dependent on my being able to arrange two seats on a flight to Liverpool in double-quick time. I told Jacqueline I would ring her back.

"I had to pull strings to get the two seats. Everyone in Aer Lingus was as excited as we were at Early Mist's victory for Ireland and they kindly provided the seats for Jacqueline and myself – on a freight plane, due to leave that evening. Jacqueline rushed by road to Dublin Airport where I was waiting for her – and I had even bought two orchids, one for each of us.

"We sat on two tea-chests with our evening dresses on our laps. We didn't have to go through Customs, as we were probably regarded as 'freight' on that flight!

"We jumped into a taxi at Liverpool Airport and, arriving at the Adelphi, dashed up the steps with our evening dresses ready to put on immediately we got to a room to change. Just as the speeches were commencing, we walked into the lounge looking cool, calm and collected. Vincent O'Brien was never one to show emotion in public but he certainly was surprised to see Jacqueline and myself arriving out of the blue."

The parties in the Adelphi were followed by homecoming parties in the Gresham Hotel and in the Kilcoran Lodge Hotel in Cahir, County Tipperary with bonfires blazing on the hillsides and bands out to lead the victory parades.

Yes, "Mincemeat Joe" had a lot to remember during the hours he spent in his cell in Mountjoy Prison . . .

He left Ireland in the early sixties after – as he put it himself – "the life and soul had been squeezed out of me by the lawyers and creditors."

"I am on the way back," said Joe about fifteen years later, no doubt convincing himself that his mother's original words would somehow come true again for him.

He even dreamed of winning a third Aintree Grand National – "to beat Raymond Teasy Weasy and the other owners who had won the race twice. Yes, I am going to win it for a third time."

He never did make it back to the big-time. Like Willie Loman he continued to live a dream that was never to be realised.

I was in the Press Room at Leopardstown racecourse on Saturday, January 11, 1992 when Neville Ring walked in and exclaimed: "Mincemeat Joe is dead."

He had died quietly in London at the age of 75.

I felt at that moment as if a close friend of mine had passed away. I had done so much research on 'Lucky' Joe for my biography of Vincent O'Brien and for this book that his life and times had come to fascinate me.

Having alerted the News Desk of the *Sunday Independent*, I left the rest of the racing behind me, once the Ladbroke Handicap Hurdle had been run, and headed for my home, just ten minutes from the course. I sat at the typewriter and fashiond my tribute to the man who for three glorious years had lived true to his mother's maxim – "Joe, it's better to be born lucky than rich." That was before the fall.

I phoned it through. Then I rooted out a head and shoulders photograph of Joe and sent it in by taxi to Willie Kealy, the News Editor. The job was done.

The paper, as we say in the business, gave it a good show on Page 2 the next morning – and there was Joe's smiling face looking out at me at breakfast under the heading, "Death Of Legendary Horse Owner".

I read through all the other English and Irish papers. Hardly a line – but then what would his name mean to the younger generation of newsmen?

At least somebody down here likes you, Joe . . .

318

PART SEVENTEEN

TOMMY O'BRIEN
The Coalminer
Who Blazed A Trail

22

"I've won so much, the bookies won't take any more bets from me."

Tommy O'Brien, known as "Tommy Coal" or "The Coalminer", blazed a trail as one of the biggest gamblers to hit the ring in Ireland and Britain in the Sixties. By today's money values, some of his more spectacular wins and losses were absolutely astounding.

He returned from Cheltenham in 1960 with winnings totalling £30,000. I checked with the Economics Department of the Central Bank to ascertain what that would represent today and the answer came back: "£385,240".

It was the year the Clem Magnier-trained Albergo won the County Hurdle in the hands of Doug Page at 7/4, the Tom Dreaper-trained Fortria (Pat Taaffe) justified 15/8 favouritism in the Champion Chase and Willie O'Grady, Edward's father, had a rare double with Solfen taking the Broadway Novices Chase (now the Sun Alliance Chase) at 5/4, ridden by Pat Taaffe and, coming out again the following day, won the Spa Hurdle (at 5/2 favourite) with Bobby Beasley in the saddle.

O'Brien waded in on these hotpots as if there was going to be no day of reckoning. He rang up his private trainer, Willie Treacy in Clonmel to tell him with glee: "I've won so much that I can't lose now, as the bookies won't take any more bets from me."

He was such a born compulsive gambler, however, that he didn't know when to stop. Nothing illustrates this better than a day at the Curragh in April of the same year

321

when his own horse, Miss MacDonald, ridden by Tommy Doyle, won the April Scurry Handicap by half-a-length from Guerco with Flower-De-Luce a further short head away third.

Miss MacDonald started 2/1 favourite and O'Brien took £22,000 out of the ring (I had moved on from *The Tipperary Star* at that point and was editing Tommy O'Brien's own paper, *The Munster Tribune* from its Clonmel office for around £10,000 a year and here was the proprietor losing in one race more than I could earn in two years).

Willie Treacy appealed to a friend of his to "take Tommy O'Brien up to the bar and keep him there until I join you."

"Of course, in the flush of winning the £22,000, he was hell bent on aiming for the moon," recalled Willie Treacy. "By the time I got from the stabling area to the bar, he had gone down into the ring not just once but a number of times. As we were driving home from the races, I remarked to him – 'that must have been one of the best days you ever had?' – thinking of the six-figure sum he had netted on Miss MacDonald. He shot back: 'A good day, did you say? I owe them £30,000.'

In the space of an hour or so, from being £22,000 ahead of the bookies, he had fallen £30,000 behind – a turnover of over £50,000. Awesome is the only word to describe it.

No wonder that Willie Treacy should say to me with a tinge of regret in his voice when we met for a long morning's conversation in Clonmel in the summer of '92: "If Tommy O'Brien could have confined himself to backing his own when we had them fit and ready to win, he would have stayed ahead of the bookies. But he was an inveterate gambler and was never prepared to shut up shop when in front."

Tommy O'Brien had another lovely touch at the Curragh in 1960 – in the Autumn Scurry Handicap.

"It was certainly a lucky race for us," said Willie Treacy. "Tommy had bought Ballymaster out of the Seamus McGrath stable and we knew he had ability. A lot of the hotpots had gone down that day and Bill Quinlan had reason to smile on his pitch on the rails. He saw Tommy moving down the line, looking now at Power's board.

'Have you a runner in this, Tommy?' he enquired.

'I have,' said Tommy.

'Do you want a few quid on?'

'What price?', came Tommy's reply.

'8/1 to you, Tommy . . . how much do you want on?'

'I'll take £40,000 to £5,000.'

'Do you want it again?'

'Yes . . . and again,' said Tommy.'

Ballymaster, with John Hunter up and starting at 4/1, won by a head from Lisburn Lad (Herbert Holmes) with Grey Sister (Garnie Bougoure), the even-money favourite three-quarters-of-a-length away third.

The addendum to that particular story – and the taking of the £22,000 out of the ring on Miss MacDonald – is that Willie Treacy once asked Tommy O'Brien: 'Why do you bet with Quinlan?'

'I know I've won when he starts moaning . . . and secondly, I know I'll always get paid when I do win.'

Tommy O'Brien, who was born in Mayo, had come back in the Fifties from England, where he had gained ample experience of mining, to re-open the Ballingarry mines in South Tipperary. By dint of hard work and a real go-go attitude, he proved that a local area could be resuscitated in an era of depressing emigration. He had soon turned it into a going concern, giving good employment in the locality.

He never asked anyone to do something that he couldn't do himself. Once he had a strike on his hands in the Ballingarry mines for increased wages. He told the men that production wasn't high enough to merit it. "If you can take out as much as I can in a day, then I'll pay you more than what you are getting at present," he told them. So he went down the mine and took out so much on the one day that it was impossible for any of the men to take him on in his challenge.

Giving him the appellation "Tommy Coal" distinguished him from the other Tommy O'Brien of Clonmel, who was a national institution from his popular radio programme, which gave so much pleasure and helped to popularise Opera throughout Ireland. Once a visitor to Clonmel stopped his car in the centre of the town to seek directions to Tommy O'Brien's house and a wit standing at the street corner, asked him: "Do you mean 'Tommy Coal' or 'Tommy Ceoil'?"

Tommy O'Brien, that is Tommy of the Ballingarry mines and *The Munster Tribune,* lived with his wife Mary – they had no family – in Woodruff House about five miles outside Clonmel. The house and magnificent estate going with it had belonged to a Mrs. Masters. Tommy O'Brien set out to create on the land the finest gallops imaginable and stabling for fifteen horses. Willie Treacy, who had been riding over the jumps for fifteen years, both in England and Ireland, became his private trainer and they would enjoy a very rewarding partnership together, landing some outstanding coups. "He was a genius in many ways, a man with a great brain who was well ahead of his time in the way he could see things," said Willie Treacy. "He would buy into a share when you couldn't give it away and in that way, I know, he cleaned up. Despite what he lost in the end through gambling, he was always comfortable and Mary didn't have to worry."

Tommy O'Brien was a man brusque of manner, with no airs or graces whatsoever. But there was a spontaneous and very generous side to his nature – seen in his kindness to renowned racecourse characters of his day like "Buckets", "Big Andy" and "The Toucher".

"Big Andy" was the intrepid card seller, who gave a racecard free, going in and collected a pound on the way out. Twinny Byrne or "The Toucher" always found his way into the winner's enclosure after big races and tendered Fox's mints to the connections while "Buckets", a rotund part-time cattle-drover was a law unto himself.

Tommy O'Brien, according to Willie Treacy, would pass no one on the road looking for a lift. One day he was returning from Leopardstown with Mary and Willie in the car and saw "Buckets" ambling along. "We will have to give a lift to 'Buckets'," he said to Mary. There and then he opened the door and shouted: "Get in 'Buckets'." He never regretted such an act and, when sundry hangers-on came in for the "kill" after he had enjoyed a successful day at the

324

races as an owner and punter, he couldn't turn them away.

The headstrong and compulsive side of his character was his undoing as a gambler. It led also to his tragic death when he was still only in his fifties.

He had sold Woodruff House and the estate and left Clonmel for Kinsale, hoping to live a quiet life in semi-retirement by the sea. The great gambling days were behind him now but there was no debt to any bookmaker.

Soon he was back running an earth moving business, not satisfied because of his nature just to enjoy the company of "the boating set". He was too down-to-earth. He needed a challenge always – like the challenge he had seen in making Bill Quinlan moan.

He loved Clonmel. One day he was heading there for the vintage car rally – the one they knew as the stone thrower's rally. But first there was a job to be done. Tommy wanted to see it completed and took the wheel of a tractor himself when there was no need for him to do so. Again his impetuous nature had got the better of him. He drove it down a sharp incline into a pit. It turned over and he was crushed under it.

He had been a High Roller in the true sense . . . long before J.P. (The Sundance Kid) McManus, Noel Furlong and Barney Curley became household names.

There are few episodes in the history of great racing gambles to compare with Tommy O'Brien's bid to clear £100,000 on the 1961 Champion Hurdle on his own horse Moss Bank – and, remember, that by today's values that would have been equivalent to taking £1 million out of the ring, if he had succeeded.

So certain was he of bringing it off that he booked a luxury cruise for his wife Mary and himself in the immediate aftermath of the Cheltenham meeting.

All through the winter he had been taking all available ante-post odds on Moss Bank, which had been bred by Frank Tuthill, then the Senior Irish Racing Judge, who sold him as a foal at Ballsbridge for 635 guineas. There was no doubting the fact that he was a horse with a touch of class. His half-brother, Gustav won the 1961 Middle Park Stakes at Newmarket.

O'Brien's confidence increased when Moss Bank, ridden by Doug Page, won the Dolphin Hurdle at the Leopardstown meeting at 4/6. Now more than ever he was going for the jugular and he laughed inwardly at the thought of the bookies going pale at the gills as Moss Bank stormed up the hill to a great "Irish roar" come Champion Hurdle Day at Cheltenham.

Willie Treacy, like a true professional, knew that no stone must be left unturned in the effort to book the best jockey available. Doug Page was already booked for Albergo but there were others who would give their right hand for the ride.

At this stage the career of Johnny Rafferty was in sad decline. He was a victim of the demon drink and there was no escape. He went down the long tunnel of despair, so distant from the time of blossoming talent when his symmetry of style in the saddle was enough to make the adrenalin course in the veins as he brought one over the last hurdle thrillingly for victory. Johnny Rafferty died young . . . and it would be kind to let the epitaph read "those whom the Gods love die young" . . . but he who had been born with a gift not given to many, had allowed it to be dispersed like chaff in the wind.

Tommy O'Brien was at a Leopardstown meeting when Johnny Rafferty told him that he would win the Ticknock Handicap Hurdle on Rouge Scot. O'Brien took him at his word. He set the ring alight. Rouge Scot ended up starting 7/2 joint-favourite and duly landed a massive gamble for "The Coalminer".

So delighted was O'Brien that he promised Johnny Rafferty there and then that he would have the ride on Moss Bank for the rest of the year. Rafferty rode the horse for the first time the following weekend when he finished second to Vulsa in the Proudstown Handicap Hurdle. Those behind included the 1960 Champion Hurdle winner, Another Flash (gave 12 lbs) and Albergo (gave 7 lbs). Some good judges felt that Moss Bank, carrying only 11-2, would actually have had to win that day if he was to justify the very short price of 7/4 he would start at in the Champion Hurdle itself.

But Tommy O'Brien was undeterred. Everything was on course for the BIG ONE and his confidence was not affected in the least.

Not so in the case of Willie Treacy. He was appalled when he learned that the ride in the Champion Hurdle had been surrendered to all intents and purposes to Johnny Rafferty when the owner told him that he would ride the horse for the rest of the year in any race over the sticks.

Treacy pulled no punches in letting O'Brien know his feelings. "Now you have really put your foot in it," he said.

When Another Flash had to be withdrawn at the eleventh hour, Willie Treacy could see that what had been a terrible mistake initially was now compounded by a situation where Bobby Beasley, one of the finest jockeys of that era and scion of a great family of born horsemen, had suddenly become available and Tommy O'Brien had tied himself to Johnny Rafferty.

In fact, Paddy Sleator brought Tommy O'Brien back to earth with a resounding thump when he said to him at Cheltenham on the day of the race: "Moss Bank would be a certainty if Bobby Beasley was up."

O'Brien came running frantically to Willie Treacy. "I'll do what you suggested initially and replace him with Bobby Beasley."

"It's too late. He has your colours on . . . you can't jock him off at this stage," was Treacy's response. He added: "All we can do is hope for the best and say nothing."

So Moss Bank with Johnny Rafferty in the saddle, wearing the familiar O'Brien Cross of Lorraine colours, went down to the start with no one outside of the owner and trainer knowing the drama that had been played out from the fateful moment when Rafferty told "The Coalminer" at Leopardstown that he would win on Rouge Scot and caused a decision to be taken in haste that in all probability killed the hope of a £100,000 gamble being landed.

The clear instructions to Johnny Rafferty were that he must avoid at all costs tracking Albergo. "We expected that Albergo would cave in when the heat was really turned on," recalled Willie Treacy. He fell at the second last. Moss

Bank had to swerve to avoid him. Johnny Rafferty had to start his run all over again. Moss Bank was eating up the ground at the finish but had too much to do and was beaten three lengths."

Victory went to the 4/1 shot Eborneezer, trained by Ryan Price and ridden by Fred Winter.

Tommy O'Brien went ahead with the luxury cruise. When Willie Treacy conveyed to him, before they parted at Cheltenham, that the losses on Moss Bank could be recouped on Antirrhinum "tried a certainty" to win the Portmarnock Handicap at Baldoyle on St. Patrick's Day, O'Brien told him: "Tell Michael O'Hehir to do the commission for me and that I want £10,000 on."

Michael O'Hehir managed to get £7,000 on at 7/1 and £49,000 was an immense amount of money to take out of the ring on one race in 1961. Antirrhinum, with Peadar Matthews in the saddle, started at 6/1 and won easily by three lengths from the Charlie Weld-trained favourite, Flower-De-Luce in a field of fifteen. Unplaced, incidentally, was Le Levanstell who later the same year in the Queen Elizabeth II Stakes at Ascot beat the 2/9 favourite Petite Etoile (Lester Piggott).

After losing the Champion Hurdle, Moss Bank was switched to the Flat for his next trip to Britain, to contest the Usher Brewery Gold Tankard at Ayr. Trying to give away the best part of a stone, he was beaten a short head by Three Wishes.

In the unsaddling enclosure Bill Williamson said to Willie Treacy and Tommy O'Brien: "I threw away the race. But I'll win the Queen Alexandra for you."

Williamson was given the ride for the Royal Ascot stamina test. He was true to his word. Taking the lead before the final turn, He guided Moss Bank with supreme confidence to an eight-lengths triumph over the Queen's horse, Agreement.

Tommy O'Brien had a very nice "touch". By now the Cheltenham losses should not alone have been wiped out but he should have been smiling all the way to the bank. However, he wouldn't confine himself to backing his own when there was money to be made; he had to play up his

328

winnings on horses from other stables that were "whispered" to him – and he was never short of information. Sometimes he would ask those "passing on the word" to put him on for a fairly substantial sum, clearly understanding that he would get paid if the horse won. But as often as not he wasn't paid. "You trust no one in this game," was the advice Willie Treacy proffered – but it fell on deaf ears.

In 1962 Moss Bank made his last trip to England for the Ebor Handicap at York. He was set to carry 9-2 and finished 5th to Sostenuto – a very game performance in the circumstances.

Willie Treacy had brought Moss Bank to Mallow for a final gallop in the countdown to the Ebor. He put in Ribena – a maiden – at level weights and, while Moss Bank duly came out best in the gallop, Treacy knew from the way Ribena had gone that she was an absolute certainty for the Slieve Mish Plate at the up-coming Tralee meeting.

He journeyed with Tommy O'Brien to Mallow where "The Coalminer" had arranged to meet a few great buddies of his, John A. Wood and Mick Sheehan. These were among the leading "heavy boys" of that era when it came to betting and it was nothing, for example, for John A. Wood to have £6,000-£4,000 on a 6/4 shot or £12,000 to win £8,000 on a 4/6 shot and, as Willie Treacy indicated to me, he could take it on the chin like a man if a hot favourite he backed went down.

Across the luncheon table in the Mallow hotel, John A. Wood said quietly to Willie Treacy: "Is this one as good as I am led to believe, Willie?"

"Almost good enough to fall down and get up and still win," came the confident reply. And then Treacy outlined to the fearless Cork punter about the Mallow racecourse gallop and how Ribena's showing that day against Moss Bank in relation to the Ebor Handicap form put her head and shoulders above the calibre of the opposition in the Tralee race.

"That's good enough for me," said John A. Wood, giving a quick glance in the direction of Mick Sheehan, who nodded his assent.

The "heavy boys" from Cork with Tommy O'Brien, wading in with them, hit the Tralee ring in a fashion that made it seem that a hurricane had descended on the Kerry track. Ribena went up on the boards initially at 6/1. By the time the boys were finished a number of boards were showing no price.

Willie Treacy had his own limit bet on of £500. Ribena, with Mick Kennedy up, won in the proverbial canter by ten lengths.

Unquestionably, the unluckiest horse that Tommy O'Brien owned – and, indeed, one of the unluckiest in the history of Irish racing – was Ballet Royal. Over a two-month period in the summer of 1959 O'Brien lost a fortune on him. Ironically enough, if he had obliged even on two of the occasions when the money was really down, there is little doubt that "The Coalminer" would have inflicted on the bookies a hammering they would not have easily forgotten.

Ballet Royal had been unplaced in four of his previous five races (the best he could do in one of them was a third, beaten 4½ lengths) when Tommy O'Brien went for a real old-fashioned "killing" on him in a six-furlongs event at the Curragh on June 10, 1959. Ridden that day by an "unknown" apprentice, one A. Woods, Ballet Royal opened at 33/1. The weight of Tommy O'Brien's money brought him down to 10/1, though on form, according to Terry Rogers, he had "no earthly chance of winning."

If he had come up trumps, O'Brien would have taken so much out of the ring that some of the bookies would have needed quite a time to settle with him. Ballet Royal was a good six lengths in front approaching the winning post when he suddenly veered right and was beaten a short head by Final Word.

At the Irish Derby meeting two weeks later, O'Brien went on a recovery mission and again the odds were right. Gerry Cooney had the ride this time. "The Coalminer" struck some massive wagers but still with four duck-eggs, a third and a second to his name in six outings, the bookies allowed Ballet Royal to start at 13/2.

Once again he was in a clear lead near the post when he

swerved violently, unseating his rider and leaving Final Word to score a bloodless victory.

Terry Rogers thinks that Ballet Royal may have been upset at the sound of the photo finish equipment as he neared the finishing post. However, Willie Treacy explained to me that Ballet Royal was a very highly-strung and excitable horse and even at home "if you lifted your hand he would glance around." The mere movement of the whip from one hand to the other in a finish or bringing the hands up head high would be enough to disturb Ballet Royal and cause him to swerve.

Now Liam Ward, one of the most accomplished jockeys of his day, with a number of Classic triumphs to his name, including victory in the Irish Derby on Nijinsky for Vincent O'Brien in 1970 and an earlier triumph on Sindon (1958) for owner, Mrs. Anne Biddle, was engaged to ride Ballet Royal at the Curragh (6f) on July 4. This time Ballet Royal, starting at 2/5, did nothing wrong but Ward's strong run from a furlong out was thwarted in exasperating fashion by Charme, which won a short head.

On then to the Phoenix Park four days later. Ballet Royal, with Liam Ward once more in the saddle, started at 3/1 in a five-furlong event. The records show that he was beaten a short head by Little Lustre.

Liam Ward, however, objected for alleged "bumping and interference" and told Willie Treacy and Tommy O'Brien confidently: "I'll get this." But Liam didn't know that, as the field split into two groups, the camera was trained on one of them and missed the moment when his mount was crossed. Ward had been fully confident that the camera would vindicate his evidence. The objection was lost.

"Jinxed, totally jinxed," was all Willie Treacy could say about Ballet Royal.

It didn't end there. Liam Browne rode him in the Howth Handicap (5f) at Baldoyle on July 22, 1959 when again looking all over a winner approaching the post, he veered left and was beaten half-a-length by Red Sovereign.

The final tragic chapter was written on the August Bank Holiday (August 3), 1959 in the Hollywood Handicap (5f) at Leopardstown. Ballet Royal, with Liam Browne in the saddle, started 11/10 favourite.

Inside the distance he broke his shoulder, dislodged his jockey and had to be put down immediately.

There was no greater supporter of Ballet Royal than Tommy O'Brien's close friend, Dan Breen, a legendary figure in Ireland's War for Independence. On one of the days when the horse threw his rider, Dan, who had left all the money he had on him that day with the bookies, remarked to Willie Treacy: "I'd better go down and see how the jockey has come out of the fall." And Treacy seeing the funny side of things in a continuing tale of disaster and woe where this jinxed sprinter was concerned, could only quip: "Have you got the gun with you, Dan!"

Mary O'Brien, a gracious lady, lives quietly today with her memories in a lovely bungalow-style home on Ireland's south coast. Talking to her, you form the immediate impression that Tommy is still very much alive for her.

But then could it be otherwise? "The Coalminer" was larger than life, one who left an indelible imprint as one of the most fearless – if compulsive – gamblers of his era.

Whenever the cards are cut in the Dunamore Club in Clonmel, they talk affectionately of one Tommy O'Brien . . . and memories come flooding back of great poker "schools" in which he was involved in long winter evenings.

Yes, the legend of "The Coalminer" still lives on.

Tim O'Toole was a gambler from Ireland's Midlands area who was not content just to aim at the moon but wanted to conquer the Galaxy. In the end this proved his undoing.

The O'Toole tragedy – with a capital "T" – lay in the fact that while he lived for nothing else really only the continuing "war" with the bookies, he eschewed the basic dictums by which the true professionals operate and he never knew when to shut up shop.

Thus, for example, if he won at the horses at Leopardstown or the Curragh, he would head straight for the dogs at Shelbourne Park to play up his winnings and from there it was nothing for him to take a flight to London to play Punto Banco in some private club.

On one occasion when both the horses and the dogs had

gone badly for him, he decided that he would try and get it all back in London. He arrived at his favourite club late. He thought he could bet at the Punto Banco table until 4 o'clock in the morning but he was told: "Tonight, Mr. O'Toole, the law states that we must end at 2 o'clock and no later."

His protests went unheeded. To placate him they laid on the Rolls-Royce to bring him to his hotel. They understood, of course, from the level of his betting, that he would probably be staying in the Dorchester, the Savoy or the Cumberland. In actual fact, not being unduly fussy where he slept, he had booked into a place in Soho that never made it to any of the "good hotel guides".

The driver of the Rolls-Royce left him at a taxi rank near Piccadilly with the immortal comment: "They'll know, Sir, where your hotel is!"

Alex Bird, as we have seen, always asserted that doubles, trebles and accumulators were "for the mugs". But that dictum of one of the most successful of all post-War professional gamblers didn't deter Tim O'Toole from investing in crazy trebles that spanned not only racing but soccer and tennis. And, contrary to all set principles, he netted £48,000 through one of them in the Seventies.

He had successfully picked Night Nurse to win the 1976 Champion Hurdle, Wollow the English 2000 Guineas that same year, and Liverpool the English Division 1 title. He admitted to really 'sweating it out' the night Liverpool met Wolves in the very last game at Molineaux to decide the Championship (Liverpool, incidentally, won 3-1 and Wolves were relegated in the process). "I didn't take any chances but laid off to ensure a profit anyway even if Wolves won," he said.

He had gone for a win of £70,000 (he showed me the docket) on another treble, and two legs came up – Flying Water winning the 1976 English 1000 Guineas, Wollow the 2000 Guineas and Malinowski, his choice to win the Epsom Derby did not run.

The Dewhurst Stakes, he told me, was the race each October that had opened the way for some of his biggest and most successful ante-post gambles. "The Dewhurst has thrown up more than one 2000 Guineas and Derby winner," he said.

Wollow's win over Malinowski in the 1975 Dewhurst convinced him that he had seen the 1976 English 2000 Guineas winner – and also the potential Epsom Derby winner in Malinowski.

The trip to Newmarket certainly paid off, as we have seen, in Wollow providing the basis for a £48,000 treble – and we can only wonder would the £70,000 treble have come off, if Malinowski had taken part in the Derby.

There is a Tipperary punter of my acquaintance who is not alone a survivor but almost invariably comes out on the right side at the end of each season.

He keeps his own system of ratings, based on long hours given to the study of the form book and he maintains that if enough time is devoted to this task, it will pay off. When his ratings show a top-rated runner to have a good deal in hand of the rest of the field, then it will represent a bet – a real bet. He is not one to be swayed by racecourse rumour but trusts his own judgement.

National Hunt racing is his first love. The Cheltenham Festival meeting is Mecca because it is about the BEST.

He prefers to keep a low profile and I respect his wishes in making him anonymous for the sake of this book. You will see knowledgeable punters seeking him out at race meetings just to get his opinion. His viewpoint always counts.

For a busman's holiday he will head for Cagnes-Sur-Mer, knowing that none of the usual "gang" from the National Hunt scene will be there. One day he met up with an English trainer friend of his who overnight had succeeded to the family title that made him a Lord.

The trainer greeted him as ever before, remarking: "I didn't think this was your scene?"

My Tipperary friend explained that it was his form of escape and then added teasingly: "And how am I to address you from this out?"

"Just call me 'Willie'."

334

PART EIGHTEEN

THE WESTERN BRIGADE
*Making The Champagne Flow
Freely At The Festival Meeting*

23

When The West Was Truly Awake – And Singing

There was never a champagne party like it during the Festival meeting in Cheltenham. And I don't think I will be part of one again in my lifetime to surpass it.

The West was truly awake and singing on that Tuesday night, March 16, 1982 when the Golden Valley Hotel housed the celebrations after the shattering seven-lengths win of For Auction in the Champion Hurdle. The winner started at 40/1.

As night merged into the dawn of St. Patrick's Day, the party was still going strong and there was not a drop of champagne left in the hotel. John Mulholland was still tinkling the keys of the piano and there were rugby men from Wales rubbing shoulders with rugby men from England and Scotland and the boys from Galway and the West of Ireland generally as we all joined in singing "Galway Bay".

The Heaslip brothers, Danno and Mick – two outstanding sportsmen – had played rugby in their time. And played it well.

I had gone back from the course with both of them and Michael Cunningham, the successful trainer. Michael Heaslip had £1,000 each way at ante-post odds of 40/1 on For Auction and backed the horse again on the course while Danno won a five-figure sum.

In addition, Danno put on another £50 each way "just for the champagne money," netting £2,000 in the process.

Before he left the hotel that same day, he had told the

336

manager to put 300 bottles of champagne on ice and he still laughs when he recalls the man saying: "Did you say 30 or 300, Sir?"

Now as he walked into the foyer of the Golden Valley, filled with the euphoria of victory, Danno was greeted personally by the manager and a member of the staff holding a silver tray with a bottle of champagne and glasses on it. The champagne corks had been popping at the course itself even before the main celebrations of the evening got under way.

As the manager congratulated him and the others in the party, Danno told him: "You can open 100 bottles of champagne to begin with. And get a piano."

"But we haven't got one down in this area," came the reply.

"Then buy one," said Danno.

They discovered they had one in a function room upstairs – "and it was like seeing a coffin being brought downstairs," recalled Danno with a laugh.

The Heaslips had lunched in a Galway pub on the Monday and then flew with a group of friends, including Pascal Conlon and Johnny Walsh in a chartered plane from Galway airport to Cheltenham, getting into the Golden Valley to have smoked salmon sandwiches and coffee in the bar at 5 o'clock.

Next day the Galway contingent went wild with excitement as Colin Magnier, wearing the light blue and white Galwegians colours, brought For Auction back into the winner's enclosure.

It was fitting that the winning colours should have been the Galwegians colours.

Danno and Michael played for many years for the Galway club and won inter-provincial honours with Connacht. Danno had played with Terry Wogan on the Crescent College Junior Cup team in Limerick before graduating to bigger things. A born character, he was a scrum-half of considerable ability who won ten Connacht cup medals while Michael was the club's hooker.

Nothing is more indicative of Danno's penchant for creating legends and being part of them himself than the story of how he travelled to Germany with a touring rugby squad and became friendly with an English No. 8 forward who told him of a horse being specially prepared for the Cambridgeshire. The Heaslip brothers decided to have "a real go" at hefty ante-post odds and backed it to win more than £4,000. On the day of the race, Galwegians were hosts to the great Northern club, Ballymena, who included international heroes Willie John McBride and Syd Millar, and on the tidal wave of enthusiasm just about everybody at the ground backed the horse. However, the match had to go ahead as scheduled but Danno got the news from the sideline that their coup had come off, and as he prepared to put the ball into the scrum he did the obvious thing as his brother was hooking. "We won – coming on your left, now!"

Little wonder then that there should have been rugby men in the gathering around the piano when the great victory party got under way in the Golden Valley Hotel. John Mulholland, who accompanied for one of the best singsongs I recall at any Festival meeting, is a character in his own right, a Galway bookmaker, Mayor of the city in his time, friend of Christy O'Connor Jnr. and son of the late Ned Mulholland, who back in 1938 was part of one of Galway's greatest gaelic footballing sides.

The late Tim Colleran was there, his wit and repartee very much in evidence and, of course, all "the gang" who comprised the inner circle of the Heaslips' friends. "John Mulholland and Tim Colleran were so good on an occasion like that that they were like professional entertainers," said Danno Heaslip.

And he was certainly right in that – and I still remember sometime after midnight John Mulholland switching into Stephen Foster numbers of the deep South and we all joining in the chorus of "Swanee". And then on to the Beatles and "Hey Jude". What a night!

We always seemed to get back to another rendering of "The West's Awake".

They sang "The Galway Shawl" and "The Fields of Athenry" and other songs redolent of the West and what it means to depart from the stone-walled fields and the dis-

338

tinctiveness that is to be found in this part of Ireland, especially in the heart of Connemara. The talent was good – so good in fact in that long evening's journey into night – that you realised why the Irish make Cheltenham and why the Festival week would be nothing without them.

The Heaslips had acquired For Auction as an unbroken three-year-old for a mere £4,000 after Michael Cunningham spotted him in a field down the road from where he trains in County Meath (in Paul Finnegan's place to be exact). They went to see him and liked him – and such is the stuff of which dreams are made.

Danno summed up: "You could never relive the moments we lived with For Auction. You may get only one horse in a lifetime like that. You may get only one chance to go for a race at the Festival meeting, knowing that you can bring it off, and when it is a race like the Champion Hurdle and it's won as impressively as For Auction won it, then you know just how lucky you have been, especially when you think of all the others who have tried to realise that same ambition and failed."

As he drank a glass of champagne, Michael Cunningham confessed to me that it was the greatest thrill of his career to win the Champion Hurdle. "It is my first Cheltenham success," said this most versatile of trainers, who won the Irish One Thousand Guineas, the Coronation Stakes and the Champion Stakes with Cairn Rouge. He really "arrived" in 1976 when he landed a famous gamble with Irish Fashion in the Schweppes Gold Trophy.

The Heaslips displayed the beautiful Waterford Crystal trophy they received as a result of For Auction's victory during the celebrations in the Golden Valley Hotel. And later in the week I had the pleasure of attending a memorable victory dinner in the Malvern View.

But they were disappointed however, that they had to return home without the imposing perpetual Champion Hurdle trophy, which normally goes to the winning owner for a year. It remained in the vaults of Martin and Co. in Cheltenham until the all-clear was given after a routine dope test – and it was some time later that Danno Heaslip received the trophy.

Danno takes up the story: "When Nigel Dimmer of Martins came into the reception at the course and handed me the perpetual Champion Hurdle trophy, I said to him that I wanted to bring it with me to the victory party in the Golden Valley Hotel and then on home to Galway. He told me I couldn't do it. I pointed out to him that if it was a problem of security, I would pay for all the security that was needed."

No, it wasn't that. The reason the trophy couldn't be handed over there and then was a sequel to the Tied Cottage saga when the Dan Moore-trained winner of the 1980 Gold Cup was disqualified on technical grounds several weeks after the race and the inscribed trophies had to be sent back to England.

"But this is MY cup," protested Danno Heaslip, fondling the Champion Hurdle trophy as he would a first-born baby.

"You can't have it," said Nigel Dimmer very politely.

"I'm taking it," said Danno. "It's mine, do you hear, it's mine."

"But you won't take it," said Nigel Dimmer, even more politely but with a finality that caused the intrepid Danno to surrender in the end.

Incidentally, there were many Irish punters that day who, while they were very happy that the Heaslips had made it a singular triumph for the "ould sod", were much poorer in their pockets as a result of the failure of the 9/4 favourite Daring Run. The money had been literally piled on this one. Not alone had Daring Run, owned by Helen Doyle from Enniscorthy, County Wexford (sporting a magnificent silver mink coat for the day – a Christmas gift from her husband, Andy) been backed to win fortunes in single bets but he was also coupled in big doubles.

The Irish punters, who had backed him as if the winnings would be like "money from America", groaned as he slipped up on the flat approaching the third hurdle from home.

Trainer Peter McCreery was left to ponder whether he would have pegged For Auction back if he had stayed on his feet.

The only certainty in racing is its great uncertainty.

The scene switches now from the Golden Valley Hotel to the Queen's Hotel at the top of the Promenade in Cheltanham, the facade of the hotel floodlit at night, the centre of the great victory dinners in the golden seasons when Monksfield – or 'Monkey' as he was affectionately known to those in the inner circle – won the Champion Hurdle in 1978 and '79.

Dr. Michael Mangan is a big man. Big in physique, in keeping with his days as a rugby player when his compatriots in Galway knew him as 'Hopper'. Big in heart and outlook and overwhelming in his generosity to his friends. A man who loves the flow of good conversation, especially when it hinges on National Hunt racing, who sparkles when good yarns are being spun and can contribute admirably himself to the fun and wit of memorable occasions. A supreme sportsman who has shown that he can take defeat in the same spirit as victory and this was never typified better than his graciousness when Monksfield was thwarted of the three-timer by Sea Pigeon and Jonjo O'Neill in 1980.

"One of the greatest races I have seen over the Cheltenham course," was how Mick O'Toole described Dessie Hughes's victory on Monksfield over Sea Pigeon in the 1979 Champion Hurdle.

Later I saw the race on television not once but a number of times. But television could never capture the sheer majesty of the climactic moments of that race as Dessie Hughes and Jonjo O'Neill went into the last and then got down to it, locked in something that was optic and beautiful in the rhythmic movement of horse and rider towards the finishing post, the perfect balance maintained by two of the greatest National Hunt jockeys of that era and yet the power they produced as they drove for victory was truly electrifying. Personally, I write it down as the greatest hurdle race finish I have seen.

It was almost– but not quite – a carbon copy of the Champion Hurdle race of 1978 when Monksfield won by two lengths. But this time Jonjo O'Neill was on Sea Pigeon instead of Frank Berry, and, of course, Dessie Hughes was on Monksfield instead of Tommy Kinane and the margin was three-quarters-of-a-length.

"A wonderful feat of training by Des McDonogh, who had the horse turned out in superb condition with a summer bloom in his coat," was the tribute from Peter Willett in the *Sporting Life*.

"It was fitness that won it for Monksfield when the chips were down in the great battle up the hill," summed up Dessie Hughes.

And again that evening the champagne flowed freely in the Queen's Hotel at the celebratory dinner as it had in 1978, Des McDonogh and his wife, Helen and Dessie Hughes and his wife, Eileen ranged on either side of Dr. Mangan and his wife, Sheila at the top of the table – with Michael Maguire again acting as M.C. as he had done the previous year. Yes, the contingent in from St. John's, Newfoundland – the close friends of Dr. Mangan – had a night they would cherish and recall by winter fires when the snow lay heavy on the ground outside.

It had become the custom of Dr. Mangan to gather with his friends in the Don Pasquale restaurant in Gloucester each year on the eve of the Champion Hurdle. It had become a lucky omen to travel out from Cheltenham and by 1980 it was now an annual event.

Only that this time – though we did not realise it then – it was to become a "Last Hurrah" gathering to honour the champion Monksfield before he surrendered his crown to Sea Pigeon.

Monksfield had £1 million in bets riding on his back. The Irish backed him at all odds down to 6/5 favourite on the day of the race itself – with Sea Pigeon going off at the very generous odds of 13/2.

This time Monksfield finished seven lengths runner-up to Sea Pigeon, which had followed him home in the two previous years.

Monksfield, however, could not be kept out of the headlines – even in defeat.

Without any prior announcement, a 200-yard up-hill stretch, taking in the area in front of the stands and behind the Tote Prices display board, had been cut out of the course over which the Champion Hurdle was contested. And immediately after the race, Des McDonogh asserted: "The changing of the track made all the difference. It meant that Sea Pigeon was able to get at Monksfield earlier. They took the short way round rather than the uphill climb in front of the stands – and this uphill climb as was shown, normally gives full play to Monksfield's greater stamina over Sea Pigeon."

Dessie Hughes, while admitting that the 200-yard stretch had to be taken into account, said frankly: "I had Monksfield in exactly the position I had him in 1979 coming down the hill and again he was with Sea Pigeon at the final flight. I am not going to make any excuses for the defeat of Monksfield on the day."

"If anything was against him, it was probably the dead ground," he added.

"The better ground and the shorter trip all helped this time," was how Jonjo O'Neill summed it up.

It would have been a fitting end to Monksfield's career if he could have joined the elite band of hat-trick winners, Hatton's Grace, Sir Ken and Persian War. But what a record he had over the Cheltenham course – he was never out of the first two in five appearances there.

Four years after the "Last Hurrah" dinner at the Don Pasquale, Dr. Tony Healy of St. Vincent's Hospital, Dublin, long-standing friend of Dr. Mangan, from their days together in Newfoundland, had arrived in Cheltenham for the Festival meeting. That year we dined with Dr. Mangan in the Bear Hotel in Stroud, about twenty miles from Cheltenham. He was in the company of a party of American friends, including famous veteran of the Second World War, Lt. General Bill Quinn, who had a third share in Herbert United, trained by Des McDonogh and which ran so well in the Waterford Crystal Supreme Novices Hurdle on the first day of the Festival meeting.

Few American Generals won as many honours as General Quinn, who served under General Alexander Patch as Intelligence Officer in the 7th Army and later under the legendary General McArthur.

But his abiding memories were of the top Germans he

saw surrender at the fall of the Third Reich.

He was there when Field Marshal Goering surrendered. What a fascinating story that was and it could make a chapter in a book in itself. What do you think Goering would ask for at the moment of surrender – a Scotch on the rocks or a Gin and Tonic with ice and lemon?

Enter now – and take a bow – the Boys from Bohola, the Durkan brothers, who had their hour at Cheltenham when that brilliant mare Anaglog's Daughter turned in an exhilarating display of jumping when winning the 1980 Arkle Trophy Challenge Chase with ears pricked by twenty lengths, beating in the process the pride of England, Beacon Light, winner of seven chases in succession. "It was a performance that has rarely been excelled by a novice over this course," wrote Louis Gunning in the 1980-'81 *Irish Racing Annual* and Louis had seen the best back to the days when Tom Dreaper and Vincent O'Brien were "kings" of the scene at the Festival meeting.

Bohola (population 298) in County Mayo boasts some very distinguished sons for a village of its size. Martin Sheridan, who emigrated to America when he was sixteen, amassed five gold, three silver and one bronze at Olympic Games in St. Louis, Athens and London in the first decade of the century. His brother, Richard was a world record holder at discus-throwing and their cousin Jim Clark was a silver medallist at the London Games in 1908.

Bohola genealogists also claim their village as the birthplace of the antecedents of the gentlemanly world heavyweight boxing champion Gene Tunney – but that claim is disputed by some family historians of the "mother" town of Kiltimagh. There can be no dispute about the origins of the O'Dwyer brothers – Bill who became Mayor of New York and his brother Paul, who was to become an internationally famous lawyer. Both were born and spent their formative years in Bohola.

After the Cheltenham Festival meeting of 1980 the Durkan brothers were the living legends of the little Mayo village. All seven of them left their father's thirty-acre farm to ply their skills as building craftsmen in the lucrative London market. They built a mini-empire in both countries which in time would embrace an hotel, restaurants and public houses in addition to the building business.

And by way of a sideshow – and a most unlikely one at that – the consortium produced a racehorse trainer whose name went into the record books as the man who sent Anaglog's Daughter to take the 'Arkle'. Bill Durkan, third eldest of the brothers, who was still at the time in his early forties admitted with disarming honesty: "I did not know much about the business of training when I started."

In the late Sixties when a survey of the housing needs of Dublin's expanding population indicated that the time was ripe to establish an Irish presence the Durkan brothers' native enterprise was launched. Its success provided Bill with the opportunity to indulge his fondness for the land and horses. He bought thirty acres of land at Glencullen, high up in the Dublin hills with the Three Rock Mountain as one of its boundaries. He built a magnificent home and a stable yard in which he soon installed two brood mares bought cheaply at Ballsbridge. The intention was to breed his own racehorses and with a view to training then himself, he laid down a fine circular gallop with a stiff uphill finish.

The prospect of the long wait for the homebred horses to make the racecourse however proved irksome and having acquired stable staff Bill decided to get into the action by buying a couple of likely jumpers. They were Paddy Tudor and Carrow Boy. Both were broken at Glencullen and a better foundation pair could hardly have been chosen to test and then vindicate the inherent skills of the tycoon-trainer. They were both prolific chase winners.

Carrow Boy was the horse responsible for bringing the name of "Durkan, Trainer" to the notice of cross-channel jumping fans when in a swoop on Ayr he won handicap chases on successive days and in another sortie abroad jumped like a stag and made all the running to win the Holiday Inn Chase at the Aintree Grand National meeting. Striking as these performances were, they paled into insignificance compared to the achievements of Anaglog's Daughter and there was nothing finer prior to Cheltenham than her ten-lengths win in the Arkle Challenge Cup

Chase at Leopardstown.

Understandably then, her fame had preceded her to the Festival meeting.

I remember still the great "Irish roar" that went up as she demolished the opposition and never were there as popular winning connections in the enclosure at Cheltenham as the "Boys from Bohola" when Anaglog's Daughter came in to renewed acclaim. Bill and Tony I found to be among the most outstanding sportsmen I have met in my time writing on racing.

Bill Durkan was quick to acknowledge the debt he owned to Ferdie Murphy, who played a vital role in the success of Anaglog's Daughter, and indeed, in all the other successes enjoyed by the Glencullen stable. In fact, team spirit was the motto of the yard.

Ferdie, who made his mark as a National Hunt rider, served his time with Phonsie O'Brien and had a very successful innings with Paddy Mullins. He showed a great flair for getting new training operations off the ground. Billy Boyers and Harrison Burcombe would testify to that. And Bill Durkan, as emphasised already, was unstinting in his praise for the man who looked after affairs at Glencullen when he himself had to shed his riding clothes and don the Chairman's pinstripe for a Company meeting.

If the year 1980 was their most memorable year of all for the Durkans, it was also a year to remember for the O'Malley brothers of Galway, Frank, Myles and the late Tony. The trio actually hailed from Louisburgh, County Mayo and their building/construction company is the biggest in the capital of the West of Ireland.

Early that summer the brothers saw their horses win a staggering seven races in a row; they saw the horse – Rare Duke – which they thought was "no good" win three times in a row including two events at the Galway Festival meeting. Most gratifying of all they saw all their nine horses in training with Paddy Prendergast Jnr. win races for them.

Their best-known chaser in the National Hunt sphere was Corrib Chieftain, a winner of many good races in Ireland and a gallant second to Anaglog's Daughter in the

Arkle Trophy Chase at Cheltenham.

But "The Chieftain", as the brothers affectionately called him, had to take a back seat when the flying two year old Cooliney Prince pulverised the opposition to win the Windsor Castle Stakes at the Royal Ascot meeting at 9/1.

The O'Malley brothers, as Jim Carney revealed in an article in the 1980-'81 *Irish Racing Annual*, named nearly all their horses (you also had Corrib Prince, Corrib Ranger and Corrib King) after the famous trout stream that flows through historic Galway city.

Tony O'Malley, who was killed in a tragic accident at a comparatively young age when out shooting during the season one day with his son, was an outstanding character who loved a bet, especially on one of his own horses, and no place in the world "turned him on" as did the Cheltenham Festival meeting. One night I saw him involved in one of the big poker schools in the open lounge area of the Queen's Hotel, before that scenario was ended, and suddenly it dawned on him that a duo of English "sharks", prowling around the circuit, had got into the game who were giving signals to each other. Like the true sportsman he was, he managed to extricate himself with grace before any real damage was done and, shrugging his shoulders at the loss of £800 on the last hand he played, he remarked to me: "It's all part of the learning process."

The racing bug was in his blood from as long as he could remember. He liked to recall the day he went to see the Melbourne Cup when he was working Down Under as a young man in the mid-Fifties. He had £50 in his pocket and intended having it on the favourite at 2/1. Just at that moment he was approached by a little Aussie old-timer who whispered the name "William The Fourth" into his ear – and was suddenly lost in the crowd.

O'Malley looked at the racecard and laughed it off when he saw that the horse had no form to recommend it. Wandering around the ring, he saw that it was quoted at 66/1. Try as he might, however, he couldn't get the little fellow out of his mind. Forgetting about the favourite, he said to himself "here goes" and had £25 each-way on the complete ousider. Fifty yards from home the favourite appeared to

347

have won it but William The Fourth finished with a late flourish to land victory right on the line.

Tony O'Malley saw the Cheltenham Festival meeting as the place where "the real action is for the jumpers." He would have gone to his grave happy if he could have emulated Dr. Michael Mangan and the Heaslips by winning the Champion Hurdle or if he could have seen the colours carried there by a novice to match Raymond Rooney's Golden Cygnet, described by Fred Rimell as the greatest juvenile hurdler he had seen win over the course after the breathtaking manner in which the Edward O'Grady-trained contender won the 1978 Supreme Novice Hurdle.

Golden Cygnet, bought for only £1,200, unquestionably looked a Champion Hurdle winner in the making and, I believe, he might have won not just one but three-in-a-row if all had gone right for him. The hopes and dreams of connections were dashed by a cruel fall at Ayr which resulted in injuries from which he did not survive.

Galway insurance executive, Raymond Rooney, an outstanding sportsman in his own right and like the O'Malleys a generous supporter of the racing at the Galway Festival meeting, talking some years on of the impact Golden Cygnet had made on lovers of National Hunt racing and of the aura he left in that unforgettable moment when he powered down the hill and we realised that this was out of a realm that we would never see repeated by another novice hurdler.

"It's a funny feeling now, looking back on the whole situation and that tragic fall at Ayr but we will never forget the reaction from racegoers throughout Ireland and Britain also who were as shocked by his death as we were ourselves," said Raymond Rooney.

"My phone never stopped ringing and there were cards and telegrams every day. It was as if a member of the family had died, and I suppose in a way that is what happened. It may be pointless wondering now about what he would have achieved but he might have been another Arkle."

"He was really something special . . . but, well, that's racing."

PART NINETEEN

THE HORGANS & THE PURCELLS
When The Big English Layers Didn't Forget!

24

The Great Leeside Sting

It has already gone into racing lore as "The Great Lee-side Sting". And it would seem appropriate that from the City by the Lee, where the Gay Future "coup" was planned by the late Tony Murphy and his racing associates, another Cork family – the Horgans – should with a colt purchased for only 19,000 guineas inflict on the big English ante-post layers a hammering that they would not easily forget.

Don't Forget Me was the name of the colt (and what an apt name!). He was trained in Wiltshire by a burly bear of a man, Richard Hannon (of Irish extraction himself) for Jim Horgan. It's history now how he won the English 2000 Guineas and the Irish 2000 Guineas in the 1987 Flat season.

The Horgan brothers started backing him for the New-market Classic at 66/1 in September of '86 and continued consistently to take all odds from 33/1 to 20/1 and right down to his starting price of 9/1.

It was estimated that they took £250,000 out of the ring. Three years on, the Horgans brought off an even greater "Leeside Sting" –only that this time they hit the big English layers even worse. The overall winnings were reported to have topped the £500,000 mark.

Tirol, purchased at the High Flyer Sales in Newmarket in September, 1988 for 52,000 guineas was the colt that did the damage. In the ownership this time of John Horgan, he was again prepared in masterly fashion for the English

351

2000 Guineas by Richard Hannon and, like Don't Forget Me, went on to complete a memorable double by winning the Irish 2000 Guineas at the Curragh.

"We all started putting money on him back in January, 1990 when he was at long odds of between 40/1 and 50/1," recalled John Horgan. "As the price came down, we continued to put money on him. There was a lot of money in Cork on the day of the race itself, as we didn't mind telling people we expected him to win.

"Everyone was backing him. It didn't change the odds as the prices were being set in England. The bookies there didn't give him the chance that we did. In the end, he went off at 9/1."

He added that the bookies in Cork got such a hammering that some of them had to close on Saturday because they didn't have the cash to pay out what they owed. "But everyone got paid on Monday," said John Horgan.

Saturday, May 5, 1990 will be remembered as "Black Saturday" by the bookmakers by the Lee.

For months beforehand Machiavellian had been the "talking horse" for the 1990 English 2000 Guineas.

Indeed, Francois Boutin confidently asserted that Machiavellian was "one of the best horses I have trained."

Little wonder then that the "inspired" money was going on him in the ante-post betting and when they went to the start at Newmarket his price was down to 6/4.

They flew across in their own plane, the members of the Horgan family and close friends. Already the champagne was on ice in The Briar Rose, the Horgans "local" in the Douglas area of Cork (adorning the walls of the bar are two fine prints of Don't Forget Me and Tirol in victory).

The fact that Tirol (Michael Kinane) had two lengths to spare over Machiavellian (Freddie Head) at the finish was academic compared with the victory scenes in the winner's enclosure. The Horgans and their connections took over the place. It was more reminiscent of Cheltenham during the Festival meeting in March after a major Irish success than the normally staid reaction you can get nowadays when a horse belonging to one of the Sheikhs wins a Classic.

"All it needed to complete the impromptu party was a ceili band," wrote John Karter in a very amusing piece in the *Sunday Times*, as he described how the connections of the winner "jigged ecstatically round the horse and trainer, Richard Hannon."

But, of course, those scenes were to be dwarfed by what was to follow at the Curragh on Saturday, May 19 when Tirol completed a great classic double by taking the Airlie/Coolmore Irish 2000 Guineas by a neck from Royal Academy – with Machiavellian and Freddie Head fourth.

"Who put the ball in the back of Freddie Head's net?" shouted one intrepid supporter and friend of the Horgans, to the heavens. The bowler hatted members of the Turf Club must have been shocked.

To cap it all they broke into the Cork anthem, *The Banks of My Own Lovely Lee.*

Yes, the Curragh – like Newmarket – will never be the same again after that famous Tirol double of 1990.

John Horgan said afterwards that he had feared Royal Academy more than Machiavellian – and he was proved right in that. Reports during the week beforehand that Royal Academy had done an outstanding gallop were reflected in the sustained support the $3.5 million Nijinsky colt received in the betting and he started at 4/1 with Tirol 5/4 favourite and Machiavellian at 9/4, having opened at 7/4.

Vincent O'Brien, aware of Royal Academy's stamina limitations, was reported to have told John Reid that he did not mind how long he held up the colt, he would not blame him if he got beat. The Ballydoyle representative had the rest of the field beaten when he led briefly inside the last furlong – but he could not repel the late surge of Tirol and Pat Eddery. It was either going to be a case of Royal Academy winning right on the line or not at all.

The tumult and the cheering had subsided and it was some months after the victory scenes at Newmarket and the Curragh when I sat with John Horgan in Cork and he recalled for me the fateful day when he went for what he thought was an ordinary medical check-up – a matter of course, so to speak, as he was taking out extra personal

353

insurance.

Before he knew what had hit him, he was undergoing a heart bypass operation in the Blackrock Clinic in Dublin.

That was in the autumn of 1987 – and his lifestyle has changed dramatically since then.

He walks now where it would have been automatic to get into the car just to go the proverbial few yards down the road. He slips away from parties to get to bed at a reasonably early hour where once, as the life-and-soul of social gatherings, it would have been nothing for him to see the dawn coming up over Cheltenham, Liverpool, his native Cork or wherever the "action" was hottest on a given occasion.

"I leave the partying to other people nowadays," he smiled – but in a way he is getting a better kick out of life, as the order imposed by the bypass operation means that he plays golf regularly, is careful with alcohol and has far more time to spend with his family.

John Horgan once stood to take a very substantial six-figure sum (he won't reveal the exact amount) out of the ring at Cheltenham on Roadway, which was carrying 10st in the County Handicap Hurdle with Tommy Carberry in the saddle. As *Chaseform Notebook* reported, "Roadway came on the scene between the last two flights looking all over a winner" but he clipped the last and that made all the difference between victory and losing in a blanket finish to Path of Peace (Jonjo O'Neill) and Prince of Bermuda. The verdict was a head and a head. Roadway started at 16/1. The Horgans got in at 25/1.

He shrugs his shoulders when he recalls what was undoubtedly one of his most fearless tilts at the ring and at the same time one of the great might-have-beens.

As the eldest of a family of twelve (ten boys and two girls), John has always been seen as the head of the clan, though Don't Forget Me's 1987 English Guineas win gave new prominence to Jim.

The family have had a unique association with the cattle trade in Ireland for more than half a century. Their great grandfather laid the foundations of the livestock business that was to see them in time extend their operations on a wide scale, finding new openings for Irish cattle exports that cut dependence for farmers on the traditional British market.

So in the glory days when you stepped into the offices of John Horgan and Company on Cork's South Mall, in which five of the brothers were involved, you knew that you were stepping into a lot of history where the Irish cattle export business was concerned.

But in time they would hit quieter days in their business fortunes – the same as in the case of the Purcells, another Irish racing family who played a key role in developing new outlets, particularly to the Middle East, including Egypt and Libya, for Irish cattle. It stemmed from the general move away from live cattle shipments and the growing tendency to process the raw material within the country.

However, the day I met John Horgan I was more concerned with talking about horses and bloodstock. I was fully conscious of the fact that for the one family to produce a colt in Don't Forget Me, that completed the English-Irish 2000 Guineas double in 1987, was a feat in itself. But for the same family to repeat that feat three years later with Tirol – and with the same trainer at that – was something that will probably never be repeated in racing history (and in that I am not allowing for the fact that they could well cement the record by bringing it off for the third time!).

John Horgan talked of his pride when his brother Jim's horse, Don't Forget Me, won the English 2000 Guineas and Jim himself said of that moment: "The money was important, of course, but winning a Classic is a dream that some people spend millions on to achieve and never succeed. It was the greatest thrill of my life. My heart was pounding all the way to the finishing line."

Don't Forget Me had always worked like a good horse at home but even so was allowed to start at 50/1 for his debut as a two-year-old at Salisbury. Richard Hannon explained: "He was not fancied but Anthony McGlone, who rode, was very impressed with the way he shaped to finish fourth. The colt ran green but Anthony got off and said 'this fellow could be a bit special'."

That was the green light for the Horgans (and Hannon) to put their betting boots on for Don't Forget Me's next race at Sandown.

"Greville (Starkey) rode and they won well at 8-1. We had gone in with our heads down," added Hannon.

But it was not until Don't Forget Me moved into the Pattern race league for Goodwood's Lanson Champagne Stakes that connections began to realise that they might have a Classic contender on their hands.

Hannon continued: "He won the Goodwood race at 7-1 and the bookies offered 66-1 about him winning the Guineas afterwards. The Horgans had a bit of that, as did John Magnier, and the odds looked a bit on the generous side after he had followed up in the Laurent Perrier Champagne Stakes at Doncaster."

Pat Eddery rode Don't Forget Me both at Goodwood and Doncaster and already rated him Classic material, but the champion jockey appreciated that his contract with Khalid Abdulla meant it was unlikely he would be available to renew the acquaintance at Newmarket. As it was, Willie Carson had the ride in the Guineas.

Three private planes had been chartered to take the 28-strong group to Newmarket. Those on board included John Magnier, Michael "Mouse" Morris, son of Lord Killanin and Tommy Stack who, of course, made racing history by riding Red Rum to his third Grand National victory at Aintree (1977) and is now a successful trainer.

Nine of the ten Horgan brothers were at the parade ring for the big event, easily outnumbering the Maktoum brothers of Dubai as one broadcaster wryly observed.

It had been a day of high drama starting at 7 a.m. when Jim Horgan took a call at his home in Douglas in Cork from Richard Hannon informing him that Don't Forget me had hurt his foot and there was a question mark over his participation in the race – but he told them to come on over anyway.

Jim Horgan went on to recall: "It was touch and go. They had been up all night with ice buckets and God knows what to get the swelling in the foot down. The horse had been unable to put his hoof on the ground the night before. It was a miracle that he responded to the treatment so quickly."

When the all-clear was given, many members of the Horgan party "waded in" to back the horse on the course at 10/1.

Jim Horgan confirmed that they cleared £250,000 at least between ante-post wagers and what was won on the course that day.

The three planes with the victorious party were back at Cork Airport at 8 o'clock the night of the race. Their subdued mood on take-off earlier that day, when they thought the colt might not run, had now changed to elation.

They adjourned to The Briar Rose and celebrated there with a massive champagne party until closing time. Then they returned to Jim Horgan's home nearby where the merry-making continued until dawn.

John and Jim Horgan could smile that night amid the flowing champagne as they reflected back to the Gay Future betting coup – the £300,000 sting that went wrong, and they knew that somewhere up there in the Great Beyond, Tony Murphy was smiling too.

There had been a moment at Cheltenham that would never be forgotten but now the "Leeside Sting" gave a new sense of satisfaction.

The Don't Forget Me sting was a straight tilt at the big English ante-post layers – and this time they certainly wouldn't forget.

"The good thing about the Horgans is that they understand losing as well as winning and they have taken enough knocks in the cattle business to know it's not all roses," said Richard Hannon.

No finer tribute from a trainer to a duo of Cork owners patronising his stable than this.

Offaly-born Seamus Purcell and his wife, Phil, who live in Dublin's southside, will always be linked with the ill-fated Buck House, champion in the true sense of the term. Tommy Carmody wore the colours of Mrs. Purcell, a sister, incidentally, of the former outstanding Kerry footballer, Micksie Palmer (a star in the Kingdom full-back line in the defeat of Dublin in the 1955 All-Ireland Final before 87,102

357

spectators), in winning the 1986 Queen Mother Champion Chase in highly-impressive fashion as Bobsline, 1984 winner of the Arkle Chase, was eclipsed.

Tommy Carmody, Michael 'Mouse' Morris, the successful trainer and Mrs. Purcell were congratulated by the Queen Mother in the winner's enclosure.

In a way Buck House's brilliance that day was dwarfed by Dawn Run's achievement in winning the Gold Cup – "the greatest chase I have ever seen," to quote John Francome – and she thus made history by becoming the first horse to complete the Champion Hurdle/Gold Cup double.

The recording of something factual like that can give no indication of the scenes that followed the unforgettable moment when Jonjo O'Neill rallied Dawn Run up the hill, after she had looked beaten at the last, and gave that triumphant arm-aloft gesture to the heavens as he passed the winning post. An "Irish roar" went up that I know I will never see equalled, no matter how many more times I go to the Cheltenham Festival meeting.

This was the stuff of which legends are created. At a moment like that it would be churlish to categorise people into nationalities. It was for the aficionados of the chasing game. And its overwhelming impact will live deep inside all of us who were there. Again it was the very essence of the challenge of Cheltenham for man and horse and it explains why we shall always return.

Already the balladeers, were singing to the tune "He's Got The Whole World In His Hands", their own happy version, "Dawn Run's Got The Gold Cup In Her Hands", It echoed out towards Cleeve Hill from every bar on the course and I heard it later that evening in the Golden Valley Hotel, as the celebrations continued into the early hours of Friday morning. Cheltenham was drunk dry of champagne before the dawn. And the bookies took a terrible hiding.

"I did not know emotion like this even when our own horse, For Auction won the Champion Hurdle," said Danno Heaslip who was among the first to congratulate Paddy Mullins.

Picture the scene if you had the misfortune not to be there on Gold Cup Day '86. Already every vantage point on the tiered terraces overlooking the unsaddling enclosure itself had been occupied, Paddy Mullins, the Quiet Man from Goresbridge, County Kilkenny standing there waiting the moment when Jonjo would bring Dawn Run back in. For years Paddy had avoided the spotlight, now he could not avoid it. Neither could his wife Maureen. Everyone seemed to want to shake their hands in congratulations.

And then it rose up from the tiered terraces, up from the milling crowd who had swarmed in past the police, the most sustained deep-throated roar that I have heard greeting a winner in my time going to Cheltenham. You felt it tingling in the spine right down to the toes of your feet. It was the final release of all the emotion that had seemed killed when Dawn Run looked beaten at the last. Jonjo, the smile of victory spreading across his countenance and obviously enjoying every minute of the adulation sweeping over him, was the unquestioned hero of the hour.

The unforgettable moments surpassed in sporting spontaneity the awkwardness and tension of Jonjo's getting through the "invasion forces" in the winners enclosure. Nothing will erase the memory of Jonjo hoisting Tony Mullins onto his shoulders and carrying him over to the presentation stand, where the Queen Mother was waiting to present the Gold Cup trophy to winning owner, Mrs. Charmian Hill . . . a gesture that brought a tremendous response from Irish and English alike.

No chaser, I am certain, will come along to stir the same depth of feeling that Dawn Run created for us in victory. It was unique, it was special. It was like the Arkle years replayed, as you replay an old documentary film from an earlier era, only it was on a more intense, adrenalin-draining plane because of the manner in which this 1986 Gold Cup triumph was forged out of the impossible. And extra special too because of all that went beforehand.

Arkle's legend was the legend of unsurpassed greatness, Dawn Run's legend was that of sheer courage and the unspoken way she conveyed to us all on March 13, 1986 that nothing can be deemed lost in racing or in life until the last crunching uphill battle to a mythical winning post is lost. And Dawn Run's heart didn't allow her to lose her final battle at Cheltenham.

She may have died in action in France but she left that outsize spirit of hers under the shadow of Cleeve Hill.

A massive crowd turned up at Punchestown on April 23, 1986 for the Great Match between Dawn Run and Buck House over two miles with £20,000 at stake. They met at level weights, with Tommy Carmody on Buck House and Tony Mullins restored as the rider of Dawn Run.

A marvellous jump at the third last looked like giving victory to Buck House. He still had the advantage at the second last. But straightening up to the last Tony Mullins asked Dawn Run for her effort and she won convincingly in the end by 2½ lengths.

On June 27, 1986 Dawn Run, bidding to win the French Champion Hurdle for the second time at Auteuil, suffered another of those strange lapses of concentration, fell, broke her neck and was killed instantly.

By the time Dawn Run died in action, Buck House had already fallen victim to colic in a field in Tipperary.

So the two outstanding Irish-trained chasers of 1986 would not be there to carry the flag for the country in the 1987 Festival meeting.

It was a terrible blow to the Purcells to lose Buck House. However, the colours of Mrs. Seamus Purcell were carried to triumph again at the Cheltenham Festival meeting on Wednesday, March 11, 1992 when My View, bred and trained by her brother-in-law, Michael Purcell in Thurles, Co. Tipperary and ridden by the outstanding young National Hunt rider Jason F. Titley won the Coral Golden Handicap Hurdle (Final) at 33/1.

A nice "touch" for the Purcells. But, frankly, the "Irish roar", as My View came over the last flight, was muted as only the connections could have been on the winner.

PART TWENTY

TONY MURPHY
The Man At The Centre Of
"The Gay Future Affair"

25

When The Bookies Were Caught With Their Pants Down

Scotland Yard might never have brought prosecutions in "The Gay Future Affair" had they not received a complaint from the Betting Offices Licensees' Association (BOLA), whose President at the time was Lord Wigg.

Most British people, who enjoyed even the odd flutter, saw the action of BOLA as cynical and unsporting. Cork builder and racehorse owner, Tony Murphy, the central figure in the Cartmel coup, anticipated a scream of pain from the bookies. However, having cleverly "caught them with their pants down" – to quote his own words – he never visualised that he would be found guilty of criminal conspiracy to defraud by a British jury who disagreed with the advice of a sympathetic judge; that furthermore, he would be fined £1,000 for his role in the coup and banned by the Jockey club for ten years from British racecourses.

Anthony (Tony) Collins from Troon in Ayrshire suffered a similar fate. However, the ban on Tony Murphy did not apply in Ireland.

Lord Wigg was in the chair when BOLA held a special meeting the day after the Cartmel race, which was run on the August Bank Holiday, 1974. That meeting was dominated by one subject and one subject only – The Coup. Lord Wigg immediately reported the matter to Scotland Yard and, pending the outcome of the police inquiries, BOLA instructed its members not to pay out on the race.

Now to the thousands of ordinary racegoers in Ireland

with a deep interest in "The Gay Future Affair", Lord Wigg may have appeared to be just another stuffy member of the British Establishment who lived for his gin and tonic before dinner and his port and Stilton afterwards and who may well have been battling the gout. Little did they know.

Lord Wigg had been in the period 1964-'67 one of the most influential politicians in Britain and that influence did not entirely recede when he became President of BOLA. He could still pull strings and he was quite adept at pulling them in the higher echelons of the political power structure.

He was nominally Paymaster-General in the Governments of Harold Wilson but, as *The Times* noted in its obituary on his passing at the age of 82 in August, 1983, his exact responsibilities in this position were never exactly defined, though efforts were frequently made to find out what they were. What was known, however, was that he was very close to Wilson, that he was responsible for keeping Wilson informed about developments within the Labour Party and that he took a particular interest in matters of security and in defence in general.

He would have seen the Cartmel coup by a group of Irishmen, led by one with the most Irish of names – Murphy – as breaching the normal near-impregnable defences of the bookies and those responsible must be brought to heel. Making it even more embarrassing for him was the fact that from the time he had first got involved in racing in an official capacity, he had made it clear that he was not going to be a mere figurehead.

From 1957 to 1961 he had been a member of the Racecourse Betting Control Board and from 1961 to 1964 of the Totalisator Board. He moved to the Horserace Betting Levy Board in 1967. He was outspoken on many occasions over the rules of the Jockey Club, which he regarded as too conservative and out of touch with modern-day thinking.

He saw himself as a spokesman for the ordinary man in the street in racing. He believed that more money should go towards reduced admission charges and improved amenities for racegoers.

He also had a passionate interest in cleaning up the

image of racing and felt that it was essential that it must be seen to operate with integrity in the eyes of the small punter.

Thus he would have set his face firmly against certain aspects of "The Gay Future Affair", especially the fact that two of the "intended" runners Ankerwyke and Opera Cloak had – as it was stated so graphically during the court hearing subsequently – "never left their grassy fields up in Scotland to go down south" and that the horse that went to the Tony Collins stable was not Gay Future, though there was no question of the Cartmel winner being a "ringer". The horse-box that came over from Ireland carried the real Gay Future and it was Gay Future who ran and won at Cartmel while the "blind" who had fooled the watchers on the gallops was a different animal altogether.

Scotland Yard would have been quite happy to have left the Jockey Club pursue the inquiries into the Cartmel coup and take what acton it deemed fit under the rules of acing.

But Lord Wigg, as President of BOLA was determined from the outset that the police should be brought into it. He wanted to justify his position as President of BOLA – to be seen as a strong man who could generate action where action, he felt, was needed. It was he who urged the members of BOLA that Scotland Yard must be informed of the coup – and his suggestion was carried through.

The recommendations emanating from the special meeting of BOLA that any pay-out on the Cartmel race be suspended was observed by a majority of the members of the Association. However, at least one prominent and highly-respected member broke ranks with the rest. Heathorn's Managing Director, Michael Simmonds (a member of the Committee of BOLA) said in a statement, released through the Press Association, that while he fully sympathised with his fellow BOLA members, he did not feel that the alleged irregularities were sufficient reason to withhold payment any longer. His firm felt that the bookmakers' image had been badly damaged by BOLA's decision to involve the police and withhold winnings.

Lord Wigg was livid at the fact that there were "rebels" in the ranks of BOLA and more livid still that they should go public and assert that there was no reason why the bets on Gay Future should not be honoured. A man like Michael Simmonds speaking for a firm with a long tradition behind it in Heathorn's carried clout with his fellow bookmakers and Wigg saw the need for quickly silencing any further breaking of ranks.

He promptly issued a statement to the media making the position clear. He pointed out that BOLA's recommendation to its members had been resubmitted to the Association's legal advisers and this had resulted in counsel repeating "in the most emphatic terms, his previous advice, that it would be wholly inappropriate to make payment until the investigation by the police had been completed."

After the jury had been out for six hours and seventeen minutes and their 'guilty' verdict was handed down on a 10-2 vote, Lord Wigg was quick off the mark again. He announced on behalf of BOLA that, on the notification of their legal advisers, they were declaring all bets on Gay Future void.

Marcel Berlins, a legal correspondent, writing in *The Sporting Life*, commented: "The facts of the Gay Future case were of a different order, never before dealt with by criminal law. The racing world is now troubled that it should create a precedent for criminal action in circumstances which up to now had been dealt with by its own institutions, especially the Jockey Club."

Another journalist wrote at the time: "The control of such matters has in the past been left to the Jockey Club. But this time because of the sums involved and perhaps at least partly because of Lord Wigg's interest in the case as President of BOLA, the law was persuaded to take a hand."

Eight years after the event, Tony Murphy was still arguing that the Gay Future coup was perfectly legitimate. "If Gay Future had lost at Cartmel, there would not have been even the mildest squawk from the bookmakers," he said to experienced *Cork Examiner* journalist, Larry Lyons for his book, *The Gay Future Affair*.

Larry Lyons revealed that Tony Murphy had written a

letter suggesting that BOLA should get those of its members withholding money staked with them, to donate it to a racing charity – but his letter was ignored.

He felt very bitter about that facet of "The Gay Future Affair", though normally he was a man who could take setbacks in gambling in the spirit of a true sportsman. Indeed, Mr. Justice Caulfield paid him the greatest compliment of all when he said in his summing up: "It would be absurd to classify you as a fraudulent man in everyday life. You are obviously a racing man and enjoy your racing. You have at least remained a sportsman to the end . . ."

A member of the Syndicate that organised the coup made the very interesting point to me that the reason why the bookmakers did not donate the money staked on Gay Future to a racing charity was that if they had done so then the *exact* amount actually invested by the Syndicate in England would have become known – and likewise how much they stood to win.

"No way did we stand to win the £300,000 to £500,000 that it was claimed in newspaper reports we would have netted," said the Syndicate member. "It suited the bookies to let the story of a £500,000 coup make headlines at the outset as it meant that it helped their case as they pressed for a police investigation and that all payment be suspended pending the outcome of that enquiry."

Tony Murphy went to his grave, after dying suddenly at home, in October, 1982 without ever revealing how much was invested, how much "won" and how much exactly paid out.

"On that score the usually communicative Tony Murphy was silent," said his friend Larry Lyons, (incidentally, the bets placed with Irish bookmakers were nearly all paid).

What we do know is that, going on the actual shares held by those comprising the Syndicate, the front-line "troops" as they fanned out from the London Tara Hotel through the West End of London had £7,000 to invest and on the S.P. returned price of 10/1 Gay Future, this would have brought in £70,000 – if every penny of it had been invested. This accounts then for the Syndicate member I spoke to asserting that the total "killing" would not have been more than £100,000 if every bet laid in Britain had been honoured.

But, apart from what they contributed in shares in the Syndicate, those tilting at the books on that fateful August Bank Holiday Monday in 1974 could have gone in with more of their own money. There was nothing wrong in that as long as Syndicate commitments were honoured.

The bets were being laid in the London area from 10 o'clock in the morning. In a military-style operation the territory had been earmarked and, according to Tony Murphy's own estimate, "about 500 to 600 booking shops were covered." And some bets were still being laid up to ten minutes past four – that is just ten minutes before the Cartmel race – though Hills had called a halt much earlier.

It's immaterial now how much the Gay Future coup would have netted. It pales before the impact it made on the minds – and hearts – of racing followers everywhere, so much so that a highly-acclaimed 75-minute documentary film, *Murphy's Stroke* was made about it by director Frank Cvitanovich.

Of course, the Cork Mafia, as they were dubbed, caught the imagination of the public. They weren't all from Cork but the principal players were from the banks of the Lee.

Tony Murphy, a popular and flamboyant personality, cut a distinctive dash by driving a silver Rolls-Royce around his native city. The silver Rolls-Royce in a way was his trade mark. But he moved easily in racing circles, among the aficionados of the National Hunt game in particular and no one could ever accuse him of allowing money to cut him off from grass-roots feelings and aspirations.

Nothing excited him more than the thought of making the bookies squirm at being taken to the cleaners by a spectacular coup.

Many people tend to forget that Murphy and his friends in the Cork Mafia had a "dry run" for the Cartmel coup earlier in 1974. It passed unheralded because it failed. The bookies never screamed in pain on that occasion because they banked at least £7,000.

There were aspects of that coup very similar to "The Gay Future Affair", if on a lesser and more straightforward level. On that occasion the bets were on doubles that became single bets rather than on trebles.

On Easter Monday, 1974 when there were no less than twelve meetings in Britain, Hindsight was entered in a Maiden Hurdle (2m) at Towcester and Golden Lancer at Carlisle. The money went on as an "S.P. job" in the offices in London in doubles on the two horses. But, of course, it was never intended that Golden Lancer would run.

As Tony Murphy related it to Larry Lyons: "It was one of the busiest racing days of the year with a choice from many meetings. Six of us stood to win £100,000 . . . we had little doubt that Hindsight would win, but unfortunately it ran into the back of another horse during the race and finished fourth at 14/1."

Hindsight, trained by Andy Geraghty (who would later train The Illiad and Destriero for Noel Furlong) hadn't been in the frame once that season but Tony Murphy and his friends got their money back at Punchestown when, carrying only 9-7 in the Mullacash Handicap Hurdle, he was a clear winner by six lengths at 12/1.

The principal lesson learned from the failed "Towcester Coup" was that next time Tony Murphy and the Cork Mafia – "went to the well", they would do so with a bumper horse that was "tried a certainty" over the jumps to win a novice hurdle. They would not rely on a handicapper.

And to avoid any suspicion that there was an "Irish coup" on, it would be best if the "job" horse was "placed" in a small stable in Britain that had no record of setting the ring alight, but the actual training would be done in Ireland. In addition, the jockey would not be a top-flight professional but an amateur who could also be trusted with total confidence to deliver.

County Tipperary trainer, Edward O'Grady was the man given the responsibility of acquiring the "job" horse – and training him. Gay Future, originally trained by John Oxx, had a good record on the flat in bumpers and as a four year old ran five times, winning once, being second twice, third once and fourth once. On the occasion he won, his rider was Mr. T. A. Jones or just Timmy Jones to those who knew him as one of the most capable amateurs in the business.

When Edward O'Grady bought Gay Future for £5,000 to pass on to Tony Collins, another piece of the jig-saw that would be unfolded at Cartmel fell into place. In July arrangements were made to ship Gay Future to the Collins stable in Scotland but now the real twist – it was not Gay Future that was shipped but another horse similar in appearance to Gay Future, that is an unnamed four year old Arctic Chevalier/Madrid Fox chestnut gelding.

Meanwhile,the real Gay Future was being schooled on the O'Grady gallops at Ballynonty, near Thurles and by the time he would go to the start at Cartmel, O'Grady and all those involved in the coup knew that, while he might be a novice in name, it was extremely unlikely that he would fail on the score of his ability to skip over hurdles.

Monday, August 26, 1974 was the fateful day. Cartmel was a long way distant in the echelons of racing from Cheltenham on Gold Cup Day, the Curragh on Budweiser Derby Day or Longchamp on the afternoon of the Prix de l'Arc de Triomphe. You wouldn't bet on any animal running there because he represented class! But now just mention "Cartmel" in the company of lovers of National Hunt racing in Ireland and nostalgia swirls in the air at the thought of how Gay Future "brought home the bacon" though the denouncement was that the bookies stopped on the major part of the payout.

There was no "blower" or telephonic link to Cartmel to enable the bookies to blow money back to the course when it was poured on in the offices in an S.P. job. So if they didn't get a man there in time to go into action and lay money around the ring, they were going to be taken out with a sucker punch. The representative of one of the "Big Four" bookmaking chains, after a hectic dash by road, arrived at the course too late to depress the price.

Edward O'Grady did not go himself to Cartmel. His very presence there would have alerted the rails' bookmakers to the fact that there was something big "on". He sent his trusted lieutenant Tim Finn, who was thoroughly experienced in every facet of the game. He was operating now under the name 'Micky Finn' and for disguise was wearing a blonde wig and dark glasses.

Tim Finn accompanied the real Gay Future over on the B+I ferry from Dublin to Liverpool and meanwhile a horse box had left the Collins stable carrying the chestnut gelding by Arctic Chevalier out of Madrid Fox. The driver of the O'Grady box was Christopher Hall and of the box from the Collins' stable Ian McAllan.

They met at a pre-arranged spot – the first layby on the left off the M6 Motorway towards Kendal, where there was an AA box.

The switch was done smoothly and professionally. Now the real Gay Future was on his way to Cartmel while the chestnut gelding would return by road and ferry to the Emerald Isle.

Meanwhile all the other pieces in the jig-saw were falling into place as planned. Apart from Gay Future being down to run in the Ulverston Novices Hurdle at 4.20 p.m. at Cartmel, Tony Collins had entered Opera Cloak to contest the 4.15 at Southwell and Ankerwyke the 4.45 at Plumpton. The jockeys named to ride the three horses were to confuse things further.

But the bottom line was that, going on the forecast price of 20/1 Opera Cloak and 16/1 Ankerwyke, the trebles involving these two with Gay Future would realise £3,200 to £1. The big bookies would naturally conclude that anyone betting on this treble on an August Bank Holiday Monday was in the realm of a "mug punter" out and out. The bookies really love to see mug punters coming and put out the red carpet for them.

But the bookies didn't know that the Cork Mafia never intended that Opera Cloak and Ankerwyke would run, so every time they took what they thought was a "mug" bet on the treble, they were actually taking "hot" money in single bets on the "good thing", Gay Future.

To make it even better, Racionzer had been put into the Cartmel race with Gay Future. He was backed on the course in such a way as to fool the bookies into thinking that the "inspired" money was coming for this runner from the Collins' stable and not Gay Future. Racionzer

371

went off at 8/1 against the 10/1 starting price for Gay Future. Racionzer was pulled up after the third hurdle.

The unsuspecting onlooker at the parade ring would have noticed that one Mr. T. A. Jones as he prepared to mount Gay Future actually tried to get into the saddle on one side and fell off the other. Some amateur! And they would have noticed also that Gay Future was sweating up rather badly. The Lux soap flakes, applied liberally in the gathering ring prior to Gay Future being saddled, had done the job well!

For the record Crocodillo, the mount of Ron Barry started favourite at 5/4 with Jonjo O'Neill's mount, Playbella the 9/2 second favourite. They might as well never have been sent to Cartmel that day. Timmy Jones, riding with supreme confidence and wearing Collins' second jockey cap, romped home fifteen lengths ahead of his nearest rival Canonbie Key.

Tim Finn watched the race in the company of Brian Darrer, who was wearing a light coloured raincoat.

Finn had given instructions that there must be no show of excitement or emotion as Gay Future left his field for dead and, of course, Finn knew that barring a fall he would leave them stone cold.

As it was, as Gay Future skipped over the last, Tim Finn could not contain himself. He threw his cap in the air and rather upset the dear old lady beside him as he exclaimed: "You little beaut!"

Meanwhile, the other members of the Cork Mafia, outside of Brian Darrer, were gathered in the London Tara Hotel waiting the word from Cartmel (it wasn't televised, of course!) that Gay Future had duly "done the business". They needn't have worried.

The eight who had booked into the hotel with shares in the Syndicate were: Tony Murphy, Pat O'Leary, Michael Rose, John Horgan, Robert Henry, Tim Horgan, Garda Supt. John McMahon and Brian Darrer. But, as we know, Brian Darrer was in Cumberland.

Two others mentioned during the trial as shareholders were Timmy Jones and Michael 'Mouse' Morris.

A few of those with smaller shares in the Syndicate had

their names in as a means of allowing Tony Murphy to have a bigger cut at Gay Future.

Tony Collins arrived for the celebratory party in the Tara, carrying out to the letter prior instructions that he walk into the bar with his binoculars over his left shoulder. As he recalled later – it was drinks all round and the laughter and the 'crack' continued into the early hours of the morning.

One of the most colourful stories of all from that amazing episode in the history of great racing coups was that a London police officer helped Tony Murphy next day as he went to collect the winnings on Gay Future in the West End booking offices.

It happened this way. Supt. McMahon had endeavoured to get in touch with an English colleague on the highly-confidential police line. At the other end they weren't certain that it was an Irish police officer who was on the line. It could be a case of a trap being laid by a group of subversives.

Det. Sergt. Henry Coates drove to the Tara to renew acquaintanceship with Supt. McMahon. There was an element of 'professional courtesy' in that call on the Tuesday morning.

McMahon, having been paged, met Det. Sergt. Coates in the foyer of the hotel. At that point the Cork Superintendent was in a hurry to go out and told his English colleague to come back at 1.30 p.m.

When Coates returned he was invited into the bar along with Constables Michael Wilson and Richard Ainsworth. They saw at first hand how an 'Irish celebration' starting on a Monday night could be in full swing again by midday next day and in racing there are no barriers between the English and Irish, especially when it comes down to those who appreciate the thrill of racing "over the sticks".

Tony Murphy confided to the English policeman that he had to go into Soho to cash-in winning dockets on Gay Future and there was so much "lolly" to collect that he was worried he might be robbed. So he was driven by Constable Ainsworth down into the West End area in the police car. Extraordinary as it may seem, as he went into the first five shops, he left the rest of the betting slips in the 'Q' car in full view of the officers. Soon the police officers got the message that there was going to be no big pay-day for Tony Murphy and he told them himself that there was no point in visiting any more shops – so they returned to the Tara.

By now Tony Collins was coming under strong pressure to explain why Opera Cloak and Ankerwyke had never got to the races.

In the final analysis, this was the one aspect of the Cartmel Coup where things had gone completely wrong. In fact, immediately Tony Murphy learned that the two horses had not left to contest their respective races he was 'not happy about it', as he told Larry Lyons. And he was unhappy about it right to the end.

In the planning of the coup, provision had been made to ensure that the clear impression should be created that they had every intention of running.

All that was needed was that they be loaded into a horse-box and a certificate got from some obliging garage-owner that the horse-box had broken down. Or to make it even more plausible, the horse-box carrying one of them could have broken down; the second horse could have arrived at the racecourse stable and developed some mystery ailment causing his withdrawal on the advice of a vet.

Granted, it would have been wrong and not in keeping with the spirit of the rules of racing. But the bookies could not have complained that there was *never* any intention whatsoever of running either Opera Cloak or Ankerwyke.

So for want of a horse-box – and if you want to add to that a mystery ailment – it all went wrong when it need never have gone wrong. And the final irony was that the difficult aspects – keeping the price of Gay Future at 10/1 and ensuring that money was not blown back to the track and also spreading the bets around the London offices – were carried out in military-style while the horse was produced at peak condition on the day and schooled to perfection to do the job he was expected to do.

The champagne that flowed so freely in the Tara Hotel turned sour when Tony Murphy, Edward O'Grady, John

Horgan and Brian Darrer were arrested at the 1975 Cheltenham Festival meeting and taken to the local Police Station. Later they were taken to Kendal Police Station and
formally charged with conspiracy to defraud. Next day
Tony Collins was arrested in Troon and similarly charged.

There was an attempt to extradite Supt. James McMahon, Pat O'Leary and Michael Rose, to England to face
charges connected with the coup.

The late Justice Denis O'Donovan refused the application for extradition in Cork District Court. The State
appealed his decision to the High Court, where Mr. Justice
Hamilton found that the District Justice's determination
was correct.

The District Justice had ruled that the particulars of the
alleged offences were insufficient to enable him to be satisfied that if the same acts had ben committed in the State
(i.e. the Republic of Ireland) they would have constituted
an indictable offence, or an offence punishable on summa-
ry conviction by imprisonment for a minimum of at least
six months.

The charges were withdrawn against all except Tony
Murphy and Tony Collins before the Crown case opened at
Preston Court on February 3, 1976.

Tony Murphy was very upset at the choice of Preston as
the venue of the trial. He would have been quite happy if it
had gone on in Cheltenham where he and the others had
been arrested in the first place. The way Murphy saw it
was that recent bombing incidents in the Birmingham area
had created deep feelings in the tragic circumstances and
he was worried about the effect on the attitude of an English jury.

The case was highlighted by the questioning and inter-
jections – often very amusing – and grasp of detail of Mr.
Justice Caulfield on the bench and gain it has to be seen as
a *cause celebre* whenever the great racing gambles and their
aftermath are discussed.

Suffice it to say that anyone sitting in the court on the
day that Mr. Caulfield addressed the jury would have
taken odds-on that there could be only one verdict – "not
guilty".

"The fact that bookmakers can occasionally lose is not something to be deplored unless their loss has been suffered because of criminal action, such as fraud," he said.

My own view is that it comes down in the end to one question – was there criminal fraud, meriting imprisonment, if Mr. Caulfield had decided to go that far?

Certainly there was no criminal act in the sense that a "ringer" was put into the Cartmel race instead of Gay Future and neither were bets laid after the time of the off when the clocks had been put back, so to speak.

Tony Collins had breached Jockey Club rules when not sending two intended runners to the respective meetings at which they were supposed to run. It could be argued that this was a matter between him and the Jockey Club. Without the police being ever brought into it, the Jockey Club would have taken the appropriate action. And they did by banning him for ten years.

After the jury had given their 'guilty' verdict, Justice Caulfield did not even contemplate imposing a sentence. If there had been a criminal conspiracy to defraud, why not?

He imposed 'a joke fine' – as it was generally agreed among racing people at the time – of £1,000 each on Tony Murphy and Tony Collins and they were each ordered in addition to pay £500 towards the cost of the prosecution. Again that £500 was a joke as the costs of the case ran into many thousands.

Ironically, Irish taxpayers had to meet the cost of the extradition hearings in Cork District Court and in the High Court because of reciprocal arrangements between Ireland and Britain. These too ran up a sizeable sum in legal costs.

Little did the ordinary punter in Ireland, who may have backed Gay Future strictly on his record, before being transferred to run in the Tony Collins colours, and wasn't in on the coup as such, realise that legal bills would be footed by the Irish taxpayer.

But then Lord Wigg was not going to be left with egg all over his face by an Irishman called Murphy from Cork, especially one who did not hide his delight at catching the big English bookies with their pants down.

In what one of the lawyers, Mr. Gray described in his

address to the jury as "the ancient war between punter and bookmaker", Tony Murphy and the Cork Mafia certainly won the battle hands down in the way Gay Future delivered at Cartmel on that August Bank Holiday Monday in '74 but I must admit that they lost the war in the sense that they left most of the winnings and their stake money behind them with the bookies.

But, what matter, it has gone into the folklore of racing as a coup that can never again in all its machinations be repeated – down to the London police touring the Soho betting shops helping Tony Murphy as he tried to collect the winnings!

They opened 'The Gay Future Cocktail Bar' in the New Victoria Hotel in Cork in December, 1981 and my great friend Larry Lyons was there in the company of Tony Murphy. Other members of the Syndicate were there also with Niall Tobin who had been in the documentary film, *Murphy's Stroke*. What a night!

The Gay Future colours worn by Timmy Jones as he powered to victory at Cartmel were on display in the bar.

The hotel has now given way to a fast food restaurant and the bar, in another part of the building, is closed – but the colours and other mementos remain exactly in place where they were on that memorable night in 1981.

Somewhere up there in the Great Beyond – in that peaceful garden that Barney Curley spoke of when giving me his vision of Heaven – I am sure that Larry Lyons is making out a treble coupling Gay Future with Opera Cloak and Ankerwyke and rubbing his hands as he tells St. Peter that the odds, if it comes up, are £3,200 to his pound.

And Tony Murphy has gone for the jugular with another coup to end all coups, the details of which I will not learn until Barney and myself join him . . . in that Field of Dreams!